Travels
in the Confederation

[1783–1784]

From the German of
JOHANN DAVID SCHOEPF

Translated and Edited
by
ALFRED J. MORRISON

New Jersey, Pennsylvania, Maryland, Virginia

PHILADELPHIA
WILLIAM J. CAMPBELL
1911

The Lord Baltimore Press
BALTIMORE, MD., U. S. A.

Printing Statement:

Due to the very old age and scarcity of this book,
many of the pages may be hard to read due to the
blurring of the original text, possible missing pages,
missing text, dark backgrounds and other issues
beyond our control.

Because this is such an important and rare work, we
believe it is best to reproduce this book regardless of
its original condition.

Thank you for your understanding.

Reise

durch einige der mittlern und südlichen

vereinigten

nordamerikanischen Staaten

nach Ost-Florida und den Bahama-Inseln

unternommen in den Jahren 1783 und 1784

von

Johann David Schöpf

d. A. W. D. Hochfürstl. Brandenb. Onolzb. und Culmb. Hof- und
Militär-Medikus, Landphysikus, des Mediz. Colleg. zu Bayreuth Rath
und der Gesellschaft naturforschender Freunde zu Berlin Mitglied.

Erster Theil.

Mit einem Landchärtchen.

Erlangen

bey Johann Jacob Palm. 1788.

ADVERTISEMENT

Dr. Schoepf, at the time of his travels in America, was in his thirty-second year. He was born March 8, 1752, at Wunsiedel, (birth-place of Jean Paul), in the principality of Bayreuth, a town of the Fichtelberg and a region of mines and quarries. His father was a merchant well-to-do, who had him educated by tutors at home, sent him to the Gymnasium at Hof, and, in 1770, to the University of Erlangen. Schoepf's studies there were primarily in medicine, but he followed lectures in the natural sciences generally; Schreber and Esper were his masters in botany and mineralogy. In 1773 he was at Berlin for work in forestry. Before taking his degree at Erlangen, in 1776, he travelled, investigating the mine country of Saxony, was in Bohemia, studied at Prague and Vienna, traversed Carniola, Northern Italy, and Switzerland. It was already plain that he would not spend his life as an obscure practicioner. During 1776, at Ansbach, he thought of going to India. The next year he was appointed chief surgeon to the Ansbach troops destined for America, and arrived at New York, June 4, 1777. After his return to Europe, in 1784, Dr. Schoepf was diligent in scientific research and held besides many positions of public trust, dying September 10, 1800, as President of the United Medical Colleges of Ansbach and Bayreuth.[1]

[1] Hirsch, *Biogr. Lexikon der hervorrag. Aerzte aller Zeiten und Völker.* Fr. Ratzel, in *Allgem. Deutsche Biographie.* Edw. Kremers, Introd., *Materia Medica Americana,* Lloyd

As much as any other man at that time Dr. Schoepf seems to have made North America his study. The following are his most important contributions touching this Continent: Ueber Klima, Witterung, Lebensart und Krankheiten in Nordamerika;[2] Von dem gegenwärtigen Zustand in Nordamerika aus dem Lande selbst, im Jahre 1783;[3] Vom amerikanischen Frosche;[4] Der gemeine Hecht in Amerika, and Der nordamerikanische Haase;[5] Beschreibung einiger nordamerikanischen Fische, vorzüglich aus den newyorkischen Gewässern;[6] Materia Medica Americana, potissimum Regni Vegetabilis;[7] Beyträge zur mineralogischen Kenntniss des östlichen Theils von Nord Amerika;[8]

Library Bulletin, Cincinnati, 1903. Rosengarten, *The German Soldier in the Wars of the United States.* Philadelphia, 1890. Pp. 91-98.

[2] In Meusel's *Hist. Literatur,* 1781; appearing also, modified, as a prefix, *Reise* II. Translation of the original pamphlet by Dr. J. R. Chadwick, Boston, Houghton, 1875, 8vo. pp. 31

[3] In Schloezer's *Staats-Anzeigen,* VII, 1785. Four articles.

[4] In *Naturforscher,* No. 18.

[5] *Ibid.,* No. 20 (1784).

[6] In *Schrift. der Berliner Gesellschaft Naturforschender Freunde,* No. 3 (1788), p. 138 ff.—"The first special ichthyological paper ever written in America or concerning American species." Goode, *Beginnings of Natural History in America,* Smithsonian Institution Report, 1897. II, 396 (Nat. Museum).

[7] Erlangen, 1787; Lloyd Library Reproduction Series, Cincinnati, 1903. The first treatise in that department, and the authority well into the nineteenth century.

[8] Erlangen, 1787—"Commonly regarded as the first work on American geology." Merrill, *Contributions to the History of American Geology,* Smithsonian Institution Report, 1904 (Nat. Museum), p. 208.

Historia Testudinum,[9] based in large measure on notes made in America or on correspondence with observers there. In addition, Schoepf had put together a manuscript descriptive of the birds of North America coming under his observation; which material was lost at sea between Virginia and South Carolina or more likely disappeared through negligence. Regarding the trees of North America Dr. Schoepf remarks, "What I saw every day and in the greatest numbers was trees, but in my travels I could the more aptly suppress my observations, the work of my esteemed friend Head Forester Von Wangenheim,[10] of Tilsit in Curland, having shortly before appeared, containing everything which it would be of use for the European reader to know." Taken together with his travels, this was a very considerable body of work entitling the author to a place in our intellectual history.[11]

On setting out from Europe, as appears from the Preface to the *Beyträge,* the young Schoepf had been counselled by Schreber to have an eye to the geological structure of the new world, Kalm having given an insufficient report in that item. The advice was followed to good purpose,[12] but the observer was able to do more,

---

[9] Erlangen, 1793-1801—" One of the earliest monographs of the Testudinata." Goode, loc. cit. cf. *Reise,* &c., I, 382-386; II, 440-444.

[10] Göttingen, 1787.

[11] Bibliography in Meusel, *Lexikon der vom Jahre 1750 bis 1800 verstorbenen Teutschen Schriftsteller,* XII (1812), 364. cf. Bock, *Sammlung von Bildnissen gelehrter Männer.* Nürnberg, 1791-1798, XV (1795)—Portrait, bibliography, and autobiographical material.

[12] cf. George Huntington Williams, *Bull. Geol. Soc. Am.,* V (1893), 591-593—" An excellent but now almost forgotten

and fortunately had the opportunity : he returned with full memoranda which are of interest today. Schoepf could talk to a member of Congress about his crops or his mines and come away with a very good idea of the man himself and his relations to the commonwealth. His work seems modern because he had a sense of humor, had trained himself to think, and also because the country he observed is still new. We learn that 'conservation' has for a long time been waiting for a chance.

Dr. Schoepf came with the other Allied Army. That was, in some respects, a different time. Authority was high, and patronage might show very excellent results. The work is inscribed to

Christian Friedrich Karl Alexander, Marggraf zu Brandenburg :
Durchlauchtigster Marggraf !
Gnädigster Fürst und Herr !

————

The dictionary found most useful has been John Ebers's— "A new Hand-Dictionary of the English Language for Germans and of the German Language for Englishmen. Elaborated by John Ebers, Professor at Halle." Halle, 1819—Prefaces dated 1800 and 1801. Dobson's Philadelphia edition of "The Encyclopaedia" (1798-), and the American edition of Rees (Philadelphia, 1810-) are recommended.

work [*Beyträge* &c] on the geology and mineralogy of the United States, south of New York, published at a time when Werner and Hutton were just beginning to be heard in the scientific circles of Europe. Many of the conclusions set forth are in the main those now generally accepted, and bear witness to the acumen of their author."

Subscribers' Names

Thomas H. Atherton, Wilkes-Barré, Pennsylvania

Baker & Taylor Company, New York

C. H. Barr, Lancaster, Pennsylvania

John Hampden Chamberlayne, Richmond, Virginia

E. I. Devitt, S. J., Washington

Eichelberger Book Company, Baltimore

H. W. Fisher and Company, Philadelphia

Worthington C. Ford, Boston, Massachusetts

Granville Henry, Nazareth, Pennsylvania

Hall N. Jackson, Cincinnati, Ohio, 4 copies

John W. Jordan, Philadelphia

Judge Charles I. Landis, Lancaster, Pennsylvania

Charles E. Lauriat Company, Boston

Dr. John Uri Lloyd, Cincinnati, Ohio

A. C. McClurg and Company, Chicago

H. R. McIlwaine, Ph. D., Richmond, Virginia

D. L. Passavant, Zelienople, Pennsylvania, 5 copies

Preston and Rounds Company, Providence, Rhode Island

Samuel N. Rhoads, Philadelphia, 10 copies

G. M. Robeson, Farmville, Virginia

J. G. Rosengarten, Philadelphia

Scranton, Wetmore and Company, Rochester, New York

St. Louis News Company, St. Louis, 5 copies

Torch Press Book Shop, Cedar Rapids, Iowa, 10 copies

Major A. R. Venable, Hampden-Sidney, Virginia

George Wahr, Ann Arbor, Michigan

Rev. Asa Watkins, Bristol, Tennessee

Academy of Natural Sciences of Philadelphia

American Philosophical Society

Berkshire Athenaeum, Pittsfield, Massachusetts

Boston Medical Library

Bowdoin College Library

Buffalo Public Library

Carnegie Free Library, Allegheny, Pennsylvania

Carnegie Library of Pittsburgh

Cincinnati Public Library

Columbia University Library

Essex Institute, Salem, Massachusetts

Hampden-Sidney College Library

Illinois State Library
Illinois State Historical Library
Indiana State Library
Jersey City Public Library
John Carter Brown Library
John Crerar Library
Johns Hopkins University Library
Lafayette College Library
Lancaster County Historical Society, Pennsylvania
Lehigh University Library
Library Company of Philadelphia
Maryland Historical Society
Massachusetts Agricultural College
Massachusetts Historical Society
Minnesota Historical Society
New York Historical Society
North Carolina State Library
Northwestern University Library

Pennsylvania Historical Society
Pennsylvania State Library
Princeton University Library
Richmond College Library
Smithsonian Institution
Society for the History of the Germans in Maryland
Surgeon General's Library (Army)
United States Military Academy
University of California Library
University of Cincinnati Library
University of Georgia Library
University of Indiana Library
University of Nebraska Library
Virginia State Library
Wilmington Institute Free Library
Wyoming Historical and Geological Society of Wilkes-Barré
Yale University Library

Preface

IT was to be expected that the last war in America would be the occasion of sundry descriptions of travels, so many and divers Europeans having been thus afforded opportunity to pass through and examine the most widely distant parts of that country. But so far this has not been the case. Only the following are known to me, as having appeared since that time :

New Travels through North America, in a Series of Letters, exhibiting the history of the victorious Campaign of the Allied Armies, under his Excellency General Washington and the Count de Rochambeau, in the year 1781; interspersed with political and philosophical Observations, upon the Genius, temper & customs of the Americans &c. Translated from the Original of the Abbé ROBIN, one of the Chaplains to the French Army in America. Printed by Robert Bell, 1783. — 8°. 110 pages.

Besides observations thrown in, touching the religion, character, and manner of life of the inhabitants, contains chiefly the history of the march of the French army from Rhode Island to Yorktown in Virginia, and of the siege of that place; the articles of capitulation; accounts of the unfortunate expedition of General Burgoyne, 1777; and an Appendix, letters of General Washington and Lord Cornwallis.

A Tour in the United States of America &c.   By J. F. D.
Smyth, Esqu., London 1784.   Vol. I.   400 pages.   Vol. II.
455 pages, large 8.

The author had taken up residence in America, and
both before the outbreaking of the war and during the
war travelled through the southern and middle provinces, as well as the regions beyond the mountains;
his accounts and descriptions, so far as I could judge
from a brief examination of the book, are good and
just, but too much interwoven with the particulars of
his own history, the persecutions and oppressions suffered by him as a Loyalist, with other events having
reference to those times.

Voyages de M. le Marquis de Chastellux dans l'Amérique
Septentrionale, dans les anneés 1780. 81. & 82.   Paris 1786.
T. I. 390 pages & T. II. 362 pages, large 8; with several
maps and views.

Of this work I have seen only an abridgment, under
the title: Voyage de Mr. le Chev. de Chastell. en
Amerique, which has appeared without indication as to
where printed, in 12 mo. 191 pages, with the date 1785.
The above title of the larger work I take from the
Götting. Anzeigen, art. 199, 1787, where several circumstances are remarked that do not help support the
credibility and exactness of observation of the Marquis.
Not to repeat the criticisms given there of the mang-
ling of German and English names, it is astonishing
how he seems to have been altogether careless even
with French names, calling the painter du Sumitiere,
(of whom I have also made mention, p. 85), *Cimetiere.*

—Whether this was a blunder or was purposely done so as to bring out a *bon mot,* he rendered himself suspect, and one will easily form an opinion how far to trust such a man in his observations of natural history.

Immediately after the war, and almost at the same time the united American states were visited by sundry learned and intelligent men who had come over from Europe with the express design of travelling through the country.   Germans, Swedes, French, English, Dutch, and even an Italian *conte,* were present to muse upon the wonders of the new states, and they journeyed almost always with pen or black-lead in their hands. But now, after the passage of several years, none of them has been pleased to give to the public the results of his observations, if I except the brief reports of Professor Martyr, in the *Physikal. Arbeiten der einträchtigen Freunde in Wien* (1st and 3rd year, and 2nd year, 1st quarter).   It may be that the others were deceived in their expectations, not finding memorable things in the hoped-for plenitude, and have done what I perhaps should have done, in this respect not less unfortunate than they, and more restricted in the items of time, circumstances, conveniences and helps.   But since it may be better to have a few contributions, rather than none, to a knowledge of the latest status of these parts, I venture now, (only since I see that none of the travellers mentioned has cared to forestall me), to give the dry observations which offered themselves to me incidentally during a journey through the United States undertaken with a different purpose in view.   I willingly admit that these notes are neither so complete nor of such importance as I could wish, but it may easily be seen in them that the putting-together of a book of travels was not really my object. To be candid, the motive of my journey was curiosity not altogether blameworthy, it is to be hoped. From June 1777 to July 1783 I had lived in America without seeing more than the small Rhode-Island, York-Island, an inconsiderable part of Long-Island, and for a very brief space the narrow compass of the city of Philadelphia, so that strictly I could hardly boast of having set foot on the main-land. It would have been irksome to me, and likely to other travellers as well, to be obliged to return to the old world without taking with me, for my own satisfaction, a somewhat more enlarged visual acquaintance with the new. But at the same time, and especially, I wished to extend in the interior of the country the collecting of natural products I had begun on the coast but which, by reason of the war, was restricted, and embarrassed enough. However, I was considerably checked in my purposes, the time allowed me for the journey falling in the circumstances at a late season of the year, and other unavoidable casualties rendering my hopes idle in many respects, so that I was very much deceived in my great expectations of examining the most remarkable natural productions of the interior country. Here as elsewhere, both plants and animals are little ready to cast themselves in the way of a hurried traveller, when, where and how he desires, he not seeking them out and unwilling or unable to wait for them. I have

therefore designedly omitted to speak at length of
matters in which I have been able to bring forward
little or nothing that was new. What I saw daily and
oftenest was—trees; and what observations I made
under that head I could the more aptly suppress in my
travels, the recently issued work of my esteemed friend
Head-Forester von Wangenheim of Tilsit in Curland
containing everything on that subject which can be of
use to the European reader.

Of certain other subjects which lay nearer the purpose of my journey, I have already given account, in
the **Verzeichnis der nordamerikanischen Heilmittel,**
(for which I had opportunity on this journey to assemble much important information), and in the **Beyträge zur mineralogischen Kenntnis des östlichen
Theils von Nordamerika.** As confirmation of the description given in these contributions, of the American
mountains lying to the south of the Hudson river, I
have been pleased to find in the *Götting. Anzeigen*
(Art. 176, 1787) a notice of Mr. Belknap's description
of the White Mountains in New Hampshire, (inserted
in the 2nd volume of the Transact. of the Americ.
Society at Philadelphia); this exactly fits with my own,
and confirms my suppositions regarding the continued,
regular, uniform course of the mountains through those
regions not visited by me.

In the item of fishes, what I had leisure and opportunity to observe in the North American waters, partly
on this journey and partly before, will be given in a
separate treatise, to appear in the *Schrift. der Berliner
Gesellschaft Naturforschender Freunde.*

I should likewise be able to give numerous descriptions
(exact as I could make them) of almost all the North
American birds that came to my notice, were it not that
I must deplore the loss of the manuscripts which, with
certain other packages, I had left at Manchester in
Virginia in the hands of an obliging fellow-countryman, Mr. Rübsaamen, to be despatched to Charleston
—but nothing more thus far has been heard of them.

For the rest, these sheets will not please him who, in
books of travel, has been used to expect astonishing
adventures or wonderful phenomena—splendid palaces,
beautiful gardens, great libraries, rich art-collections,
collections of natural curiosities, antiquities &c., fab-
ricks, and other public institutions worth the seeing, all
of which help fill the note-books of travellers in older
settled countries,—these as yet are not to be found in
America, and one might perhaps, not to give the matter
a bad turn, tell as much of what America is not as of
what it is. But I have been content to put down, aside
from the chief objects of my journey, what I saw and
learned, and if it is no more, it is not my fault. I relate
simple facts and give dry observations, without seeking to embellish them by the refinements of speculation
or by edifying considerations. I shall therefore hardly
be charged with having industriously described the
Columbian States, (where I am persuaded also that
many people live very happily) merely in their bright-
est aspects; as a critic has guessed, not unreasonably,
of the author of the famous *Lettres d'un Cultivateur
Américain,* noticing the latest Paris edition of that

book, which however contains much that is beautiful
and true. If perhaps there may be asked of me more
detailed and circumstantial information regarding
moral, political, œconomical, and mercantile conditions,
I can offer apology for incompleteness in no other way
but that these subjects were not precisely a part of my
plan, and that the period of my travels—immediately
after the war—when judgments and opinions were still
uncertain, statistical accounts unreliable, and peace and
order, especially, had not yet been firmly re-established,
the time, I say, was not the most opportune for these
things. Besides, there is no lack of writings giving
trustworthy information in the items of the agriculture,
trade, exports and imports of the former British colonies—but the changes arisen in these matters during
and since the war were as yet hardly to be determined
with certainty. Just as during the period of my
journey all manner of plans were making and institutions beginning, and everything was still in a ferment,
so it will be easily understood if certain of my intelligence comes too late and appears superfluous because
of newly hit-upon changes—what I have learned in
this respect I have made note of, and the rest may serve
to show how matters were at that time.

I hope I shall not bring upon myself by any of my
remarks the reproach of having blamed without reason
or maliciously, and where there may be the appearance
of such a thing it should be known that every thing I
say here I myself gave expression to in America, where
freedom of thought, of speech, and of the pen are

privileges universally allowed; moreover I am confident that I have not said many things, have left the reader to form his own judgments, where citizens of the United States themselves would freely and without hesitation have given their opinions.

Regarding many things not touched upon by me, information may be had from Professor Kalm's report of his travels, whose relations I have everywhere found to be true and exact, so far as I have examined the same territory. The travels of this learned and diligent observer (as much of them as have been published) having been from Philadelphia and New York towards the North, and mine being from thence towards the West and the South, the two may be placed together—in that respect only—giving as they do a continuous survey of the state of the eastern half of North America, with the exception of the New England and Nova Scotian provinces.

The reckoning in miles is the English throughout, just as all the other measures and weights given, as used in America, are the same as those customary in England, and in consequence need no further explanation.

The money-reckoning in the United States is various; throughout, the pound is 20 shillings and the shilling 12 pence, but these by the different currency standards are of different values, and the best comparison is to be had from the value of Spanish dollars or piastres and of English guineas.

The worth of	a Spanish dollar	an English guinea
In New Hampshire, Connecticut, Rhode Island, and Virginia	6 shillings	1 Pd. 8 sh.
New York and North Carolina	8 shillings	1 Pd. 17 sh.
New Jersey, Pensylvania, Maryland, and Delaware	7 sh. 6 pence	1 Pd. 15 sh.
South Carolina	1 Pd. 12 sh. 6 pence	7 Pd. 7 sh.
Georgia	5 shillings	1 Pd. 3 sh.

But since the war, in the last two states, the basis has mostly been sterling, the dollar at 4 shillings 6 pence, and the guinea at 21 shillings.

Accordingly a pound current is in Virginia &c. = 3¼ Span. dollars; in New York &c. = 2½ Span. dollars; in Pensylvania &c. = 2⅔ Span. dollars.

I should mention also that of the so-called carnivorous elephants, (p. 266 ff. of my Travels), beautiful representations of which are given in Buffon's *Epoques de la Nature,* remains have been found outside America, in other parts of the old world. In Germany a molar tooth, kept in the cabinet at Erlangen, has been found very similar to that coming from the Ohio; and there lies before me a drawing of bones and teeth which were discovered in the year 1762 at Gruebberg between Untergrafensee and the Gruebmühle, near Reichenberg in Bavaria, the figure showing molar teeth altogether like the American, with partly sharp, partly worn apophyses.

And it is worthy of remark that the complaints made

by the country people of several regions (p. 213, 228),
that new-made dams and mill-ponds are the cause of
intermittent fevers, less frequent previously in those
parts, have been confirmed by Dr. Rush in a treatise of
his to be found in the 2nd volume of the *American
Philosophical Transactions* (vid. *Gött. Anzeigen*, art.
176, 1787) who likewise believes the causes of the increasing bilious and intermittent fevers in Pensylvania
to be the greater number of mill-ponds, the clearing-
off of the forests which had been a protection against
the exhalations from standing water, and the far more
frequent rains of the past few years.

Bayreuth, 11th January 1788.

Journey Through Jersey
July 1783

TRANQUILLITY was now in some sort re-es-tablished in America. Ratification of the Peace had not yet come over from Europe, but under the guarantees of the provisional truce, there was already a certain intercourse opened between New York and the United States. Business and curiosity tempted a number of travellers from the one side and from the other. For near seven years I had been confined to the narrow compass of sundry British garrisons along the coast, unable until now to carry out my desire of seeing somewhat of the interior of the country. The German troops were embarking gradually for the return voyage; and having received permission, July 22 I took leave of my countrymen at New York, in order to visit the united American states, now beginning to be of consequence.

In the evening at five o'clock, with Mr. **Hairs**, an Englishman who accompanied me for a part of the journey, I went on board a **Petty-Auger**,* from and

---

* Petty-Augers are a sort of craft, used to any extent only in New York waters, where they were introduced by the Hollanders. They are half-decked boats, of five to ten tons burthen, flat-bottomed, so as to be navigable in shallow water. Flat-built, they would in the open bay, with wind, waves, and currents, make too much leeway unless counter-equipped—on each side a large board, oval-shaped, which may be let down

for Elizabethtown in New Jersey. As we were on the point of pushing off, our Jersey skipper was threatened with the necessity of taking with him a lading of blows consigned by a man of the King's party who fancied the skipper had injured him in Elizabethtown. The skipper defended himself by keeping to his cabin, with his musket cocked. The matter was for the time adjusted and we got loose, but not without fear, and the risk, at least of experiencing on the other shore something of the law of reprisals. We were however hardly under sail before the skipper began to assure us of everything agreeable on the part of his countrymen, and in particular promised us great respect in our capacity of British officers, which he no doubt took us to be. I mention this little circumstance because our friends in New York were uneasy for fear we should meet with a sorry reception among the still irritated American populace and on that account sought to discourage us from the journey. The sort of evil entreatment with which they alarmed us in New York was attributed in prospect solely to such Tories as had ventured again among their former countrymen and were by them recognized. Pride often overcomes a desire of vengeance; at least that was my explanation of the skipper's over-busy courtesies, shown us after his own rude experience in a British garrison at the hands of British subjects.

---

or taken up at the side of the vessel. This board is let down against the wind (on the lee side); the so-called Lee-board, then, hangs in the water several feet below the bottom of the vessel, and the greater resistance so gained balances the effect of the side wind which would otherwise tend to bring the vessel too much out of its course.

It was one of the warmest days. Light breezes and calm lengthened our short way. As we moved slowly over the Hudson and through the bay towards Staten Island, there was opportunity to enjoy for the last time the splendid view which is offered at a certain point between the city and the islands. The Hudson opens for several miles in a direct north line; its fine breadth, its high, precipitous banks adorned with bush and forest growth, and a number of vessels at the time busy gave to the stream a magnificent appearance which bore a softer coloring by reason of the now sinking sun.

Two little islands standing in the midst of the bay towards Jersey, however inconsiderable formerly, within a brief space have become trading places of importance. While traffic between the United States and New York was still not entirely free and unrestricted, the Americans grew accustomed to take from these islands what they hanker after yet and will always—English goods, which had been secretly expedited from the city.

One of these islands, from its excellent oyster bank, has gained the name of **Oyster Island**, formerly so rich in oysters that from it alone the city and all the country around could be supplied with this pleasant provender by which a great part of the poorer people lived. But for several years the most and the best oysters have been brought from the southern coast of Long Island, from Blue Point, where (as formerly around Oyster Island) the oyster is found in extensive beds, lying one above the other and many feet deep. Strong, curved, iron rakes are used to fetch up the fruit which never lies deep, preferring the shallower but somewhat rocky or stony spots. Oysters may be

had in more or less quantity everywhere around New
York; the reason is not known, but they are not everywhere of an equal size or pleasantness of taste. The
salt water product is always better than that which is
deposited in the fresher water near streams. Often
oysters climb so high on the beach, clinging to stones,
roots of trees, &c. that at ebb-tide they are for many
hours exposed quite to the air. The oyster of the rocky
shores of the northern parts of America is universally
larger and better than what is produced on the more
sandy coasts south of New York. A method of fatten-
ing oysters is resorted to here and there—they keep
them in cellars and set them up in sand, frequently
sprinkling with salt water. There was formerly a law
prohibiting oyster-fishery during the months of May,
June, July, and August, regarded as the spawning
season, when the eggs appear, small, thin scales, deposited on stones or on the shells of the older oysters.
During the war this restriction was not observed.
Quite apart from any regulation in the interest of the
oyster banks, oysters during the hot season have a
worse taste, are more slimy, and decay so rapidly that
any taken then must be largely lost.

Oysters are eaten raw, broiled on coals, baked with
fat and in other ways; they are also dried, pickled,
boiled in vinegar, and so preserved and transported.
The American edible oyster is in form quite unlike the
oval-shaped European, being oblong and almost
tongue-shaped. In America one finds shells from eight
to ten inches and more in length, and from three to
four inches wide tapering somewhat towards the hinge,
generally straight, but often a trifle curved; the exterior of the shell, which is of a layer formation, is

rougher than the European. It happens not seldom
that one oyster makes several mouthfuls. At times
incomplete pearls are found in the shells. In certain
regions the shell now and then has a diseased appearance, whitish, half-transparent, and glassy, but such
oysters are eaten in quantities and without injury. Indeed, people of a sickly, weak habit of body find that
fresh oysters are good for them, and here as well as in
Europe Tulpius's ✚ oyster-cure is often prescribed. In
York they burn for lime the shells of oysters, clams,
and other muscles, because there is no limestone in that
region. Lime prepared in this way makes an especially
good white-wash, but for building it has not the best
lasting qualities.

Oysters, Clams (*Venus mercenaria L.*), and **Pissers**
(*Myae species*)* are the most usual shell-fish brought
to market in this region. In the country the range of
choice is wider, and a sort of cockle [Jakobsmuschel]
is there eaten. Of the Buccina a rather large and a
very small variety are relished by a few fastidious
palates. Even the **King-crab** (*monoculus Polyphemus
L.*)† is not despised by some of the inhabitants.

---

* Probably *Mya arenaria L.*—They live on the beach and
are betrayed by a round opening in the sand. If slightly
pressed they spurt with considerable energy a clear stream of
water. Their flesh is coarse and tough, but makes a strong,
nutritious broth.

† These, from their shape, are commonly called Horseshoe-
crabs, and are found on this coast only in the summer months.
Often left on the beach by the tide, they are sought after
greedily by hogs, which thrive on them. As a matter of fact
they belong among the larger insects. Some of them, including the tail, are three feet and more in length. They live
several days out of the water.

Of the crayfish order, these waters furnish for the kitchen only the **Lobster,** (*Cancer Gammarus L.*), and a Crab. Before the war lobsters were numerous, but for some years have been seldom seen. The fishermen's explanation was that the lobster **+** was disturbed by the many ships' anchors and frightened by the cannon fire. How much ground there was for this theory I will not attempt to say, but it is true that since the war lobsters have this year shown themselves for the first time in the Sound.*

We were compelled to spend a few hours of the night at Staten Island, in order to catch the flood tide, for light winds had brought us on so slowly that the ebb from Newark Bay was already against us. The tide coming in by Sandy Hook finds several channels of varying length and breadth in which to distribute itself; in consequence the rise and fall take place at different times in the East River, the Hudson, and Newark Bay, although each of these is filled and emptied through the same channel.

The distance between York Island and Staten Island is scarcely more than nine English miles. Staten Island and the west end of Long Island are separated by a channel only three miles wide at a point called the **Narrows,** which is the chief entrance for ships coming to York. The channel between the island and East Jersey is of varying width, but navigable only for smaller craft. Staten Island is sixteen miles long and

---

* Elsewhere they change their habitat with the season; in Sweden they are found at midsummer (*um Johannis*) six fathom deep, in July at a depth of from eight to ten fathoms, and later in the autumn at a depth of fourteen or fifteen fathoms.

from eight to eleven miles wide; the northern part is
hilly and stony, the land becoming flat and sandy towards the south, similar in character to that portion of
Long Island lying opposite. Staten Island forms a
county of the province of New York, called **Richmond,**
which is the name of the village in the midst of the
island. Free entrance into the harbor of New York
depends upon the possession of this island, since the
harbor may be completely covered by works placed on
the steep hills near the Narrows. Further than this,
Staten Island is to be distinguished in nothing from the
neighboring country. In the morning at two o'clock
we arrived at **Elizabethtown Point** in **Jersey,** a prom-
ontory where vessels coming from York tie up. The
whole region is low, salt-marsh land exposed to the in-
flow of sea water. In summer such districts grow
somewhat more dry, and in addition the effect of broad,
deep ditches is considerable. In the dry season these
salt-marshes go by the name of salt-meadows, but
produce only a short hay, coarse and stiff, for the
most part rush, the usual meadow grasses not growing
on such lands. Horses do not like this hay, and the
milk of cows eating it rapidly sours. There is, however, one variety of salt-meadow grass, to wit *Juncus
bulbosus L.*, known as **Blackgrass** and the best forage
for cattle. This is seldom sown, although the use of it
would make the handling of such tracts very profitable.

Surrounded by millions of **Musquetoes,** (*Culex
pipiens L.*), we were obliged to spend the time until
daybreak on the deck of the little vessel. These marshy
coasts are the favorite sojourning places of musquetoes,
more than usually numerous this year as a result of
moist and rainy weather, and grown to an unusual

2

size. Whoever has made the acquaintance of these
small enemies of the nights' rest will know that the
buzzing of a few of them is sufficient to banish sleep
for hours. I had covered myself with a cloak and a
thick sail, and the night being extremely warm I suffered as in a perfect sweat-bath, but the musquetoes
found their way through. The complete stillness of
the night gave them liberty to swarm about at will, for
in windy weather they do not appear, and when high,
cold winds set in from the northwest such regions as
these are for a time swept of musquetoes, either be-
numbed by the cold or carried out to sea.

After daybreak we were taken to the house of the
man who owns the ferry, the only ferry thereabouts, a
few hundred yards from the landing place but not beyond the territory of the musquetoes. Before the door
stood a great vat, in which a wet-wood fire was kindled ;
the musquetoes were kept off by the smoke in which
the people of the place were making themselves comfortable. The owner of the ferry was a Doctor, no less,
and admitted with the greatest candor that he had
chosen such an infernal situation solely with the praiseworthy design of making, that is gaining, money.

At this place I made the acquaintance of an American Captain. The day before, on his way to New York,
he had been arrested at Staten Island by a young
British officer, roughly handled and sent back because
he had no pass to show from the Governor of New
York. He was telling his story to the company in the
smoke, which had by degrees become more numerous,
and there was anger and vengeance in his words and
gestures. I found myself in a similar position, the
other way about ; I was now in the jurisdiction of the

United States without permit from them. So I turned
to this irritated American, and without circumlocution
told him how I had come from the English army, like
him had no pass from one side or the other, intended
to travel through the country, hoped I should meet with
no difficulties, and so forth. The answer which I was
looking for followed. The Captain seized with pleasure the opportunity which I offered him to show himself magnanimous. He volunteered to take me to his
Excellency Mr. Livingstone, the Governor of New
Jersey, and went with me to his country-seat in the
neighborhood of Elizabethtown. However, we had
not the pleasure of finding the Governor at home, which
I the more regretted because my companion had taken
trouble on the way to give me a high opinion of the
man with the noble Roman nose (for that was the
chief ground of his argument). Instead, I was taken
before certain other officers and furnished with a letter
of recommendation to a member of the Congress, near
Princetown. Meanwhile, I regarded this unexpectedly
polite behavior as a good omen, causing me to hope for
pleasant treatment farther on, and in this I was not
deceived.

Elizabethtown is a market town of middling size
which to be sure has no particularly large trade, but on
account of the passing between Philadelphia and York
many strangers are to be seen in the place. Opportunity was afforded us here of seeing a female opassum with four young, which had recently been caught
in the neighborhood. It is remarkable that these animals are found no farther north than this, and never
on the east shore of the Hudson. Only in recent years
have they been seen this side the Delaware in Jersey;

they crossed that stream on the ice, it is probable, for they are said not to swim. In a similar manner these animals, intended originally for the warmer provinces only, might find their way still farther north, where it is true they would miss even more their favorite food, the fruit of the Persimon (*Diospyros virginiana L.*). It is commonly believed in America that the false bag of the female is a matrix as well, although there is ample proof to the contrary. It is the fact, however, that the young are produced very small and unformed, and sustain themselves in the bag through the nipples there found. It is claimed that the young of the opassum have been observed as small as a large bean.*

When the greatest heat of the day was over, we set out towards evening on the road to Brunswick. Five miles from Elizabethtown we came to **Bridgetown**, a neat little place on the **Rariton** river, where I visited the father of one of my American friends. He, as one of the King's party, had been obliged to leave his former residence in Jersey and come to Bridgetown because he expected and found more quiet in a place inhabited chiefly by Quakers, who seek to do good to every man or at the least make no use of opportunities to do evil. The Rariton at Bridgetown is still an inconsiderable stream, but large enough to float unladen vessels, built in the neighborhood, of ten to thirty tons. The shipwrights do not restrict themselves to the banks of the stream but set up the framework before their dwellings, perhaps a mile or two from the river, and bring the finished skeleton to the waterside

---

* This fact among others was stated to me by Mr. Forster, a skilful anatomist and surgeon in the English army.

on rollers, oxen hitched before, which animals are much used in this region for draught. We passed on through a very pleasant country of low hills, and already began to encounter the red soil of Jersey, known generally by that name in America. On the surface this appears to be a weathered ferruginous clayey-slate * showing certain veins. Farm and manor-houses were numerous on the road, in appearance kept in good order, and bearing evidences of attention and industry, more so indeed than we had been accustomed to see about York and on Long Island. Mr. Morgan who formerly spent much time, more to the north, as a land surveyor assured us that he had often seen dogs after baiting hedgehogs stuck through, muzzle and ears, with the quills of those beasts, and that the hedgehog it is believed has the faculty of looseing its quills in emergencies, but that it is not true, as asserted, that the beast can shoot quills forth at distant objects. On account of their exceeding smoothness and the force drawing together the wounded parts both in men and animals, the hedgehog quills, it has been observed, find deep lodgment in the cellular tissue, and often must be taken out with the knife.

From **Bridgetown** to **Brunswick** it is 16 miles over a gentle succession of pleasant valleys and hills. Everywhere a rather vivid green adorns the soil, which in this region for the most part of the year presents a

---

* Vid. Kalm. *Reise.* P't 2, p. 367 who calls this soil red limestone very much resembling that found in Sweden at Kinnekulle and probably *marmor stratarium* of Linnaeus. But this Jersey soil does not effervesce under acids, and does not contain the *petrificata copiosissima* of Linnaeus' description; and besides the surface is not harder than the subsoil.

dark red appearance. But this is hardly a distinguishing mark of Jersey, for it is pretty generally observed, even in other countries, that grass on red soils has a particularly green color.

Brunswick. Here for the first time we underwent a general questioning—on the part of the landlord at the Queen. There are no people in the world of more curiosity than the inn-keepers throughout the greater part of America. It is told of Dr. **Franklin** (but it may have been anyone else) ✚ how on a journey from Boston to Philadelphia, he became so tired of the insidious tavern-catechism, that on arriving at an inn he had the whole family assembled and made it clear to them once for all what his name was, where he lived, what he did for a living, where he was going, and then asked that no further queries be put. At the inn in Brunswick nothing was to be had until it was known where we came from and whither we were bound; I asked for a room and the woman of the house bade me in a most indifferent manner to be patient; she was unwilling for us to escape too soon from the curiosity of her husband, who in the meantime was looking up slippers of every calibre, kept for the traveller's convenience.

Brunswick is pleasantly and advantageously situated. The Rariton even here reaches no great breadth, probably ten to fifteen feet; but with the help of the tide, which ascends two miles above the town, tolerably large vessels come up, and in former years the place has exported directly to the West Indies flour, bread, Indian corn, timber, and the like. Brunswick therefore has great hopes of renewing its trade, since at one time the town carried on more business than **Perth-Amboy,**

which is really the port and capital of East Jersey, lying
ten miles farther down at the mouth of the Rariton, a
safe and commodious bay where notwithstanding few
ships put in. Recently when a peace was looked for,
a company of English merchants offered to employ a
considerable capital, sufficient for the purpose, in re-
establishing the trade of Amboy; by reason of untimely
animosities the project was abandoned, and Amboy *
will have, as before, only an insignificant traffic with
foreign ports. New York on the one side and Philadelphia on the other long since drew to themselves the
trade of Jersey, and without great exertions and the
capital assistance of rich merchants, this established
course of trade is not to be altered. The produce of
Jersey is the same as that of both the adjoining provinces, and the Jerseymen find a better market and
longer credit in those two cities than in their own.
Thus, free to choose the best markets, it will not likely
happen that the people will deny themselves. In
Brunswick the royal barracks still stand, for which
there are no soldiers, and an English church remains
for which there is no congregation. The Quaker meeting-house and the market-house, as well as many other
buildings, are in ruins. This section of Jersey, and
especially Princeton, Woodbridge, Newark, Bergen,
Elizabethtown, &c. suffered the most during the war,
from the troops of both parties.

From Brunswick we proceeded down the Rariton
through an incomparable landscape. A still stream,

---

* Latterly the State of Jersey has declared this a free port
and flatters itself that in this way the trade of Amboy will be
the more easily revived, since the neighboring states have
placed heavy taxes on shipping.

fairly broad ; narrow reaches of green bottom-land bordered by gentle hills ; neat country-houses scattered here
and there, the buildings forsaken and half-ruined ; and
as background for the whole, a range of mountains.
Colonel **Steward's** house, on a rising ground by the
road, like so many others in America is thinly built of
wood, but after a tasteful plan. The construction of a
house, if the appearance is pleasing, need not worry
the traveller, since it is the owner who must contrive
how to offset the rude northwester streaming through,
and making cold quarters for winter.

Two miles from Brunswick we again crossed the
Rariton, over a wooden bridge, and after a few miles
down that stream reached **Boundbrook** and **Middlebrook.** The whole region about Brunswick consists
of a red earth, but towards the mountains the soil
changes. At Boundbrook we visited Dr. **Griffith,** a
practicing physician whose skill and upright character
made him free of the general persecution which other
royalists were exposed to.

Beyond **Boundbrook** appears the first of those chains
of rather high mountains which in Jersey lie inwards
from the sea. In the company of Dr. Griffith and a few
other gentlemen we made an excursion towards the
mountain country where formerly Captain Mosengail
and Mr. Rübsaamen had establishments for smelting
copper, the first in America. In this region the stone
is a species of **dense, grey, quarrystone**, very similar
to that used in New York for tombstones. The road to
the old smelting-house is through a wide gap in the
first chain of mountains, the range being made up of
several chains one behind the other. Here, as farther
on in the winding valley, I saw what I took to be sure

marks of powerful dislocations at one time sustained. Stones appeared as if pulled apart and again cemented together. In other places the declivities seemed as it were composed of plates lying one over the other but fast bound together.*

In this narrow valley we were unspeakably oppressed by the heat and the company insisted on returning, earlier than I should have liked. At the same time, in Dr. Griffith's house, the thermometer stood 94° Fahr. in the shade, and I am convinced that in the valley at midday and with no wind we suffered a temperature of at least 120°. We all groaned for refreshment, but there was nothing to be had except brook-water, and water alone did not suffice.

The first chain of mountains in this region is distinguished from those lying behind it and running in

---

* Later, in Philadelphia, I came upon the Abbé Robin's *New Travels in North America*. The Abbé came through Jersey with the army of Count Rochambeau and cast a cursory glance, only in Jersey, at the mountains. ' I was at the trouble,' says he, ' to inspect the summits of the high mountains (not high) of Jersey, and I find that they consist chiefly of granite of several varieties, closely associated; aqua fortis causes no effervescence—Mica is also found in great quantity —If these mountains, which must be reckoned as primitive, owed their origin to a vitreous mass, several thousand years in that state, they would necessarily be homogeneous, but I do not remember having seen here a mixture of various substances brought together in grains of regular figure and differing color. However that may be, these mountains must certainly have undergone a great revolution, for in many places they have been burst apart, and fragments of appreciable size are found at some distance from their first position.' The Abbé had doubtless read shortly before the *Epochs* of Buffon and attempted, but in vain, to discover traces of fire.

the same direction by the name **First Mountain**, extending under this appellation from **Newark**, where the stone is of a sort like granite, as far as **Pluckamin**, about 28 English miles, a country richly supplied with copper. **Van Horn's** mine has more than once been profitably worked. The ore is red (Ziegelerz), flecked with grey, and often contains fibres of pure copper. Duely worked and refined this ore yields, it is claimed, from 60 to 65 lb. the cwt. of the finest copper. The veins run up from the southeast, (i. e. from the coast inwards), to the mountains, and continue there rising and falling, wave-fashion—like most superficial veins; but far on in the mountain the veins suddenly plunge and are lost in water, so that these mines cannot in the future be worked without low stopings. After getting through the grey rock, in which the ore lies, a red stone is encountered which extends to unexplorable depths.

In the year 1772 the smelter near this mine was begun, but on account of various difficulties, lack of a suitable stone for the smelting-furnace and the proper alloy, it was not until 1774 that work could be undertaken with a reasonable hope of success. The owners of the land and of the mine agreed to bear all expense until the business should be self-sustaining at a clear profit; on the other hand, the condition was that the managers, Messrs. Mosengail and Rübsaamen, should take two thirds the income for their trouble in establishing and keeping up the smelter. Later the owners ran short of money and credit, and the work was for some time interrupted, but by a new arrangement was again vigorously prosecuted. Then the need of skilled workmen was felt, the raw copper not being saleable in

America unless first prepared in sheets under the hammer for the use of the coppersmith. In former years it had been necessary for such establishments to send to England either the ore, (of no great value), or the unrefined copper. On this basis the dealer gained very much at the expense of the mine-owner. So rolling machines of a nice construction were brought from England, of a sort which could not be cast and fitted in America. Such an apparatus (two smooth iron rollers working horizontally) made it possible to get out the copper with more convenience and expedition than under the hammer. In a short time nearly four tons of sheet copper were got ready for market, as fine as any ever brought from Europe; and by the use of the roller it was found possible to prepare 2½ tons a week. The first specimens of this Jersey-made sheet-copper were brought to Philadelphia precisely, at the time when the Congress had passed the non-importation act of 1775; and there was so much pleasure taken in this successful and really fine product of the country that without any hesitation a price was offered 6d. in the pound higher than for English sheets, quoted at 3s. 8d. to 4s. Pensylvan. Current. But the war coming on, the work once more came to a stand; the workmen were scattered, and finally the establishment was burnt by American troops, merely to get nails from the ashes. The mine has since gone to ruin; we made a search for ore in the rubbish, but could find only a few insignificant pieces.

On the same mountain, near **Pluckamin**, other mine-prospectors at one time sunk a shaft, and followed up a good vein of grey copper ore. But water swamped the work, which was given over because there was no inclination to install hydraulic machinery.

About 26 years ago another copper mine was opened near Brunswick, in a hill consisting of the red soil (red-shell) mentioned above, which from the color, it was believed, must certainly be copper-bearing. A vein located by the wand (ausgehender Gang) nearly four inches wide was a sufficient guaranty, but it was found that it fell away almost perpendicularly. Solid copper was taken out in quantity, lying in a brown mould containing copper as well. However, it was a low hill and the Rariton was too near; the shaft filled with water and could not be kept clear by a small hydraulic apparatus. The owners became discouraged and gave up the works, after taking out probably two tons, mostly solid copper, at an outlay of more than 12,000 Pd. Current.

From Boundbrook we came, by way of a beautiful plain, hard by the mountain where Washington's army camped in 1779; and further through an extremely well-cultivated region along the **Millstone River** which falls into the Rariton but, a narrow stream, is not navigable. These waters contain a multitude of fish, pike, gold-fish, and suckers.* Formerly shad also, in numberless schools, came high up this river; but dams, of which many have been built in recent years, keep back the shad and contribute appreciably to the provisioning of the inhabitants along the banks. In the Rariton, however, a law compels millers to leave a 40-yd. passage way over dams during the running of the

---

* Suckers are found also in the Delaware; I have seen none about York. They belong to the species carp. Forster ✚ has given the first exact description of them, from a specimen caught in Hudson's bay, under the name *cyprinus catostomus*. See *Beyträge zur Länder und Völkerkunde*, III, 270.

shad. These fish (*Clupea Alosa L.*) are found in millions every spring in all the rivers north from Chesapeake Bay and the Delaware, ascending high enough to be certain of depositing their eggs in fresh water. In the Hudson they follow the main channel and tributaries for a distance of 150 miles from the coast. They come, if the weather is mild, early in April; cold weather often holds them back until later; but by the end of April or the beginning of May, the mouths of all the rivers are generally full of them. At this season fishermen line the riverbanks, cast their seines with the flush tide, and at times catch during a running several hundred pounds' worth. The many thousands taken (in all the rivers, inlets, and creeks) amount to a very small part of the host, which apparently begins to be diminished only when, far inland, the danger from nets cannot so easily be escaped in the narrower and shallower streams. That they are all caught is not to be believed, although few are seen descending, and those thin and often dead. They are, at their first coming, pretty fat and fullbodied, and it is claimed that as they ascend the better they grow to the taste. They are sought after when the season is young, and the first to appear are costly morsels, but as they become more frequent are seen no longer at fastidious tables. They are also salted * and with careful handling resemble

---

* Salted shad are exported to the West Indies as rations for the negroes, but are not greatly in demand there on account of the careless preparation. Herring appear on the coast somewhat later than shad; they are like the European herring but come neither in as great numbers as shad nor do they ascend the streams so far; they are caught and handled in the same manner as shad.

the herring in taste ; and again, only superficially salted,
they are split and air-dried or smoked and so served at
respectable tea-tables.

Red soil and loam continued until we had passed the
Millstone River, by a bridge not far from **Black-horse**,
where the sandy loam began again such as is found
about York. In the tavern at **Black-horse** we found
quarters for the night, on a little slope near the river
not far from a mill and several other houses as little
worthy of remark. Our landlord was loquacious and
extremely occupied, and in truth a man could be no
otherwise who did as much. He told us, without any
boasting, how many different occupations he united in
his small person—' I am a weaver, a shoemaker, farrier,
wheelwright, farmer, gardener, and **when it can't be
helped**, a soldier. I bake my bread, brew my beer, kill
my pigs ; I grind my axe and knives ; I built those stalls
and that shed there ; I am barber, leech, and doctor.'
(*Tria juncta in uno,* as everywhere in Germany.) The
man was everything, at no expense for license, and
could do anything, as indeed the countryman in
America generally can, himself supplying his own
wants in great part or wholly. From this man's house
we set out the following morning along the sandy banks
of the Millstone River and came, by a stone bridge, to
Rocky Hill which was not idly named. A few houses
stand upon and around the hill. The landscape, after
we got out of the red soil, was much less green and
agreeable, the woods rougher and the bottom lands
more broken, more like the soil of York and southern
Long Island, thin and unfruitful, that is. But there
met us everywhere a pleasant balsam odor, from the
great profusion of pennyroyal (*Cunila pulegioides L.*)

which grew in the dryest places along the road, and on these warm days, was the more perceptible.

It was surprising, just at midsummer, to find everywhere in the woods leaves red or deadened, particularly on the oaks. To be sure, towards the first of the month (July) there had been a hoar-frost, seen on little standing ponds and moist spots, on the mountain near Middlebrook and elsewhere.* But this cold could not so easily kill oak leaves, certainly not particular oak leaves. Others, with as little probability gave thunderstorms and lightning as the reason; but the best explanation was that the leaves had been killed by a sort of grasshopper which comes every seventeen years and just this year had been conducting operations.

Rocky Hill once had the hope of being one of the richest and most productive hills in America. Ignorant of its value a countryman found a fragment of grey copper-ore, of nearly 100 lb. weight. This occurrence inspired several people, who had informed themselves of the worth of the copper discovered, to set about establishing works in the liveliest spirit of enterprise. The ground was leased, the mine to be opened was divided into eight shares, miners were brought from England, and everything necessary was undertaken with enthusiasm. When the first shaft was sunk they came upon a rich stock-work of similar ore, but not quite so pure. By this time the shares were selling at 1500 Pd. Current. Through the manager's ignorance, or perhaps with a set purpose to damage the owners, the ore brought up was packed in barrels, and in less than four

---

* At the same time we had several very cold days in York, and one morning the thermometer sank to 42° Fahr.

months 1100 barrels were filled with what was denominated saleable ore.   This was sent to England at a
dead expense of at least 1000 Pd. Sterling.   The ore
was tested and appraised in London and the price fixed,
considering its quality as crude ore, was not sufficient
to pay the freight.   The undertakers were alarmed at
this unwelcome news and the works were given over
at a great loss.   Several of the workmen offered, at
their own cost, to take out the ore still on the holdings
and that in the shaft, (easily done) wash it, stamp it,
and send it to England.   The venture proved an excellent one, but none the less this happier outcome
aroused no further interest among the speculative, and
the establishment was closed.

This is no doubt the most suitable place to insert the
remaining mineralogical observations which I assembled in regard to Jersey and several other parts adjacent.   It was not my intention to give much time to
the various mines and foundries of this province,
richly supplied with them, and until now worked with
especial industry.   I had resolved to visit the more distant mountain country of Pensylvania and Virginia,
and since the summer was waning I could waste no
time.

Almost every hill and mountain of New Jersey contains ore of some sort, at any rate ore has been found
in greater quantity in this province, as a consequence
of greater effort.   A line drawn from about the mouth
of the Rariton to the lower falls of the Delaware marks
the south-eastern limit of the ore-bearing region, beyond which no further traces of ore have been observed
by me.   Thence northwesterly a series of hills and
mountains make up the rest of the province, which lies

east of the Hudson and west of the Delaware. This advantageous proximity to both rivers, with their tributaries, adds no little to the convenient working of the mines and transportation of the product.

One of the largest and most famous copper mines in all North America was until recently that of the **Schuyler** family, on **Second River** in Bergen county. The metal was found associated with a good deal of sulphur and was therefore easily fusible. For forty years and more these works were carried on to great advantage, and from their productive yield a very numerous family became well established, highly regarded, and honored. The ore was of the grey variety, yielding with good management 70-80 lb., and in one of the best years as much as 90 lb. in the hundred weight. About twenty years ago a fire-engine * was installed to control the water. This had to be brought from England, and when set up in running order had cost 10,000 Pd. Current, but a few years later was itself destroyed by fire. A second engine met the same fate, the owners were somewhat thrown back by these misfortunes, and the mine, overrun with water, could no longer be worked. Mr. **Hornblower,** from county Cornwall in England, (who was the manager of the mine), after these two mishaps made a contract with the owners some twelve years ago by which he paid down so much of the clear income and received permission to knock out the holdings, which yielded him from 7 to 15 tons pure copper annually, sold in England at 70-80 Pd. sterling the ton. Proof of how carelessly the ore had been worked. The war put a stop even to these operations. When

---

* Pumps set in motion by the steam from boiling water.

3

the mine was first given up to the water, the abandoned vein was six foot wide.

On the banks of the Delaware, about twenty miles up from Trenton, a copper-bearing slate stratum comes to the surface. The slate runs in beds of varying width and is flecked with grey copper ore. A friend, whom I must thank for these items, found that this ore merely at the surface contained 36 lb. copper in the hundred-weight. By the accounts of people resident there, it appears that similar spots are found higher up the river.

The following list of several other noteworthy copper and iron mines was given me at New York in May 1783:

"**Suckasunny Mine**; **Iron**; in a hill on the east side "of **Suckasunny Plains**, in Morris county, 13 miles "from Morristown. The veins, like all in that region, "run almost northeast to southwest, and are from six "to twelve foot wide. Many thousand tons of bar iron "have been made from this ore at sundry works. The "ore is especially valued because of its easy flux and "rich content.

"**Hibernia** or **Horsepond Mine**; **Iron**; 12 miles "north of Morristown, in a high hill, a continuous "vein which has been opened from the bottom to the "top of the hill, and found to be from three to eleven "foot wide. Only 600 paces off is the furnace attached "to this mine, called **Hibernia Furnace**. The sow of "this ore is good; the iron excellent; easily workable "in the furnace.

"**Ogden's Mine**, 16 miles northeast of Morristown. "The vein is only from one to five foot wide. Bar iron "from this ore worked in the furnace is better than

" any other bar of the region. However, the mine does
" not advance so rapidly as the two mentioned above.

" **Yale's Mine,** 3 miles northeast of the Suckasunny,
" probably the continuation of that vein, 3-8 ft. wide.
" The ore fluxes well and, like the Suckasunny, is
" highly valued.

" **Ogden's Newfoundland Mine,** 25 miles north of
" Morristown, 7-20 ft. wide, also produces good iron.

" **Pompton Bog,** 20 miles northeast of Morristown
" A bog-ore lying perhaps 12 inches deep and dug out
" of the water. Under the ore there is a ferruginous
" sand. The surface layer having been removed, in
" about 20 years a new layer is formed, a precipitate
" from the water quite as good if not better than the
" first.

" **James Young's** copper mine, near **Musknecuneck**
" in the county of Sussex.

" **Deacon Ogden's** copper mine, near to the head-
" spring of the Wall-Kill, in the same county.

" **Tennyke's** copper mine, in the county of Somerset.

" **Ritschall's** copper mine in the county of Somerset.

" The two last are situated on the southeast side of
" **First Mountain,** three miles beyond Boundbrook
" and Quibbletown, on the same ridge (a little to the
" north) as Pluckamin, Bluehill, and Van Horn's mine,
" which all yield copper of about the same quality and
" temper, lying very nearly at the same depth. Hence
" it is conjectured, and not without reason, that this
" whole ridge, 12 miles and more in length, is traversed
" by one and the same vein of copper. The ore occurs
" for the most part in veins, generally superficial, in-
" termixed with loose strata of earth and stone and
" easily excavated. Notwithstanding, no vein has been

" discovered workable to advantage, with the price of
" labor customary now in Jersey and the uncertain sale
" of the ore in the English markets. Every copper vein
" in New Jersey has the same surface direction—from
" northeast to southwest; and each plunges in very
" nearly the same manner, that is to say, making an
" obtuse angle towards the east. The veins grow
" broader at a depth, and the copper better. It is still
" unknown how far to the southeast the veins underlie
" the surface, for although several mines have been
" worked for 60 years, there is no instance of a vein
" having been exhausted.

In the county of **Morris** alone there are a great number of iron mines, high furnaces, bloomeries, and forges.
Most of these were the property of a private English
company which long ago had already spent a great sum
on them. At such a distance, and under the super-
vision of managers, these works as early as 1773 had
consumed a capital of 120,000 Pd. sterling and nevertheless did not pay interest. A certain Johann Jakob
Faesch, ✝ from Germany, was formerly one of the
managers of this company's works, but relinquished
the business and set up his own furnace, equipped with
a particularly advantageous mechanism.

The business of the mines and foundries, in New
Jersey as well as throughout America, cannot be said
to be on as firm a basis as in most parts of Europe, because nobody is concerned about forest preservation,
and without an uninterrupted supply of fuel and timber
many works must go to ruin, as indeed has already
been the case here and there. Not the least economy
is observed with regard to forests. The owners of
furnaces and foundries possess for the most part great

tracts of appurtenant woods, which are cut off, however, without any system or order. The bulk of the
inhabitants sell wood only in so far as to bring the
land they own into cultivation, reserving a certain acreage of forest necessary for domestic consumption. The
Union, a high furnace in Jersey, exhausted a forest of
nearly 20,000 acres in about twelve to fifteen years, and
the works had to be abandoned for lack of wood. This
cut-over land was to be sure divided into farms and
sold, but was of trifling value merely because the wood
was gone. If it does not fortunately happen that rich
coal mines are discovered, enabling such works to be
carried on, as in England, with coal, it will go ill with
many of them later on. In and around this mountain
country, the forest trees are generally leaf-bearing, oak
for the most part, and, what is to the purpose, this tree
does not seem of a very rapid growth in America.

Because at the beginning in the nearer, and latterly
in the farther regions of America, wood has been everywhere in the way of the new planter, people have
grown accustomed to regard forests anywhere as the
most troublesome of growths ; for if crops were to be
seeded it was a necessity to cut down the trees and
grub the roots,—a great labor, and if the forests could
only be blown away, then certainly few trees would be
there to give more trouble. A young American going
to Europe happened to land on the west coast of Ireland, where in certain parts not a bush is to be seen for
many miles. He exclaimed in astonishment, ' What a
wonderful country ! What a lucky people, with no
woods to plague them.' ' We are plagued,' they answered him, ' precisely because we have none, and we
are planting as fast as we can.'

In America there is no sovereign right over forests and game, no forest service. Whoever holds new land, in whatever way, controls it as his exclusive possession, with everything on it, above it, and under it. It will not easily come about therefore that, as a strict statutory matter, farmers and landowners will be taught how to manage their forests so as to leave for their grandchildren a bit of wood over which to hang the tea-kettle. Experience and necessity must here take the place of magisterial provision. So far there is indeed no lack of wood, except in particular localities or for particular purposes. Only in towns is the price high, and for the reason that the charge for cutting and hauling is four or five times the value of the wood on the stump.

Since I am in the mining region, I shall ask permission to bring together a few additional mineralogical items. On the Hudson, in many places, there are found surface indications of ore, about which in its weathered state nothing certain can be determined, for the heat test would not be trustworthy in the case of minerals decomposed by the action of sun, rain, and frost. At **Haverstraw**, province of New York, it is claimed that traces of tin have been discovered, near the former country-seat of Mr. **Noyelle.** Twenty odd miles from New York, at **Phillips' Manor**, silver was enthusiastically worked at in the years 1772-73. Solid silver was found scattered in fluorspar. An amalgam-mill was set up, which got out a regulum of silver, some twelve ounces, worth to the operators 1500 Pd. York Current—and with that, digging and amalgamating came to an end. The Schuyler family, already mentioned, long ago worked a silver mine in Jersey, and very profitably. The discoverer is said to have been a negro. The mine lasted only a short time, and I have been able to get no further information regarding it. I have been told that dollars were struck from the metal, but I have seen no specimens of them. There have been traces of precious metals found still farther north. Forty and more years ago, near Boston, there was a silver mine, but worked with little profit, nobody understanding the business, it is supposed. Judging by several circumstances the ore was a silver-bearing lead ore. At **Middletown** in Connecticut lead ore was once mined, found associated with a yellow copper ore, and yielding three to four ounces of silver in the hundred-weight. Although this content was determined by a goldsmith in New York, who tested specimens, it appears that the trick of separating the metal of the ore was not sufficiently familiar, and this work also came to a stand. At the beginning of the late war the Connecticut Assembly took up this mine again, for the sake of the lead, but could neither manage the refining properly nor make enough bullets to shoot every Englishman, (a hankering after any little silver left was also in vain), and for a second time the business was abandoned.

From these few items it will be clear enough already that North America was by no means forgotten of nature in the matter of mineral wealth. Even now, when the shell of this new world has been explored in the most superficial way, in a few places only and there, for the most part, by chance, the most useful metals have been found in quantity, and there are at least traces of the precious metals. Several important reasons may be given why mining has not been generally more successful.

In former times the English government sought to hinder as much as possible all digging after gold, silver, and other metals, so that the working hands of a country still young might not be withdrawn from agriculture, the one true source of the peopling of a country, of its trade, and of its wealth. The export of unwrought as well as of wrought copper from England to America was always a considerable article of trade, and in discouraging American mines it was a subsidiary purpose of the government to bolster that trade. There were and still are few capitalists in the country rich enough to furnish on speculation great outlays of cash in the slow and sure establishment of works. This side the mountains, (beyond them conditions are still less known), sundry minerals have been found, particularly silver and copper, but sporadic and so an allurement and at the same time a discouragement.— There was a lack of capable miners, for among the English such are found only in Wales and Cornwall. Vagrant Germans were employed, at times efficient and again only pretenders; who, as the case was, failed for lack of support or aroused false hopes. Finally, the greatest difficulty lay in the scarcity of laborers, and the high wages in a country where the people, it must be said, are not the most industrious; moderate outlay therefore seldom left the undertakers a profit. From these several reasons taken together, it has happened that no establishments, besides iron mines and furnaces, have kept active. The more general use of that metal, and the greater ease in handling the raw material, made sales and profits surer, notwithstanding the fact that the English government admitted crude American iron duty-free, in exchange for which was taken wrought iron.

Princetown. From Rocky Hill, where I broke the thread of the narrative, the road lay for some distance over a sandy-loam, and through long reaches of woods. The red soil appeared again only in the neighborhood of Princetown, 8 miles this side. The whole way I missed the smilax, which about New York takes possession of all open land.* **Princetown** is a little country-town of only one considerable street in which few houses stand, but its elevated site makes the place especially agreeable, the view from it being splendid, out over the lower country as far as the **Neversinks** and other parts of the coast. There could, I thought, be no finer, airier, and pleasanter place for the seat of the Jersey Muses— for in 1746 under Governor Belcher, an academy was established in this province, and given the privilege of bestowing the same degrees as Oxford and Cambridge. The College, a not uncomely building, stands in the middle of the town, but is at this time in bad condition. The British troops, in the winter of 1776, used it for stalls and barracks, and left a Presbyterian church near by in a state equally as bad. At the present time only 50-60 young students are in residence, partly within, partly without the College; and only *humaniora* and philosophy are taught. Among the professors is Dr. Witherspoon, a Scottish clergyman, widely known not only for his learning but for the zeal

---

* About York several sorts of smilax grow with extraordinary vigor. These are so lasting and pliant, bear cutting so well, and grow together in such an impenetrable shrubbery that certainly nothing better could be found for live hedges around fields. They keep their leaves late into the fall, and would be an ornament as well. The only objection is they spread too fast.

with which he championed the cause of the Americans.
Recently Princetown had the honor of being for a while
the place of assembly of the American Congress——
after a handful of indelicate soldiers, demanding such
a trifle as back pay for five or six years, had frightened
the Congress from Philadelphia.

The unbearable heat prevailing kept us from going
forward except slowly, and was the reason why we
spent several days in coming from New York to this
place.   Within a short space two men have died
suddenly at Princetown, seeking refreshment in cool
drinks when overheated.   A **diligence,** known as the
Flying Machine ✚ makes daily trips between Philadelphia and New York, covering the distance of 90 miles
in one day even in the hottest weather, but at the expense of the horses, only three times changed on the
journey.   Thus, the last trip two horses died in harness
and four others were jaded. These flying machines are
in reality only large wooden carts with tops, light to be
sure but neither convenient nor of neat appearance.
They carry from ten to twelve passengers with luggage, are drawn by four horses only, and go very fast.
The charge for this journey is 5-6 Spanish dollars the
passenger.   Besides **flying machines** there are in the
country other excursion-machines, neither coach nor
cart, run for the behoof of visiting families ; these hold
commonly six to eight persons and are probably much
like the sort of vehicle which in old prints is represented as conveying Dr. Luther to Worms.   In the
towns, however, there is no lack of fine carriages,
phaetons, and chairs (a two-wheeled cart or chaise) ;
throughout America almost every house is supplied
with a chaise, in which the farmer takes his broken
plow to the smith or his calves to market.

I had the pleasure of meeting two members of the
Congress, agreeable and worthy men, and congratulated myself especially upon taking dinner in the company of General Lincoln. I found in him a man of
great intelligence and open-mindedness, although, since
the surrender of Charleston, his military talents seem
less brilliant to the more unreasonable among his
countrymen. He possesses a considerable landed property in New England whither he returns to tranquillity
and the brewing of excellent beer, now that he has
resigned his place as War Secretary, which office he
administered with approbation.*

Wheat in America suffers almost every year from
the mildew. It is remarked that usually the disease
attacks the wheat between the 1st and the 10th of July.
On that ground General Lincoln proposed a method of
prevention. Granted that at the season mentioned
wheat is at a stage of growth the most favorable to the
origin and spread of the mildew, it follows plausibly
that the disease might be kept off if the wheat could
be more quickly carried through that stage of its
growth, (when it is nearly mature), or on the other
hand if the period of maturity could be retarded. In
the middle and southern colonies this method could be
put into effect by procuring seed-wheat from the more
northern provinces, where the characteristic of the seed
is to make wheat of an earlier maturity, the several
stages of growth being rapidly passed through ; and
consequently, sown in a warmer climate there would
be formed a stronger grain, to defy the mildew at a

---

* He has lately assumed command again—of the New England troops against the rebels of that country, and has made
an end of the disorders.

time when the indigenous wheat begins to be most susceptible to the disease. Several experiments of this sort have already been attended with good success. With the maize-crop this method would not be of such advantage, for the reason that seed from the more northern regions developes more rapidly indeed, but produces smaller and lighter grain.

This summer the wheat harvest in Jersey turned out very moderately. There had been too little rain in the fall, and the winter was too mild and open. The farmer is well pleased, therefore, if his winter wheat, towards the end of December or in January, is covered with snow and thus protected against rain and frost, by which (when snow fails) the tender, exposed sprouts are killed or are pushed out of the freezing ground. Here as in the other middle provinces almost no spring wheat is sown, but that is not the case more to the south and more to the north, as for example in Carolina and in Massachusetts. Winter grain does not thrive in the southern provinces, because of the warmth of the autumn, the mildness of the winter, and the lack of snow, which very seldom falls; the young sprouts therefore grow faster, and a frosty winter night often kills off entirely the soft, exposed seed. What with extreme cold and early winters, spring wheat also does better in the colder provinces.* It is the custom here to call a bushel of wheat 60 pd. English weight; for each pound more or less, a penny, Pensylvan. Current, is added or subtracted in the price. The average price

---

* People here and there on Long Island have begun to sow spring wheat, since winter wheat has often failed on account of the uneven winter temperature.

is at present 5-6 shillings current, i. e., about three shillings sterling. About one bushel is seeded to the acre (43,600 English feet in the square), and people expect 10-12 for one on the poorer lands, 15-18 for one on better lands. In Jersey as in the other middle colonies wheat is a considerable article of trade.

In New England the common barberry is in evil repute. There is laid to its charge that its proximity is injurious to the growth of wheat and other field-crops. Whether it is a positive or a negative injury, that is, whether it works damage actively, corrupting the atmosphere, or merely exhausts the better juices of the soil, nobody has been able or willing to determine. However, a strict law has been passed against the poor barberry, making the inhabitants responsible, with no further judicial process, for the carrying out of the death sentence imposed upon both varieties of this shrub, (elsewhere harmless) whenever it makes its appearance—if any man extends protection to the shrub his neighbor has the right to enter and destroy, and can bring action against the slothful or unbelieving condoner for damage and trouble incurred. But the New Englanders are known for other strange beliefs and practices as well, and it was among them that witch trials, at the beginning of the century, were so grimly prosecuted.

It is said that petroleum is found in or on the **Millstone River**, not far from Princetown. Petroleum occurs in many other parts of America, especially, I am told, in and about the **Oneida Lakes.**

By General Lincoln's account a piece of solid copper weighing 2078 pounds was found some years ago on the summit of a mountain near **Middlebrook,** in the

sand under the roots of a tree. A copper mine near
Brunswick yielded ore containing silver, but not enough
to warrant the expense of separation. The same thing
was told me by Mr. Peters, ✚ (a member of the Congress) in regard to a lead mine in Pensylvania, a share
in which he owns.

In the evening, not without regret, we took leave of
these agreeable Congressmen, so as to reach **Trenton**
that night, ten miles from **Princeton.** The road lay
through a country at intervals well-cultivated. The
wheat harvest was over almost everywhere. Maize we
found nowhere in Jersey so advanced as that we had
left on Long Island and about York. Is it perhaps true
that the red soil of this region does not produce corn
so well? Six miles from Princeton we came to **Maiden-
head,** a hamlet of five or six houses. There are in
America a number of such places called **towns,** where
one must look for the houses, either not built or scattered a good distance apart. That is to say, certain districts are set off as **Townships,** (market or town districts), the residents of which live apart on their farms,
a particular spot being called the **town,** where the
church and the tavern stand and the smiths have their
shops—because in one or the other of these community
buildings the neighbors are accustomed to meet. And
when later professional men, shop-keepers, and other
people who are not farmers come to settle, their dwellings group themselves about the church and the shops.

The thermometer at high-lying **Princeton,** in a large,
airy room stood at 91° Fahr., and even late in the evening the weather was extraordinarily close. After sunset
we arrived at **Trenton,** a name familiar enough from
the history of the late war. This is a not inconsiderable

place, standing on uneven ground, through which flows a brook, crossed by a stone bridge. In view of the fact that the town is perhaps no more than fifty years old, Trenton contains very many buildings and among them several of good appearance. The landlord here permitted us to go to bed unquestioned being not yet done with several other guests arrived shortly before, and we not disposed to wait for him. The taverns on the way were in other respects very good, all of them clean, well-supplied, and well-served.

A mile from **Trenton** brought us to the banks of the Delaware, over which the passenger is set, very cheaply, in a flat, roomy ferry-boat. A large brick house and several other houses, all in ruins, stand here as a token of the war. A little above the ferry there appears a reef, standing diagonally across the stream; at low water this is uncovered, and through the many breaks the stream hurries with a swifter current and a certain uproar. This is what is called the **Lower Falls of Delaware**, the limit of shipping inland. That is to say, little shalops and sail boats come up as high as this place, but nothing ascends beyond. In the spring and in the fall, when either rains or melting snows swell the stream, and these rocks with others in the channel are under water, there come down residents of the upper country in large, flat boats, from a distance of 100-150 miles, bringing their wheat and other products to market. Throughout America these swellings of the rivers are called 'the freshes' and are of great importance to the more distant inhabitants. The tide comes up to this fall some 200 miles from the sea, but brings no salt water with it.* Judging by the

---

* The tides bring salt water hardly half the distance from

high-water marks the stream must often rise many feet. The depth of the channel is very variable here. Some 12-15 miles above there is another fall, called the **upper** fall.

Just above the lower fall there is a little island on the Jersey side. Some one had formed the project of building a dam there and running a deep ditch as far as the ferry, intending to erect a mill at that spot. The ditch is to be 12 ft. deep and 20 wide, and will require time and expense enough in the digging. At a depth of no more than two to three feet below the surface nothing but rock is found, for the most part a hard, blueish sort of stone,* (with fragments of incomplete granite), which also appears at the surface of the water along the banks, and seems to be the material of which the reef is composed. Above this stone, at the side of the ditch, were to be seen loose rounded stones of several sorts, the whole covered with the common sandy, reddish soil. On the Pensylvania side, at some distance, we were shown several houses belonging to a forge of Colonel **Bird's.**

It was not my purpose to spend time in Jersey, which (beyond its mines already described) has nothing especial to show as between the adjoining provinces, New York and Pensylvania. The products of the country, its climate &c. are the same. Among the natural curiosities the beautiful waterfall of the **Pequanok**, or **Passaik**, deserves mention. Over a wall of

---

the sea to Philadelphia. In the Delaware, on account of its length, there occur two flood-tides and two ebb-tides, at fixed times but varying for different places.

* Seems to be similar to trap?—does not strike fire on steel—is not affected by acids—has a very fine grain.

rock 70 ft. high the stream falls straight away, 60 yards wide. The roughness and wildness of the spot should markedly heighten the loftiness of the scene, which I did not visit. New Jersey was earlier settled and cultivated (by Swedes) than the neighboring provinces, and formerly was called New Sweden. At present the inhabitants consist of the descendants of the Swedish settlers, with Hollanders, Germans, and English— whether the number (including blacks) is actually 130,- 000, as the Congress gave out before the war, might need further proof. Those parts of Jersey toward the sea are infertile, sandy, swampy flats, grown up in pines and red and white cedar. Along the coast itself are few settlements, and those for the most part inhabited by fishermen. Larger ships do not willingly approach this flat coast, which is cut by many inlets.

This province is divided into two parts, East and West New Jersey, the boundaries of which are still a matter of dispute. East Jersey is made up of the counties Monmouth, Middlesex, Sommerset, Essex, and Bergen—West Jersey of the counties Cape-May, Cumberland, Salem, Gloucester, Burlington, Hunterdon, Sussex, and Morris. Of the latter division, **Burlington** on the Delaware, 18 miles above Philadelphia, is regarded as the capital, a town known for its good tap-houses. **Perth Amboy** is the capital of the eastern division. Among the more considerable places may be reckoned Bordentown, Mount Holly, Freehold, Shrewsbury, Greenwich, and Salem. Salem and Greenwich, on the Delaware, formerly had a good trade.

The administration of this province is through a Governor, a Legislative Council, and a General Assembly. Each county sends a member to the Council, an estate

4

of 1000 Pd. and at least a year's residence in the province being required for eligibility. Each county sends three members to the General Assembly, and an eligible must have lived a year at least in the county, and be possessed of realty to the value of 500 Pd. In order that a law shall be valid, both Assemblies must agree to its passage. Freeholders who have been a year resident in their county, and possess real estates to the value of 50 Pd., are entitled to a vote in the election of members of both the Assemblies. The Assembly reserves to itself the right of proposing and authorizing all taxes and imposts. In this matter the Council has no authority. The two Assemblies in common elect a Governor for the term of one year, who constitutes the chief executive power, presides over the Council, is Chancellor, and is also Commander-in-chief of the militia and other provincial forces.

The Governor and Council (of which 7 members are a *Quorum*) are the highest court of appeal in all matters at law, and are empowered as well to pardon condemned criminals, if the case warrants.

Judges * of the Supreme or General Court, which sits but twice a year at each capital, continue seven years in office. Judges of the Inferior Court of Common Pleas for the several counties; Justices of the Peace †; Supreme Court, Inferior Court, and Quarter

---

* Judges—Among the most highly regarded of public offices. The judges are chosen from among the most experienced and most learned lawyers. By one or more of them the several courts are held; they hear plaintiff and defendant, prove the grounds and evidence brought forward, give their opinion as matter of law, but leave to the Jury the final decision.

† Justices of the Peace—are charged with the keeping of

Session Clerks; the Attorney General; and the Provincial Secretary remain in office five years—the Provincial Treasurer only one year.   After these terms, however, if nothing is charged against them, these officers may be again elected—the two Assemblies elect and the Governor confirms them.   Courts of Common Pleas are held monthly in the Court House of each county, and have jurisdiction merely in criminal cases, personalia and realia, not of great importance.   Quarter Sessions Courts are held in like manner in the county Court Houses, once each quarter, and their jurisdiction is wider.   The General or Supreme Courts receive appeals from these lower courts and pass on them; criminal processes also are brought before the General Court, which may exercise original jurisdiction in all suits whatever involving amounts exceeding 25 Pd.

Those residents of each county, eligible as electors, choose among themselves yearly a Sheriff * and one or more Coroners †; the same persons may be chosen three years in succession but not longer.   After another space of three years, these persons may be again elected. The choice is announced to the Governor for confirmation.

---

good order and peace in their district or county; commonly intelligent and upright men are chosen by the people to this office.

The titles and duties of all the officers enumerated are, without much difference, the same as in England and in the other North American states.

* His office is to execute the commands and judgments of the courts, and to see that the laws are obeyed.

† Whose office it is to make examination and determine the cause, in cases of accidental, sudden, or violent death.

Towns and villages elect yearly their Constables,* and also three or more honorable and intelligent freeholders before whom the residents bring their reasonable or imaginary troubles, in the matter of unfair taxation, and must abide by the decision rendered without further appeal. All criminal offenders have, in regard to witnesses and counsellors, the same rights and privileges as their prosecutors. Every man has the liberty of serving God according to his own will and conscience. No man can be compelled to any sort of worship. No man can be forced to pay tithes, taxes, or other levies for the building or maintenance of any church or house of worship soever, or for the support of ministers, except as he himself is willing.

No religious sect is to be given preference over any other. No Protestant is to be denied any civil right or liberty on the ground of his religion, but all persons of whatever protestant sect, who peaceably conform to this mode of government, are eligible for election to any magisterial or other office. To obviate all suspicion of extraordinary influence or corruption on the part of the legislative assemblies, no Judge of the Superior or Inferior Courts, no Sheriff or other person holding lucrative office under the government, shall be admitted a member of the Assembly ; and if such person is elected his former post is to be regarded as vacant.

---

* Subordinate officers whose duty it is to see to the keeping of the peace in their districts, and to arrest and bring to jail all criminals, debtors &c.

Pensylvania

After we had descended a little slope (on the Jersey side) to the river, we had to ascend another gentle rise beyond. The road then lay for four or five miles through continued woods, and here and there we came upon a wretched block-house. But the thoroughfare cut out of the forest is broad, and in dry weather, as now, very good. The country is level, but sandy and sterile. We had the Delaware to the left, a little way off, and through the forest openings fine perspectives were often presented. Two miles beyond the Delaware there was another small ferry to pass, over the **Shamany**; the ferry-boat runs on pulleys working along a stout tackle made fast at either side of the stream. It was yet early in the morning when we reached

Bristol, a pretty little town on the banks of the Delaware, which although not to be likened to the Bristol of the old world, on account of its mineral waters is known in the new. Situated in a hollow, at the foot of a large, high-lying, natural embankment, is the spring, the waters of which are used as well for bathing as for drinking. The water contains iron, and is of no especial strength. There is built over the spring a light structure of wood housing the saloon, or long-room, in the middle, a bath at one end and the pump-room at the other—that is, the water is brought up through pumps and dispensed to visitors in this room, and here the rules to be observed and the schedule of charges

are posted on boards. Professor Rush of Philadelphia
has written a pamphlet on this water, giving the results of his experiments; he himself says that it is but
very lightly charged with particles of iron, but, for the
rest, is a very pure and pleasant water. He does not
recommend it in special cases, but merely for its general curative properties—for this spring is not superior
to many other iron springs in Pensylvania and indeed
throughout America. At Gloucester, at Abington &c.
in Pensylvania, there are iron springs; the Abington
spring is said to be especially strong, depositing much
yellow ochre and therefore commonly called the Yellow
Spring. The habitual drinking-water of Philadelphia
contains much iron. The metal is so general over the
whole surface of America, and particularly in the wilder
parts, that it is impossible iron springs should be infrequent. I have come upon them in Rhode Island, and
on York and Long Islands. The especial excellence of
such springs lies in the more or less purity and very
agreeable taste of the water. Bristol must attribute
the honor done it more to its fine and convenient situation, only 20 miles from Philadelphia, than to anything else. At the usual seasons all manner of guests
come hither seeking health and diversion, and more
would come if the people of Bristol were willing to devote themselves to matters of entertainment and service.

From Bristol to the Sign of General Washington, a
lonely tavern, is 10 miles through a somewhat hilly
country, for the most part sandy, here and there reddish. The traveller comes by two walled bridges (a
sort still rarely seen) to the village of Frankfort, a
handsome little place five miles from Philadelphia;
from that point to the city the road is quite level, over a

light, sandy soil. The nearer one comes to the capital, the freeer of woods is the landsscape, and there are more people and more farms. Wheat and oats had been everywhere got in. Here also the corn was no-where so good or so advanced as about New York. The cattle which met us on the road were not of a sort particularly fine. Between Bristol and Frankfort, and elsewhere, churches stood by the road either quite isolated or placed in a shady grove. The construction of these was peculiar, invariably more height than length. The design may have been to build on at some time and bring the whole into proportion. The whole way from New York to Philadelphia not a foot-passenger met us. Few passengers met us at all, but in every case riding or driving. To go a-foot is an abomination to the American, no matter how poor or friendless; and at times he hits upon a means—he steals a nag from the pasture or borrows one without asking.

In New York there had been an opinion that the Americans, as a result of the war, were suffering for lack of clothes and other necessities; on the contrary, we found on the road that everybody was well and neatly clad, and observed other signs of good living and plenty. On the 26th of July, in the evening, we arrived at the pleasant city of Philadelphia.

Philadelphia. Who in the fatherland has not heard of Philadelphia? And to whom should not this pre-eminent city of America be known? It is not indeed a city such as it can and ought to be, but none the less it is a remarkable place in more respects than one. William Penn, sufficiently known in history, founded the city in 1682, and in the space of 100 years it has grown to a notable size. The houses today are 2400

in number, for the most part of two storeys.*   It is to
be regretted that there is no thorough and impartial
history of this city, and it is especially deplorable that
no such history is to be had for this province, of which
the rise and wonderfully rapid growth would form so
valuable a contribution to the history of mankind.   The
historical fragments which exist are but the prejudiced
accounts of political quarrels, neither instructive nor
interesting.   The stedfast spirit of enterprise of the
honored founder, his amiable and philanthropic plan,
his unwearied efforts and conscientious fairness in the
acquisition of land from the aborigines, the wise, toler-
ant laws of the colony, the rapid increase of the population and of its trade, the advance of the arts and
sciences, the gradual betterment of taste and morals,
the harmony among so many religious sects, and indeed the rise of new sects—all this would supply fruitful and rich material for a history of wide acceptance.
There is no lack of men in Philadelphia who would be
entirely capable of this work, but these few are at this
time overwhelmed with other business.   From predilec-
tion for his religious principles, and deluded by his
own goodness of heart, the first design of the founder
seems to have been to establish a colony free of earthly
authorities, free of soldiers, of priests, of individual
property, and also, it is said, free from doctors of
medicine.—Quite after the manner of the Golden Age,
all this, and as Voltaire ✚ remarks, not to be found anywhere in the world outside of Pensylvania.   Penn, as
it seems, felt and sought to avoid all the hardship which
inequality among men entails, those conditions de-

---

* In a recent news item the number is given as 4600.

scribed by Rousseau, in so masterful a fashion, only
long after. But experience soon taught that universal
love may be easily imagined and preached, but, in a
growing colony, may not so easily be practiced. However, the world had to be told in this way to what
lengths brotherly love may go—of which all hearts are
not equally capable, and over which self-love still holds
dominion. Certainly, laws would be necessary in a
society of saints, and perhaps would be nowhere more
needed than where people so easily become habituated
to think excentrically—The history of England at that
time, and the individual history of the immortal Penn,
must be read in Smollet, Raynal, and others, since so
many circumstances were united to give the founder's
plans and achievements the directions which they took.

Philadelphia lies under Latitude 39° 57′ and Longitude west 75° 20′, and so, nearly at the middle of the
United States—the city, if not greatly beyond others in
America in wealth and number of houses, far surpasses
them all in learning, in the arts, and public spirit. The
plain on which Philadelphia stands is elevated ground
between the magnificent Delaware and the romantic
Schuylkill. Granite is the underlying rock, which
shows itself particularly along the banks of the Schuylkill. The distance apart of the rivers, in the neighborhood of the city, is not quite two miles ; three miles
below, they unite, and the tongue of land so formed,
called the Neck, is for the most part lower and swampier
than the site of the city. The plan of Philadelphia is
fine and regular, but not wholly faultless. The larger
and smaller cities of America have this advantage, that
they have not grown from villages by chance but were
planned from the beginning and have been enlarged by

a plan. By the original chart Philadelphia is fixed
within a rectangle from the bank of the Delaware to
the Schuylkill and a little beyond. But at the present
time not a third of the plan is filled in, and one must
not be led into the error of thinking it complete, as
represented in certain maps both of Philadelphia and
of Pensylvania. For nothwithstanding the swift push-
ing-back of the city, centuries yet must go by before
the ground plan is built up. The streets cross at right
angles. Those along the Delaware run nearly North
and South and are parallel, as are those running East
and West, or from the Delaware to the Schuylkill.
Along the Delaware the line of houses, including the
suburbs, extends for some two miles, and the breadth
of the city, including the suburbs, is not quite a mile
going from the river. Water-street, next to the Delaware, is narrow and considerably lower than the rest
of the city. In this street are warehouses chiefly.
Commodious wharves, for ships of as much as 500 tons,
are built in behind the houses, and here a few feet of
land, often made land, yield rich returns to the owners.

The remaining streets parallel with Water-street and
the river, are called in their order First or Front-street,
Second, Third, Fourth, Fifth, Sixth, Seventh; so many
at present—the three last are still short. The cross
streets running from east to west are the most elevated,
and in their order from north to south are: Vine, Race,
Arch, Market, Chesnut, Wallnut, Spruce, Union
From these a number of alleys traverse the chief
quarters. Market-street is the best street and the only
one 100 ft. in breadth; all the rest are only 50 ft. wide.
Were all the streets as wide again the town would be
by so much the finer and more convenient. It is easily

seen that Quakers drew the plan, and dealt frugally with the space. Market-street is disfigured and the city is deprived of the view, otherwise splendid, towards the river and the Jersey side, by reason of the market-stalls, two long, open buildings set in the middle of the street and extending from First to Third-street.* It is droll how the upper part of these buildings makes so extraordinary a distinction between East and West, rear and front. That is to say, the upper part of the Market-house is the Court-House, and built at either end are balconies, of which that at one end is the place where newly elected Governors are introduced to the people, and at the other end are the pillories for rogues.

It is a pity that when the town was laid off, there was such a total neglect to provide open squares, which lend an especial beauty to great towns, and grassed after the manner of the English, or set with shrubbery, are very pleasing to the eye. In Philadelphia there is nothing but streets all alike, the houses of brick, of the same height mostly, and built by a plan that seldom varies; some few are adorned outwardly by a particular pattern or are better furnished than the general within. Throughout the city the streets are well paved and well kept, highest down the middle, but next the houses there runs a footway sufficiently broad, and laid with flat stones; this side-way is often narrowed by the ' stoops ' built up before the houses, or by the down-sloping cellar and kitchen doors. There being a superfluity of space, it would have been easy, at the foundation of this new city, to avoid the inconveniences of old ones. At night the city is lit by lanterns placed on

* And lately still farther.

posts diagonally alternate at the side of the footway, but the lanterns are sparingly distributed and have no reflectors. The streets are kept clean and in good order by the householders themselves. Water and filth from the streets are carried off through conduits to the river. Appointed night-watchmen call out the hours and the state of the weather. Behind each house is a little court or garden, where usually are the necessaries, and so this often evil-smelling convenience of our European houses is missed here, but space and better arrangement are gained. The kitchen, stable, &c. are all placed in buildings at the side or behind, kitchens often underground. Vaults I do not remember seeing in any house. The attempt is made to avoid everything detrimental to the convenience or cleanliness of dwellinghouses. In the matter of interior decorations the English style is imitated here as throughout America. The furniture, tables, bureaux, bedsteads &c. are commonly of mahogany, at least in the best houses. Carpets, Scottish and Turkish, are much used, and indeed are necessities where the houses are so lightly built; stairs and rooms are laid with them. The houses are seldom without paper tapestries, the vestibule especially being so treated. The taste generally is for living in a cleanly and orderly manner, without the continual scrubbing of the Hollanders or the frippery and gilt of the French. The rooms are in general built with open fire-places but the German inhabitants, partly from preference and old custom, partly from economy, have introduced iron or tin-plate draught-stoves which are used more and more by English families (as a result of the increasing dearness of wood) both in living-rooms and in work-rooms. Here especially there are seen **Franklins** (named in honor of the inventor), a sort of iron affair, half stove, half fire-place. This is a longish, rectangular apparatus made of cast-iron plates and stands off from the wall, the front being open, in every respect a detached, movable fire-place.* ✛ The comfortable sight of the open fire is thus enjoyed, and the good ventilation is healthful; moreover, the iron plates warm a room at less expense of fuel than is possible with the wall fire-place, from which most of the heat is lost.

In so warm a climate the inconveniences arising from the narrowness of the streets were felt at this time and must be whenever the weather is hot. During three days, June 23, 24, 25, Fahrenheit's thermometer stood constantly at 93-95 degrees. The city is so far inland that no wind from the sea brings coolness; round about is a dry, sandy soil; and in addition narrow streets, houses and footways of brick strongly reflecting the sun's rays—everything makes for a high degree of dead heat in the city. During these three days, not less than 30 sudden deaths were announced in the Philadelphia newspapers, martyrs to the heat by the coroners' returns, and also, very probably, victims of an indiscreet imbibition of cold drinks. But as everywhere else, not until after the event, were the people warned by public proclamation to keep clear of cold drinks.

The number of the inhabitants was placed at 20,000 as early as 1766, before the war at 30,000, and at present (counting strangers) is fixed at 30-40,000—with what certainty I am not prepared to say. On account

---

* Description and drawing of which, to be found in Dr. Franklin's Collected Works; there is a German translation.

of the many distinct religious sects, no exact register is so far kept of births and deaths, which if attempted might not be reliable. A strict enumeration of the inhabitants is difficult in America, (and merely political calculations are untrustworthy,) where people are continually moving about, leaving a place or coming in.

I remember once reading in some book of travels that Philadelphia was a city of Quakers and beautiful gardens. Brief enough, and for the time probably true. Quakers from the beginning have been the most numerous, the most respectable, and the richest among the inhabitants; in the government of the state they have had an important, perhaps the weightiest, influence; and their manners, through imitation, have become general among the people. Quakers purchased and peopled the country; they made with the aborigines peaceable treaties, as Voltaire observes, the only treaties between Indians and Christians, unsworn-to and not broken. The greatest part of the useful institutions and foundations owe their origin to this sect. By it chiefly was the police organized and maintained. This temperate and originally virtue-seeking brotherhood takes no part in impetuous and time-consuming pleasures which worldliness and idleness bring other, baptized Christians into. Their religion, giving them a coat with no buttons or creases, denies them play and the dance. Thus they gain much time for pondering useful regulations which do honor to their society and are advantageous to the community. For the same reason, where circumstances are equally favorable, Quakers are invariably better-off than their neighbors, because they bring order into their domestic affairs, undertake nothing without the most careful forethought, and prosecute everything with constant zeal. In Philadelphia the large Hospital and the Workhouse are standing examples of their benevolent views. Also, the field of the sciences has them to thank ; the American Philosophical Society was founded by them, and their sect furnishes to it many worthy members. For gradually the Quakers are giving over their former depreciation of the sciences, since they find that increased intelligence does not injure the well-being of a community, and that everything is not to be expected from immediate revelation. In their outward conduct, and in their relations with their fellow-citizens of other beliefs, they are beginning to recede from the strict attitude of an earlier time. No longer does the hat sit quite so square, and many young Quakers venture to half-tilt the round hat, gently, so that the brims are brought into a position, doubtful as yet, half perpendicular and half horizontal. But the ' Thou ' and ' Thee,' which in our title-seeking Germany was the chief hindrance in the spread of Quakerism, they still find it well to retain.

It is against the principles of the Quakers to take part in any feud whatsoever, because as Christians they consider it their duty to love their enemies. Hence, neither in former wars nor in this last war would they let themselves be placed in ranks and companies with murderous weapons in their hands, although the Jews themselves have not in America declined such service. In former times it was the easier to abjure all participation in war, since the Proprietors, the Governors, all the more important citizens and officers of state were of that sect. Besides, it happened that the unbaptized blood-shy Friends stayed quietly at their plantations or their towns in lower Pensylvania while in the farther regions the poorer, baptized Christians were being murdered and scalped by the Indians or the French. To be sure they did not cease to deprecate these grewsome contrivances of jealous and land-hungry monarchs; but they excused themselves on the ground that the Brotherhood never waged war, and would the rather suffer everything at the hands of an enemy insatiable. How long a state could exist, composed entirely of Quakers and therefore inimical to war, may be easily imagined. Adjoining states must be Quakers as well or the supposed state less rich than Quakers commonly are. The leaders of the now free American states very clearly perceived that by the virtues of Quakerism no victories could be won: so, during the war the Brotherhood was left in undisturbed inactivity, but was doubly taxed. But the Quakers resisted payment of these taxes because they regarded them as mediate contributions in the effecting of bloody designs—for which they professed an absolute hatred, but the results of which were entirely to their liking. In the circumstances, a part of the property of those refusing to pay was seized, and sold below value in the name of the state. Eventually, most of them became amenable. if only to preserve the appearance of the peace-loving and non-paying Quaker, and when the tax-gatherer came, (in America the farmer does not seek him out), they fell into a custom of laying a piece of gold on the table, which could be taken for tax—the part of conscience or duty, perhaps also the part of wisdom. Those Quakers within the compass of the royal English army conducted themselves in like manner during the war. They never gave a horse, or a wagon, or a servant, or anything which might be demanded of them for the maintenance of the troops, but they looked on unconcerned if without further question such things were taken as needed.

During the late war, however, certain of the Quakers permitted themselves to be led astray by the spirit of schism and took an active part in the war : but these, with their friends and adherents, were excluded from the meetings of the genuine, orthodox Quakers. Upon that, they built themselves a meeting-house of their own, in Arch-street, between Fourth and Fifth-street, where they will, like the others, quietly await the moving of the same spirit. Their number is not large and they are distinguished by the name of **Fighting Quakers**. It might perhaps have been possible, by compliance on either side, to avoid a separation ; but since this is never the case in matters of opinion and faith, and since the break has gone so far as the erection of a new meeting-house, there will be no re-union, if only because the building would then have been raised to no purpose : and so Philadelphia gains a new rubric in the list of its sects. A certain Matlock ✚ is one of the most conspicuous of these fighting Quakers, or quaking fighters, and made no scruple of accepting a colonelcy in the American army. He had always been an enterprising genius, and as a consequence had debts. When he was just made Colonel, and with his sword at his side, was walking the streets, an acquaintance met him—' Friend, what doest thee with that thing at thy side ?' 'Protecting Liberty and Property,' (two words very current in England and America), answered the Colonel. ' Eh,' said his friend, ' as for property I never knew thee had any, and liberty, that thee hast by the indulgence of the brethren.'

5

After the separation took place, the old and the new-school Quakers sent formal notice to every of the other religious sects, who were pleased at the schism because hitherto the Quakers had reproached them with the twists and quarrels prevailing among them.

Many of the younger Quakers, who have travelled in Europe, begin to find pleasure in the joys of the world, and bringing back to Pensylvania a freer way of thought, more pliant manners, and a modish dress, the example is effective. The Quaker coat is hung on a nail for a while, but with advancing age is at times hunted out again; with it there return other Quaker ideas, and the old-time customs, imposing little restraint, are willingly followed—they serve as welcome excuse to a frugal man.

When one of the Brotherhood by his behavior loses the confidence of the society or deserves punishment of them, he is not perhaps excommunicated, but ' they disavow him '; he is not recognized further as a member of the Society.—The Society of Quakers does not now increase, as formerly, through numerous proselytes. They are now circumstantial and critical before admitting new members, who besides offer themselves less frequently than at one time; and since by marriage, travel, and in other ways members here and there are lost or resign, the number rather diminishes than increases, and it is likely that with the course of time and the changes resultant in manners and beliefs, the whole sect will become if not extinct at least decayed: the case, it is said, in England where there is a marked falling-off among them in comparison with former times.

Pensylvania, and in consequence Philadelphia, as-

sures freedom to all religious sects; men of all faiths
and many of none, dwell together in harmony and
peace. Tolerance, the advantages of which are only
now beginning to be felt in several of the kingdoms of
Europe, has been for a hundred years the foundation-
stone of this flourishing state. Whoever acknowledges
a God can be a citizen and has part in all the privileges
of citizenship. Whoever is a member of any of the
Christian congregations is eligible to petty office, and
can be elected also to the Assembly, to the governor-
ship, or to the Congress. Inspiration is left out of the
account, except among the Quakers who look for
everything from that source, and without it a man
may be a good citizen and senator of Pensylvania. By
such laws as these the Jews enjoy every right of citizenry and, provided they own property enough, vote
for members of the Assembly. This everywhere oppressed and burdened nation can here and throughout
America follow any civil business, and is restricted in
hardly any way. The spirit of tolerance has gone so
far that different religious sects have assisted one another in the building of houses of worship. At the
present time there are in Philadelphia more than thirty
such buildings, which if not all equally of a size and
comeliness are in every case of a simple and neat construction; costly and artistic decoration is not to be
found in them. Of these churches and meeting-houses,
the Quakers own five, including their new meeting-
house—there are three churches, using the English
liturgy and ceremonies, which formerly were under
the care of the English bishops—there are two Scotch
Presbyterian churches—two German Lutheran, of
which the one in Fourth-street is large and handsome

—one German Reformed church—two Roman Catholic chapels, the one directed by a former Jesuit from
Ireland and the other by a German priest, the two par-
ishes numbering probably more than 1000 souls—there
is a Swedish church at Wikakoa near the city—there
is a synagogue—and there are other meeting-houses
belonging to the Anabaptists, Methodists, Moravian
Brethren, &c.

In the German Lutheran congregation there are baptized yearly some 400 children, and perhaps half as
many burials are made. This difference is due to the
fact that people living at a distance from Philadelphia
bring in their children to be baptized, on occasions of
market or other business; but with the dead the case is
that they are buried quietly in the country, behind the
houses they have lived in—for many landowners in
America have a family burying-ground in their gardens.
The priesthood gains nothing by the dead, unless their
services are desired at burials. You may (if the father
in the case consents) be born for nothing, and you may
die gratis—as you like; only while you live must taxes
be paid.

Among the churches, Christ Church in Second-street
has the best appearance and the finest steeple. The
east side is well-embellished, the building, however,
stands too near the street. Christ Church has a beautiful chime of bells, which makes a complete octave and
is heard especially on evenings before the weekly markets and at times of other glad public events. The bells
are so played that the eight single notes of the octave
are several times struck, descending, rapidly one after
the other,—and then the accord follows in tercet and
quint, ascending; and so repeated. On certain solemn

days, there is repetition to the thirteenth time, that sacred number. At Philadelphia there is always something to be chimed, so that it seems almost as if it was an Imperial or Popish city. The German Reformed church, at the corner of Third- and Arch-street, has also a fine steeple.

Among the other public buildings must be mentioned especially the **State House**, a large but not a splendid structure of two storeys. The façade is of tiled brick, with no particular decoration, but in comparison regular and handsome. In this case also the providing of a large square in front has been neglected, and this would have lent distinction. The lower storey contains two large halls, one of which the Congress formerly made use of. Here they assembled for the first time on the 2nd of Sept. 1774, and here they announced the Act of Independence, 4th July 1776. Three times the Congress fled from this place—first, to Baltimore, in the autumn of 1776, when the English army stood on the banks of the Delaware in Jersey; then, in the summer of 1777, to Yorktown in Pensylvania, when General Howe landed in Maryland; and recently, before their own troops, to Princetown in New Jersey, June 1783.

The other hall, on the ground floor, is for the use of the Supreme Court of Judicature. Above, there are two halls, for the General Assembly and for the Governor and Council. Two wing-buildings are joined by archways to the main building. A pretty large collection of books which belongs to a Library Company was formerly installed in one of these wings but several years ago was removed to a special building in **Carpenter-street**, and at present the War Office occupies this wing. The left wing is used as the office of the Comptroller General.

The **new Jail** is a large, but quite a plain building, where the British prisoners of war found no great cause to praise American philanthropy and magnanimity. This building cost about 30,000 Pd. Pensyl. The old jail stands, unattractive in design, in Market-street, which is thus disfigured; it is proposed to tear it down,* since at all events there is sufficient room in the new jail for the good and free citizens of the state.

At a little distance from the city stands the **Pensylvania Hospital,** for the indigent sick and insane. This is not yet complete, only one wing being built at the present time. The whole will be extensive and according to a fine plan. Meanwhile the space to be covered is surrounded by a wall. There are only two sick rooms, one for women above, and one for men below. These rooms are high, airy, and long, and will be kept, like the whole establishment, in a very cleanly state. Half underground are the closed cells for madmen. There is a small medical library in the Overseer's room. The Hospital has its own apothecary's shop; a young student attends to it, for which he receives board and other perquisites. In an upper, corner room, there is a splendid collection of anatomical engravings and paintings, for the most part obstetrical, the gift of the famous Dr. Fothergill ✚ of London, who was a Quaker and greatly interested in this establishment undertaken by his fellow-believers. In addition, there are three excellent metal-moulded designs, to be used in obstetrical demonstrations also.

---

* This has since happened, and the space has been filled with other, newbuilt houses.

This Hospital formerly had a fund of 10,000 Pd.
Pensyl. Current, for maintenance.   But the war, and
especially the paper-money, entailed a considerable loss,
so that at the present time the established number of
sick cannot be cared for.   Six Philadelphia physicians
take upon themselves the care of the hospital, without
charge, two every four months; but by the arrangement
during two months, one of the two is to give his particular oversight, and the other may at his pleasure,
but both of them must be present at the reception and
discharge of a patient.   A little old man from the
Neckar country paid down a moderate sum 23 years ago
and bought a berth for life in the hospital.   He is now
in his 98th year, having eaten out his franchise three
times over, and will live to be a hundred.   I never saw
such dazzling, pure white hair as this ancient's,—
beard, eyebrows, the minute growth on the cheeks;
which, with his costume of nothing but white, gave
him a very strange appearance.

Not far from the hospital is another public building
which in its plan and noble purpose does honor likewise to so young a state.   This is the Bettering or
Working House, called also the House of Employment—not intended for malefactors but for the old, the
poor, and the maimed, where those still capable of work
could ply their several trades, and be useful to themselves and the community as spinners, weavers, knitters
&c., earning in this way a part of their keep.   And
everything before the war was in the best of order, a
number of looms being kept constantly employed in
the house.   Afterwards it was turned into a lazaretto
by the American troops who, more than the English,
were superstitious about desecrating churches by using

them for the sick. At the time I saw the house several rooms were fitted as a hospital for women lying-in &c. This building also is not complete, standing as two separate wings, with adjuncts, between which the corps de logis is to be raised.

The two buildings last mentioned stand a little way from the city on the so-called ' Commons,' a region included by the plan in the proposed limits of the city. Formerly this Common was the property of the **Penn** family which leased the ground, little by little, necessary for the building of these houses ; and so, as late as the year 1778 the tract was a desolate pasture grown up in bush. But since the independent state has taken over the proprietary rights, these Commons have been divided into lots and sold, the necessary streets having been indicated. The **lots** are for the most part enclosed and for the time, are cultivated in vegetables and grain ; here and there preparations are going forward for raising houses on these lots, so soon, apparently, as a peace shall be declared. Formerly as many as 200-300 houses have been built in a year : house-building is carried on rapidly and lightly, so that now and then there may be seen two-storeyed houses conveniently en promenade on rollers, brought from one end of the city to the other, according as it seems best to the owners to live in this quarter or that.

North of the city, in a part corresponding to Thirdstreet, stand the barracks * built by the English gov-

---

* No American city has walls and ramparts ; before the war Philadelphia was not in any way fortified. Nor do there exist the drawbridges and gates shown in Plates 6 and 12 of the *Allgem. hist. Taschenbuch* for 1784.

ernment for the troops stationed here at one time.
The building is in a miserable condition, because the
American troops which occupied them, (the rule held
throughout), were not the most orderly lodgers.

Promotion and furtherance of the sciences have long
since been a care with the state of Pensylvania. In the
year 1754 a College was founded for the instruction of
the young. The building stands at the corner of
Fourth and **Arch-street,** and intended for a different
purpose, is not of the distinguished, handsome appearance of the College at New York. Particular attention
was given to the English language. A special teacher
imparted to the young the principles of their mother-
tongue, and disciplined them in correct reading and
pronunciation, not a superfluous exercise among youths
sent from such different provinces of the British Empire. At the same time capable men gave instruction
in the Latin and Greek languages, Geography, Mathematics, Logick, Rhetorick, History, Natural and
Moral Philosophy. Later a school of Medicine was
added. At the yearly public Commencements certain
ceremonies are observed. The Rector or Provost begins these with several collects from the English liturgy, and there follow sundry public exercises, partly
short speeches, partly disputations, in English or in
Latin. The Latin, here as with Englishmen everywhere, is so mangled, the vowels and consonants pronounced according to their own usage, that it is not to
be understood by unanglicized ears. By an Act of the
Assembly, confirmed by the Congress, this College was
raised to a University in the year 1780. The University consists of two departments, the Academy or
lower preparatory schools for younger students, and

the University proper, where the higher sciences, Philosophy, the Mathematics, and Medicine are taught. There are as yet no Professors of Law and Theology, and the appointment of such will not easily be brought about. Since no one religion is to be counted prevalent here, none may be preferred through the choice of a Professor. If a young man intends studying theology, and has got a knowledge of the preparatory sciences he can do nothing but travel to Europe, or betake himself to a minister of his religion and learn the necessary through private instruction; and it is so likewise with students of the law. Among the trustees of this University, besides other learned men, there have been chosen ecclesiastics of these several religions,—English, Presbyterian, Catholic, Lutheran, and Reformed, since the young from all parts are received as students here, where nothing is taught respecting God and the saints. Meanwhile, the University makes Doctors of Theology, by diploma—Dr. Kunze, Professor of the Oriental and German languages, was the first so created, and very recently. At the same time General Washington received the degree of a Doctor of the Law, which he had so stoutly fought for.

The pay of the Professors of Philosophy, Languages &c. is 300 Pd. Pensyl. Current. They call it, however, a miserable pay and justifiably, because it is in arrears.

I made the acquaintance of Dr. Ewen, a meritorious and learned man, who is the Professor of Natural and Moral Philosophy. Mr. Davison is the Professor of History, and his brother a Tutor in the Latin Language. Dr. Smith, an erudite clergyman, who performed valuable service in the organization and endowment of the college, was in some way wronged, and is now at the

new-established **Washington College** in the State of
Delaware. He is a skilled natural philosopher, and
gave lectures with much approbation on the experi-
mental physics at the time when the English army was
at Philadelphia.

The science of Medicine has the most Professors.
These are at present Drs. **Bond, Shippen, Kuhn, Morgan,** and **Rush.** None of them has a fixed salary, but
they earn considerable sums, according to the number
of those attending their lectures. They do not lecture
during the summer, but, hitherto, only in the five winter
months, three or four times weekly. They have determined for the future to restrict their lectures to a
term of three months, but to hold hours daily, and for
the reason that there are many practicioners coming in
from the county to hear lectures who cannot remain
long from home, and besides many young students
dread the expense of residence. Ordinarily they read
their lectures, and in the English language, in which
also examinations and disputations *pro gradu* are held.
For here it is regarded as superfluous to twaddle bad
Latin from a desk for an hour (or to listen), and to
muddle many hours with a language in which, later,
there is no occasion to palaver. Besides, most of the
books appearing in England on medical subjects are
written in English and it is these that are used in
America almost exclusively. At the creating of a Doctor, in whatever faculty, all the Professors are present
and sign the patent. Candidates for the degree of Doctor in Medicine, it is said, are exactly and strictly examined, and several have already been refused; but,
with the degree, the practicioner has no advantage, in
honor or remuneration, over other practicioners and

bunglers, except as he himself chooses to make much of his diploma.*

In America every man who drives the curing trade is known without distinction as Doctor, as elsewhere every person who makes verses is a poet—so there are both black doctors and brown, and quacks in abundance.†

Since this University lies nearer the West Indies than any of the European universities, it is hoped that young students from thence will now resort to Philadelphia rather than take the longer way to England. But this will probably not come about at once. In the University building there is a collection of books neither large nor complete, containing however several

---

* "In a quarrel of the Connecticut Doctors with the huddlers and quacks of the colony, it was the purpose of the Doctors to allow no ungraduated person, unless first examined by them, to visit the sick or to prescribe medicines. The Assembly of the province declared against the Doctors, calling their Association a monopoly which was enriching the learned. To the reply of the Doctors the Assembly, of 1766, returned no answer but the following: 'Medicine can effect nothing without the blessing of God. The quacks do not prescribe unless a minister has first prayed for a blessing, whereas the Doctors ascribe all the good to the medicine and none to the blessing prayed for.' Every person, as before, had the liberty of healing disease." Vid., *Beyträg. zur Länder und Völkerkunde* (Neuest. Zustand von Connecticut), II, 197.

† According to late advices, the physicians of Philadelphia have come together in a society (after the manner of the London and Edinburg Colleges of Physicians), the chief object of which will be to contribute to the diffusion of medical knowledge through the publishing of their observations and discussions. The same has happened in New York, and perhaps the good example will be followed by the physicians of the other states.

fine works and mathematical and physical instruments. The most conspicuous work of art here is the Planet-system or Orrery * of the famous Mr. **Rittenhouse,** a detailed description of which is to be found in the Transactions of the Philosophical Society. I had not the pleasure of seeing the whole of this Orrery; only that part was there showing the course of the moon. Mr. Rittenhouse had taken apart the remainder and transferred it to his house, in order to make certain improvements.

Public Schools and Academies are established also in several of the other provinces: at **Cambridge** near Boston, at **New Haven** in Connecticut, at **New York,** at **Williamsburg** in Virginia, and in Delaware a new college called **Washington College**; however Philadelphia can boast of an advance still more considerable in the prosecution and diffusion of the useful and beneficent sciences. That is to say, there is established here a **Philosophical Society** which owes its origin to the industrious and fruitful genius of Dr. Franklin, known for science and statecraft equally.

More than twenty years ago Dr. Franklin with certain of his learned friends founded a society of like character. But a number of members getting in who were pretty ignorant but proud enough to desire a place among the philosophers, the society fell into a decline. So in the year 1769 a new plan was formed, and without recourse to all the members enrolled at that time. Those excluded, out of revenge began to

---

* Lord Orrery was the patron of a certain Rowley who prepared the first apparatus of this sort in England; hence the name given all similar apparatuses.

recruit for themselves at the same time and elected members indiscriminately, so as by a majority (among which it was hoped a few good names might have been fished in) to get the start of the new society. After some time it was found that in behoof of the sciences it would be better to form a union, and so it happened; but the spirit of party once aroused was not to be checked immediately—by a majority of votes useless members again got in, and several of the older members felt injured and resigned. Notwithstanding these unavoidable circumstances the progress of the worthy undertaking was happily not stopped. In the year 1771 appeared the first volume * of the Transactions of the American Society, in quarto, containing several pieces on the subject of natural history. Of many other papers ready for the press, nothing has so far appeared, the war having prevented; but the Congress, still *inter arma* and of an undetermined sovereignty, did not neglect to cast a glance at these *musas silentes,* and by a solemn act was pleased to give the society confirmation and new life.†

The President is Dr. **Benjamin Franklin,** but the

---

* The second volume of the Transactions of this Society appeared in 1786.

† Extract from a communication from Philadelphia, 1787— " Another society has recently been established here, which concerns itself with political enquiries. Its objects will be the elucidation of the science of government and the furtherance of human happiness. This society is regulated on the norm of the European philosophical societies; its papers and contributions will be published annually so as to preserve many valuable works which otherwise would be lost in the public prints. The honorable Dr. Franklin is President of this society."

Vice-President is Dr. **Bond,** a meritorious Hippocratic, in his 70th year of great cheerfulness and activity of mind, who has for many years practiced his art at Philadelphia with much success. I had several times the pleasure of enjoying his society. He was at one time the appointed Health-Physician at Philadelphia. The duty of this officer was to inspect all ships bringing in servants and adventurers from Europe. For the greed of skippers often tempted them to stopple too many passengers together, thus giving cause for dangerous maladies whereby very many of these poor people were done for without ever seeing the land for which, in the hope of better fortune, they had given up home. Dr. Bond assured me that on several occasions ships had come to port with so much malignant tinder stowed in that no one could have stayed on board 24 hours without falling a sacrifice. But by precautionary measures the spread of such poisons was prevented. No person was allowed on land until he had first been cleansed and all his old clothes thrown away; and then those landing were sent to an isolated spot on shore for a short quarantaine. Contagious diseases are extremely rare in America, almost entirely unknown indeed, not reckoning the small-pox and what follows the gallantries of armies and fleets. In the country the people live scattered, among shade trees; in the towns there is no crowding, almost every family living in its own house, and everything very clean. However, Dr. Bond once observed a contagious fever in Philadelphia, which had its origin in a space between Water-street and the Market where some dead sturgeons and other filth had been left neglected by the inefficient police of that time. This fever, although extremely contagious, was neither vehement in its attacks nor dangerous, and spread no farther than the square in which it began, but within that space nobody easily escaped who was exposed as much as six hours.

In the year 1761 Dr. Bond observed a sort of influenza which followed a regular course almost throughout America—a fever with an itching of the skin, accompanied by a cough and an acrid running at the nose and eyes. It showed itself first in some of the West India islands, then in the Bermudas ; in the spring it appeared at Halifax, and thence came down to Boston, and so to the south, through Rhode Island, New York, Philadelphia, Baltimore &c, visiting all the larger towns along the coast without being affected by any dissimilarities of wind or weather, appearing to stop in North Carolina not before July of the same year. It was remarked that at the same time horses were attacked by a similar fever, with running at the nose and eyes, but with happier results, since the smiths made cures more quickly and surely than the physicians were able to do. The cure for the horses was, they were tied and burning sulphur held before the nose for 15 minutes, by which treatment they all got completely rid of the disease.

Among many other observations of this worthy man the following account of an extraordinary worm is the most astonishing. A horrible monster some 20 inches long and on an average as thick as a man's wrist worked for 18 months no small mischief in a woman's body, ate its way through to the liver where it contrived a measurable cavity, continued through the *ductus hepaticus* and the *choledochus*, taking leave shortly after by the fundament—whereupon the woman died

suddenly. Dr. Bond has described the entire worm and
its history for the London medical commentaries.

Dr. **Benjamin Rush** is the Professor of Chymistry,
and is a very favorite practicioner—a man whose agreeable manners, oratorical fluency, and flowery style abundantly recommend him to his fellow-countrymen. He
is the author of several opuscula of a medical nature,
but also appears frequently as a political writer. Several sheets of his on the newest methods of inoculating
for the small-pox and of treating that disease have
appeared recently in a German translation. During
the war he was for a time Physician-in-Chief of the
American army and frequently had occasion to observe
the fatal course of the lockjaw ✚ in cases of insignificant wounds, although opium was administered heavily. This led him to the opinion that the cause might
be found in an extreme weakness of the body. Therefore his treatment was to administer Peruvian bark and
wine, at the same time making incisions in the wound
and applying a blister of Spanish fly. Results were
incomparably better. He intends himself to publish,
with other material, his observations and conclusions in
this matter, unless publication of them is managed
earlier in some other way. The idea is confirmed by
the comparisons made between the wounded of the two
armies, British and French, after the siege of York in
Virginia. Most of the wounded in the French army,
but especially those of West India regiments, were attacked with the lockjaw and died, although their injuries may have been slight, whereas in the British
hospitals a fatal outcome was seldom remarked. It is
a known fact that soldiers from the West Indies always
show a weak state of health, and the remainder of the

6

French troops, (having made in the height of summer a long and tedious march from New England to Virginia), must have been in a weakened condition. Lockjaw was not frequently the case at Philadelphia, and was as seldom seen at New York, among the British troops.

Some time ago an Irish woman made several fortunate cures of blood-spitting, by the use of common kitchen-salt. She recommended for patients suffering with this malady a teaspoonful of salt every morning, to be gradually increased to a tablespoonful several times a day. In the more positive cases of blood-spitting, several doses must be given, often repeated until the symptoms cease, which will unfailingly happen in a short time, it is claimed. Dr. Rush about thirty years ago learned of this treatment, and has made use of it since in more than thirty cases, and invariably with good results. The cure is effectual also in bleedings at the nose and in floodings, but is excellent for blood-spitting. Only in two cases was there no good effect, to wit, with a man who was an old and incorrigible drinker, and with another who from distrust of so simple a means, would not take the salt in sufficient quantity. Something similar has been long known respecting saltpetre and sal-ammoniac, but these being not so generally at hand, the practice with kitchen salt deserved mention.

The French physicians and surgeons, here as well as in the West Indies, were very much disinclined to give bark in cases of intermittent fever. The Americans were always sooner done with their patients, whereas the French showed a preference rather for enfeebling theirs to the skeleton point; finally indeed brought

them round, but very slowly and at the risk of frequent
relapses and stoppages of the bowels, sequelae of long-
standing fevers very much more certain to occur if
bark is not given in time. Dr. Rush learned of a quack
doctor the use of blistering plaisters for obstinate cold
fevers, or agues, and his experience convinced him of
the value of the treatment. The blisters are applied to
both wrists and seldom fail of effect. (Several bands
about the hand have long been used by our German
country-people.) Dr. Rush in this way cured a Virginia doctor of a tertian which he had been dragging
about for three months, and he in turn used the treatment again in Virginia with good results.

Dr. **Morgan** is Professor of the Practice of Medicine, a man no less agreeable than well-informed. He
is a Fellow of the Royal Society at London and of
several other learned societies, and has travelled in
France and Italy. Chiefly through his efforts the medical school at Philadelphia was established. At the beginning of the war he was Inspector General of the
American hospitals, but as a consequence of intrigues
resigned this place; however, not before bringing upon
himself rude treatment on the part of the Congress. He
was one of the first men who at that time ventured to
expose the assumed infallibility of the Congress, his
action springing from the stedfastness of his character
and the consciousness of his own rectitude. At his
house I saw a collection of great bones brought from
the Ohio, which Mr. Peale was just then painting,
natural size, for Counsellor Michaelis.

Dr. **Kuhn**, of German origin, is the Professor of
Botany + and Materia Medica. He is a disciple of the
lamented Linnaeus, who named an order of plants in

his honor, the *Kuhnia,*—which Dr. Kuhn himself has not seen, although it exists in Pensylvania. The professorship of Botany is an empty title, since throughout the summer there is neither lecturing nor botanizing. That the Congress can be obstinate in small matters also, Mr. Kuhn has reason to know. During the war he was for a time absent from America, and coming from St. Thomas in the West Indies, a neutral island, landed at New York from an English ship. The Congress, to whom this scarcely seemed the most direct way, would not permit him to come to Philadelphia, and he was obliged to sail back to the West Indies, and make the return voyage in an American ship.

Dr. **Chovet**, a learned old man of much reading, and in his 79th year full of life and enthusiasm, although not a Professor has at times lectured on Anatomy, his favorite study. He is particularly known for his beautiful wax-work collection, ✚ largely his own fabrication and designed to illustrate the parts of the human body. He has, in addition, a considerable number of fine anatomical preparations and a notable and rare collection of books.

I should tax the patience of my readers by an enumeration of all the Aesculapians and learned men of Philadelphia. Those mentioned are the most conspicuous of the number there, where the labors of the physician are as richly rewarded as at any place. The yearly in-take of the most of these men is reckoned at several thousand pounds Pensyl. Current. But their greatest profit arises from the private dispensation of remedies ; * to which end each physician of large prac-

---

* There are, besides, several apothecarys and dealers in

tice has a select stock of drugs and keeps a few young men at hand to prepare prescriptions and assist in visiting patients. By private reading or academical instruction, these young men contrive to increase their knowledge and so fit themselves for practice on their own account.

I must mention here two worthy men of whom Philadelphia boasts.

The name of Mr. **Rittenhouse** is known throughout America, as it deserves to be. He is perhaps 50 years of age, of modest and agreeable manners, open and engaging. His parents or grandparents came from Germany to Pensylvania; he himself was apprenticed as a watch-maker, but without the least assistance he has made himself a complete astronomer, by his own brains and industry. In the Orrery already mentioned as at the College in Philadelphia he has given a generally admired proof of his mechanical talents. Another work of this sort prepared by him is at Princeton. He has sketched a new plan for a third, a much improved and simpler apparatus, but he himself does not know whether he can ever bring it to completion. They have made him a Collector of the Revenue and so have quite snatched him from the paths of science.

Mr. *du Sumitiere,** of Geneva, a painter, is almost

---

drugs at Philadelphia—among others a German shop where the 'Pensylvania-Dutch' farmer, to his great comfort, is supplied all the silly doses he has been accustomed to in the fatherland.

* He has since died, and his collections are broken up. The Assembly of Pensylvania threw out the bill for purchasing them for the University, although the sum necessary would have been very moderate.

the only man at Philadelphia who manifests a taste for
natural history. Also he possesses the only collection,
a small one, of natural curiosities—and a not inconsiderable number of well-executed drawings of American birds, plants, and insects. It is to be regretted that
his activities, and his enthusiasm for collecting, should
be embarrassed by domestic circumstances, and that he
should fail of positive encouragement from the American publick. In his collection of curiosities, which is
adorned with many specimens of North American
fauna and a few Otaheitian, the Americans take most
pleasure in a pair of French courier-boots and a Hessian fuseleer's cap.

There had been begun in the so-called **Fish House,**
beyond the Schuylkill, a very respectable collection of
the natural products of America, but this was quite
destroyed in the year 1777 by the British army, at that
time passing.

Libraries also Philadelphia possesses, those institutions contributory to the general enlightenment. A taste
for reading is pretty wide-spread. People of all classes
use the library in Carpenter-street, of which I have
already made mention. Dr. Franklin, supported particularly by Quakers, began this library as early as
1732 by the foundation of a Reading-society. The
rooms are open to the public twice a week in the afternoon, but the members of the society have access every
day. Books may be borrowed on the deposit of a read-
ing-fee. The number of books is not very great, but
there are in the collection many fine English works and
also some Latin and French books. Two librarians are
installed who, however, could not always find books
named in the catalogue. It was not the misfortune of

this collection to be plundered and scattered by soldiers,
the case with the library at New York and with that
in Rhode Island. In an adjoining room several mathematical and physical instruments are kept, as also
a collection of American minerals, but with no indication of name or place of discovery.

Another fine collection, especially rich in medical
books and in the Greek and Latin authors was given to
the public, in 1752, by Mr. Logan, a Quaker, who had
been at great pains and expense in the gathering of it.
At this time, I know not why, this library is kept under
lock and key, and is used by no one.

Notwithstanding, of writers of books, as well as of
other manufacturers, there are still few in America, but
there is no lack of printers at Philadelphia who are at
the same time book-dealers. I learned of the following:
Messrs. **Aitkin, Bradford, ✚ Hall & Seller, Dunlap,
Cruikshank, Baylie, Towne, Bell** (who is besides an
antiquary and frequently holds auctions)—Mr. **Cist**
and Mr. **Melchior Steiner ✚** print in German. The
chief business of these is the printing of newspapers,
announcements, political brochures, and Acts of Assembly. There appear 8-10 newspapers, weekly sheets in
large folio; of them all the **Independent Chronicle** is
the favorite on account of its freedom in regard to public affairs. Liberty of the press was one of the fundamental laws which the states included, expressly and
emphatically, in the programmes of their new governments. It arouses the sympathies to see how often the
Congress is mishandled in these sheets. The financier,
Bob Morris, recently found himself slandered by an
article in the Independent Chronicle and vigorously began process at law, but the public at large supported

the printer and as free citizens asserted their right to communicate to one another in this way their opinions and judgments regarding the conduct of public servants.   Since not all transactions (even of private citizens) come under amenability to the law, zealous patriots can use the press as a terrible scourge, for giving timely warnings, for bringing officials to their duty, for criticising abuses and shortcomings, instructing their fellow-citizens in all manner of things—when elsewhere they would be free scarcely to whisper the burden.   But it must be said that through the misuse of so special a privilege great harm may arise.   How many upright and innocent characters are roughly and prejudicially treated under this shield of the freedom of the press.

English books are reprinted here, but are very little cheaper than the originals, and besides are often very badly executed.*   Reprinting therefore is restricted to new books the authors of which enjoy a great *honorarium,* that is to say, dear books.   Books of edification, school-books, bibles &c can always be had cheaper from Europe, since paper and wages stand at a high price in America, and the Americans have a fancy for well and finely printed books, such as the English commonly are.   Books brought in from England are all bound (they may not be otherwise exported) and form a very considerable article of trade.   German religious books come especially from Frankfort on Main.   Since the peace, Dutch and German ships have brought in a great quantity of all manner of publications.

From what has been set down here it will be readily

* Types, ink, paper &c are had from Europe.

seen that the sciences are known and valued in
America, and that efforts are making to further them,
although no one anxiously studies as a means of livelihood. The fine arts, on the contrary, have not yet made
a significant progress. Amateurs and connaisseurs
hitherto have had adequate opportunity to supply themselves with works of art, paintings and copper-prints,
from Europe. The genius of America, however, is
beginning to show itself in these matters. Philadelphia
possesses in Mr. **Peale** an artist, native-born, who may
be placed alongside of many in the old world. In an
open saloon at his house, lovers and students of art
may examine at any time a considerable number of his
works. This collection consists for the most part of
paintings of famous persons: Washington life-size,
with the British standards at his feet—Franklin, Paine,
Morris—most of the Major Generals of the American
army—all the Presidents of the Congress; and others
distinguished in the new states are to be found here.
Several painters and artists of mark born in America
have settled elsewhere. Mr. **West,** and Mr. **Du-
chesne** ✚ were particularly mentioned to me, and a
young man of promise, Mr. **Copley.** America as well
as the old world has its geniuses, but these hitherto
(conditions having been such as to assure easier and
richer returns in trade and agriculture) have remained
unknown and undeveloped.

America has produced as yet no sculptors or en-
gravers. But stone-cutters find a pretty good market.
Mr. **Bauer** and Mr. **Häfelein,** at Philadelphia, make
a business of preparing tomb-stones, chimney-pieces,
and other heavy decorative work, using the common
marble of those parts. A foot of worked marble costs

8-12 shillings Pensyl. Current. Mr. Bauer also makes mill-stones, which are split in Salisbury Township, Bucks county, of a rather rough grain, extremely hard. A stone 10 in. in diameter and 14 in. thick costs 20 Pd. Pensyl. Current. He showed me a beautiful brownish-yellow marble, diversly flecked, which came from the region about Easton on the Delaware.

Music was before this last war still quite in its infancy. Besides the organists in the towns and the schoolmasters in the country there were no professional musicians. A darky with a broken and squeezy fiddle made the finest dance-music for the most numerous assembly. Piano-fortes and such instruments were in the houses of the rich only so much fashionable furniture. But during the war and after it straggling musicians from the various armies spread abroad a taste for music, and now in the largest towns concerts are given, and conventional balls. In the item of dancing-masters France has supplied the necessary.

During the first days of my stay at Philadelphia, I visited among others Mr. **Bartram,** the son of the worthy and meritorious botanist (so often mentioned by Kalm) who died six years ago at a great age. Bartram the elder was merely a gardener, but by his own talents and industry, almost without instruction became the first botanist in America, honored with their correspondence by Linnaeus, Collinson, and other savans. He was to be sure more collector than student, but by his enthusiasm and love for plants many new ones were discovered. He made many long journeys on foot through the mountain country, through several of the provinces, and (with Kalm and Conrad Weisser *)

---

* A German universally known and loved among the Indians,

into the interior of Canada. After the peace of 1762, when both the Floridas were apportioned to Great Britain, Bartram received a commission from the King to visit those two provinces. Contrary to his own purpose his journal was published, but Bartram should not be judged by that dry record. Whoever wishes more information regarding him may find it in Hector St. John's Sketches of American Manners. The Bartram garden is situated on an extremely pleasant slope across the Schuylkill and not far from its junction with the Delaware. An old but neat house of stone, on the river side supported rather than adorned by several granite pillars, was the residence of this honored and contented old man. The son, the present owner of the garden, follows the employments of his father, and maintains a very respectable collection of sundry North American plants, particularly trees and shrubs, the seeds and shoots of which he sends to England and France at a good profit. He is not so well known to the botanical world as was his father, but is equally deserving of recognition. When young he spent several years among the Florida Indians, and made a collection of plants in that region; his unprinted manuscript on the nations and products of that country should be instructive and interesting. In the small space of his garden there are to be found assembled really a great variety of American plants, among others, most of their vines and conifers, species of which very little is generally known. The Sarracenia and several other marsh growths do very well here in dry beds—

---

and therefore at one time indispensable on all important occasions as interpreter and coadjutor.

confirmation of what I have often observed with astonishment, namely, that American plants grow anywhere with little or no reference to the place of their origin.*

Bartram senior in his travels had collected as well all manner of rocks and minerals which are now kept in a box without any system intermixed with European specimens, especially Swedish, sent over by Linnaeus Archiater. The son showed them me when I was a second time at Philadelphia and able from my own knowledge to distinguish what was American; but Mr. Bartram was not to be persuaded to sell me these at any price, cherishing in them the memory of his father's industry.

Nearer to Philadelphia, but also on the farther bank of the Schuylkill, there lives a botanist who is the equal of Bartram neither in knowledge nor spirit, although he makes more a-do—Mr. **Young,** by birth a Hessian, who in a strange way has gotten to himself the title of Botanist to the Queen. His father lived at this same place, by what he could make on his bit of land; the son was frequently in Bartram's garden, and found amusement in the variegated blossoms. One day, (so I was told at Philadelphia), he sent to London a paquet of plants which he had collected in the garden, with a letter addressed **To the Queen.** He had placed the paquet unobserved in the bag which is usually kept open at the Coffee-house by ships shortly to clear. Arrived at London the skipper was in a quandary

---

* Since my return I have seen American trees and shrubs more than once, in England and Germany, thriving on dry soils, whereas in America it had been my observation that these varieties were to be found only in swampy places.

whether to deliver the paquet, of which he knew nothing, what it contained or who had sent it; but after
consultation with his friends despatched it as directed.
The Queen, supposing this to be an extraordinary hopeful lad, had the youthful Young brought to London
and placed under the care of the well-known Dr. Hill.
300 Pd. Sterl. was appropriated annually for his use,
and after a time Young came back to America, with
the title, with a large peruque and a small stipend, and
fulfilled none of the hopes he had aroused. Some
years ago, indeed, he had printed at Paris an exhaustive
catalogue of plants presumably in his garden; but I
found that his garden is very extensive—if this or that
plant of the catalogue is not to be found in his garden
he answers with his customary bombast that all
America, field and forest, is his garden.*

The taste for gardening is, at Philadelphia as well
as throughout America, still in its infancy. There are not
yet to be found many orderly and interesting gardens.
Mr. Hamilton's near the city is the only one deserving
special mention. Such neglect is all the more astonishing, because so many people of means spend the most
part of their time in the country. Gardens as at present
managed are purely utilitarian—pleasure-gardens have
not yet come in, and if perspectives are wanted one
must be content with those offered by the landscape,
not very various, what with the still immense forests.

---

* Recently Mr. Humphrey Marshall has made himself known
by his American Grove, ✚ or Alphabetical list of all North
American trees and shrubs, published at Philadelphia in 8vo.
1785. He lives in Pensylvania, in Chester county, and offers
to furnish at a moderate price collections of seeds or of living
plants noticed in his catalogue.

The fruitful warmth of the climate obviates indeed very many difficulties which we have to contend with in securing garden-growths—and makes careless gardeners. So long as people are content merely with the customary products of northern Europe, these may be had at small pains; but with this management the advantages are lost which would be afforded by a better, that is to say, many of the products natural to a warmer climate might be had with a little care. Most of the vegetables and flowers of northern Europe have been introduced. Many of these do well and have even been improved, but others grow worse under careless management. American gardening has nothing of the characteristic to show, beyond several varieties and dubieties of pumpkins, squashes, and gourds, the cultivation of which was usual among the Indians. Several of our vegetables were first introduced by the German troops, e. g. kohlrabi, broccoli, and the black raddish. But certain of our good fruits are lacking, (or at least are very seldom seen and then not the best sorts), such as, plums, apricots, walnuts, good pears, the domestic chestnut, gooseberries, and others, and for no other reason but neglect to make the proper efforts, with patience and attention—for the American cares little for what does not grow of itself, and is satisfied with the great yields of his cherry, apple, and peach trees, without giving a thought to possible and often necessary betterments. They know little or nothing of grafting and inoculations, or use such practices very seldom. Much, without sufficient ground, is charged to the disadvantages of the climate, and people have let themselves be too easily frightened away from gardening, when the trouble was that nothing of the first quality has been produced, because of thin soil, bad seed, and unskilful cultivation.

The taste for garden-flowers is likewise very restricted; however, a few florists are to be found. Dr. Glentworth, ✚ formerly a surgeon in the army, has a numerous collection of beautiful bulbs and other flowers which he maintains by yearly importations from Holland. But as a rule one finds in the gardens nothing but wild jasmine, flower-gentles, globe-amaranths, hibiscus syriacus, and other common things. The beautiful gilliflower, the ranunculus, auricula &c., of these they are little aware. At Dr. Glentworth's I saw another strange phenomenon, which I mention here in passing, i. e. a cross between a cock and a duck. The beast was a perfect hen in the forepart, but in the rear constructed like a duck; its feet were half-webbed and set far back, so that its walk was a waddle, penguin-fashion, almost upright. A person present told me he had seen two similar bastards in the West Indies. They are, however, rare, notwithstanding many cocks seem to show a preference for ducks.

Deformities and misgrowths, especially of the human species, are rarer in America (where everything is truer to nature) than elsewhere. An American dwarf exhibited himself recently at Philadelphia; I had already seen him at York. He was born in Jersey, was 23 years old, and his height 3 ft. 4 in., London measure, with the exception of the head pretty well formed to scale. It is worth the trouble to be a dwarf in America: he showed himself for not less than a half-dollar Spanish for grown people, and the half of that for children.—Another rare phenomenon is an adult with an immoderately large head, so heavy that he can never raise it; he lives in Jersey near to the Passaik Falls and has lain 27 years, his age, in the cradle.*

The present Governor of Pensylvania, Mr. **Dickinson**, is known as a man of keen intellect, although his enemies of which he has many, (governors of a republic may have them without much trouble), prefer to paint him in dark colors. He showed his spirit and capacity, politically, by a collection of **Letters** under the fanciful name of **An American Farmer** but these are not to be confused with another collection, of a similar title, **Letters of an American Cultivator. +** I desired to make him my duty, and in order to be received by him I had recourse to a physician of my acquaintance, who excused himself on the ground that he had been against the Governor at the last election. I then went to an American Major with the same request, and he likewise excused himself because at the last rising of the troops he had had some difficulty with the Governor over their pay. I betook myself therefore to a Quaker confidently believing I had come to the right man since Dickinson himself is of the Society of Friends; but my Quaker assured me he had nothing to do with the Governor, and that my intended courtesy was superfluous. Finally I sought out another doctor who also thought my proposed visit unnecessary and told me the Governor was ill. So I let the matter stop

---

* " His name is Peter van Winkle, born 1754, from the feet to the chin he measures 4 ft. 5 in., from the chin to the poll a foot precisely, from the chin to the root of the nose 7 in., thence over the head to the neck 25 in., round the temples 32 in." Further information has been published by Counsellor Michaelis in *Med. Beyträg.* ———— Michaelis, *Med. prakt. Bibl.* I, 91.

with that, but regretted I could not meet one whose
vainglory, not satisfied with the government of so considerable a province as Pensylvania was at the same
time putting in for another, that of the state of Delaware. But this may have been from lofty patriotism.

The inhabitants of Philadelphia seemed to me to
have retained something of that suspicious reserve
which policy compelled them to adopt at the beginning
of the war, and while it lasted, in their dealings with
strangers—behavior due in the first instance partly to
fear, partly to aversion for political dissentients. It has
been said for a long time of Philadelphia that one
might not gain a footing in houses there so easily as
in the neighboring York, the explanation of which was
chiefly that the Quakers excluded all but their own
particular friends, and this behavior, imitated among
the bulk of the inhabitants, has in some sort remained a
characteristick. The war, however, which must be
thanked in America for so many things, and the number of Europeans present in the country (especially the
French) have worked already a positive revolution in
America. Burnaby remarked with regret that people
were not very courteous and hospitable to strangers;
he would have less cause to say as much now. But I
must acknowledge that those among the Philadelphians
who have visited foreign countries are incomparably
more engaging and polite than others who hold courtesy to be reserve; those who have travelled have
learned by experience how obliging even the smallest
attention is to a stranger, and they practice what elsewhere has pleased them. Not so, those entirely home-
bred. Two of my friends, Englishmen, came from
York to see Philadelphia and found rooms in a house

7

where strangers were customably taken in. It so happened that an American traveller, by the exchange of a room, made place for the two Englishmen. The lady of the house promised that the matter would be so arranged, but at the same time unreservedly remarked, ' you know,' (as if a thing of common knowledge in Philadelphia), ' you know that people do not like to inconvenience themselves to oblige a stranger.'

The behavior of the Philadelphians is for the rest only one among the consequences of the spirit of freedom, a British inheritance strengthened by removal to American soil and still more by the successful outcome of the war. From of old these were strong and active republicans. Freedom has been, since many years, the genius and the vow of Pensylvania and of all the North American states. Many and various as have been the reasons assigned for the outbreak of the war and the separation of the colonies from the mother-country, it has seemed to me that the true and only reason has been overlooked. There was a set purpose in America to make the land free and any pretext would serve. England might have removed one burden after another, might have given encouragement after encouragement, but fresh excuses would have been constantly sought and found so as to bring about a final breach. It is a matter of wonder to me, in this connection, that nobody mentions the prediction spoken of by Kalm * ✚ who heard it as early as 1748 during his stay in America and gives it as a thing well-known. "I have often, he remarks, heard it said openly by Englishmen, and not only by those born in America but

---

* Reisen. Deutsche Ausg. II, 401.

also by those recently come from Europe, that the English plantations in northern America would in 30-50 years form a separate kingdom, quite independent of England."

People think, act, and speak here precisely as it prompts them; the poorest day-laborer on the bank of the Delaware holds it his right to advance his opinion, in religious as well as political matters, with as much freedom as the gentleman or the scholar. And **as yet** there is to be found as little distinction of rank among the inhabitants of Philadelphia as in any city in the world. No one admits that the Governor has any particular superiority over the private citizen except in so far as he is the right hand of the law, and to the law, as occasion demands is respect paid, through the Governor; for the law equally regards and deals with all citizens. Riches make no positive material difference, because in this regard every man expects at one time or another to be on a footing with his rich neighbor, and in this expectation shows him no knavish reverence, but treats him with an open, but seemly, familiarity. Posts of honor confer upon the holder merely a conditional superiority, necessary in the eyes of every discreet man as a support of order and government. All rank and precedence is for the rest the acquirement of personal worth. Rank of birth is not recognized, is resisted with a total force.

Luxury, which is unavoidable in enlightened free nations, prevails here also, without, however, any dispossession of industry and thrift, being largely restricted to the luxury of the body; virtuosity, sensibility and other manifestations of soul-luxury are not yet become conspicuous here.

The taste in dress is chiefly English, extremely simple, neat, and elegant. The finest cloth and the finest linen are the greatest adornment. Only a few young gentlemen, especially those of the army, approximate to the French cut, but they by no means give themselves over to the ostentatious frippery by which, here also, certain Frenchmen are distinguished. The women, as everywhere, seeking to please allow themselves more variety of ornament. Every year dressed dolls are brought them from Europe, which, silent, give the law of the mode. However, distinction of rank among the feminine half, is not striking as a result of any distinct costume; in the item of dress each selects according to her taste, means, and circumstances.

The women of North America have long since been the subject of particular praise, ✚ regarding their virtue and good conduct, rendered them by both travellers and the homekeeping. It is not easy to find a woman, remarks one of their panegyrists, who makes a parade of unbelief, although they are not always members of any particular sect. Gallant adventures are little known and still less practiced in this last refuge of virtue pursued. Conjugal disloyalties, on either side, are punished by ineffaceable infamy, and the culprit, however protected by wealth, position, or other advantage, soon finds himself without honor, distrusted. This is no extravagant praise, and the **Abbé Robin** himself admits that his countrymen did not in America meet with their habitual good fortune in affairs of gallantry. The feminine part of America is none the less made for pleasure and partakes, and Rochefoucault would have likely assigned another reason for their virtue. Thus, a traditional practice of **bundling,**

the vogue in certain parts of America,* especially New
England, ✚ might well give our European fair another
idea of western restraint.   That is to say, it is a custom
there for young men to pay visits to their mistresses ;
and the young woman's good name is no ways im-
paired, so that the visit takes place by stealth, or after
they are actually betrothed ; on the contrary, the parents are advised, and these meetings happen when the
pair is enamored and merely wish to know each other
better.   The swain and the maiden spend the evening
and the night undisturbed by the hearth, or it may be
go to bed together without scruple ; in the latter case,
with the condition that they do not take off their clothes ;
and if the anxious mother has any doubt of the strict
virtue of her daughter, it is said she takes the precaution of placing both the daughter's feet in one large
stocking, and in the morning looks to see if this
guardian is still properly fixed, but the inquiry is commonly superfluous, the circumstance having rarely any
other consequence than in regular betrothal, which is
the object had in view in allowing the meeting.   When
it is said in praise of America that there are seldom
other consequences due to the intimate association of
the sexes, it must be remarked that people there generally marry with less forethought and earlier, and that
in almost every house there are negresses, slaves, who
count it an honor to bring a mulatto into the world.

Philadelphia boasted once of its especially good police,
and knew nothing of tumultuary and mutinous gather-

---

* Burnaby noticed it in Virginia.   Vid. Travels through the
Middle Colonies of North America. p. 170.   [Burnaby's note
is in regard to a different custom. cf. reprint, 3d ed., New
York 1904, p. 142]

ings of the people which were not seldom the case with their more northern neighbors. This advantageous character (due, like everything else good, to the peaceful principles of the Quakers), was lost during the war, when mobs often took possession of the city and particularly mishandled the Quakers in their quiet houses.

To be industrious and frugal, at least more so than the inhabitants of the provinces to the South, is the recognized and unmistakeable character of the Philadelphians and in great part of all those inhabiting Pensylvania. Without boasting, I daresay it is the fact that, in conjunction with the Quakers, the German-Pensylvania nation has had the largest share in the forming of this praiseworthy folk-character.

The German nation forms a considerable part, probably more than a third, of the state of Pensylvania. The Quakers, who at first gave the tone in political affairs, strove for that reason to win to their side the Germans, who were scattered about the country and commended themselves by their retired, industrious, and frugal manner of life. The Quakers have never gone very far from Philadelphia, individual members of the sect not liking to settle far from the rest, but preferring to draw together in little colonies. It was therefore a policy with them to be on good terms with the outlying inhabitants and they found it the easier to come by their ends through a good understanding with the Germans, since these together outnumbered any one of the other nationalities among the colonists, English, Scottish, Irish, and Swedish. The ancestors of these Germans came to America all in similar circumstances, as indeed many have come during and since the war. That is to say, they left the fatherland

out of poverty or in the hope at least of finding better
fortune, able to grow rich with less trouble. Many of
them, indeed very many of them, have seen their desires fulfilled, although at first they were obliged to
bind themselves out for a term of years so as to pay
the cost of the voyage, if, as it often happened, they
did not bring with them property in that amount. From
very insignificant beginnings the most of them have
come to good circumstances, and many have grown
rich. For here the poor man who is industrious finds
opportunities enough for gain, and there is no excuse
for the slothful. Where a German settles, there commonly are seen industry and economy, more than with
others, all things equal—his house is better-built and
warmer, his land is better fenced, he has a better garden, and his stabling is especially superior; everything
about his farm shows order and good management in
all that concerns the care of the land. The Germans
are known throughout America as an industrious
people, but particularly those of them that come over
from Europe, and in all the provinces it is desired
that their numbers increase, they being everywhere
valued as good citizens, and I daresay that Pensylvania is envied for the greater number of them settled
there, since it is universally allowed that without them
Pensylvania would not be what it is. The greater part
of the German emigrants were originally of humble
origin and meagre education, nor have they or their
descendants greatly changed in their principles of action. On the whole they show little or no zeal to bring
themselves up in any way except by small trade or
handicrafts or farming. To use their gains for allow-
able pleasures, augmenting the agreeableness of life,

this very few of them have learned to do, and others
with a bad grace. The lucre is stuck away in old
stockings or puncheon chests until opportunity offers to
buy more land which is the chief object of their desires. In their houses, in the country especially, they
live thriftily, often badly. There is wanting among
them the simple unaffected neatness of the English
settlers, who make it a point, as far as they are able,
to live seemly, in a well-furnished house, in every way
as comports with the **gentleman.** The economy of the
German farmer in Pensylvania is precisely the same as
that customary in Germany—even when his next neighbor every day sets him a better example. A great
four-cornered stove, a table in the corner with benches
fastened to the wall, everything daubed with red, and
above, a shelf with the universal German farmer's
library: the Almanack, and Song-book, a small ' Garden
of Paradise,' Habermann, **+** and the Bible. It is in vain
to look for other books, whereas in the cabins of the
English there are not seldom seen, at the least, fragments of the *Spectator,* journals, magazines, or dictionaries. The highest delight of the German countryman in Pensylvania is—drink. He drives many miles
to Philadelphia to market, sleeping in his wagon, living
on the bread and cheese he takes along, but having
made a good sale, he is certain to turn in at some grog-
shop on his way home—drinks in good spirits a glass
of wine, drinks perhaps a second, and a third, recks
no more and often leaves his entire wallet at the bung.

They give their children little education and have
no fancy for seeing their sons parading in the pulpit
or the Court-house. Not until this last war, (when
several regiments were raised among the Pensylvania

Germans), have any of them been seized with a passion
to appear in a better light, by going about after posts
of honor.   Their conversation is neither interesting
nor pleasing, and if so, it is because they have had a
better bringing-up in Germany or, native-born, have
become English quite, and thus they are no longer
Germans and withdrawn by their own wish from intercourse with their people.   In the towns there prevails an altogether different tone among the German
families.   They feel that no distinction of rank imposes
any restraint on them, and behave as if farmers turned
lords.   I met at Philadelphia only one or two agreeable and intelligent women of German origin, but they
spoke German very little and did not owe their breeding
to their own people.

There is a striking contrast between the untaught
class: German and English.   In the same circumstances
and with the same faculties the Englishman invariably
shows more information; the German has the advantage in superstitions and prejudices and is less intelligent in political matters.   However, the German
country-people are extremely jealous of their liberties,
and of their rights in the matter of sending members to
the Assembly, although they find it difficult at times to
get capable men.   For it often happens that members
chosen from among the German farmers and sent to the
Assembly are not sufficiently equipped with the English
language, and so make but dumb chair-fillers and never
dare to give their opinions openly—and, when questions are to be decided, discreetly range themselves
with the majority, sitting quietly by until they see
which side has the numbers.   Really they often know
nothing of what the question is before the Assembly,

because of the very slight tincture they have of the language. The story is that once an honorable German member heard that the business was whether to Move the House,* which he literally took to mean whether the house should be removed. He said nothing, but went out to the door and entirely around the large Assembly-house, then came back shaking his head and gave it as his opinion that it would be no easy matter. Just this year an old German countryman, no doubt an oracle among his tap-house friends, was elected to the Assembly from his district and sent to Philadelphia, where he was welcomed and congratulated. 'Ey,' said he, 'I wish they had let me alone—what do I understand of all that chitter—I wish I was at home looking after my things.' I have since seen members of that cut, in blue stockings and yellow-leather breeches, sleeping off boredom in the Assembly.

The lack as yet of numerous good schools and of capable teachers for the people; the further lack of educated and disinterested Germans who might by their example inspire imitation; the prevalent policy under the former régime of bestowing conspicuous office mainly on the English, European or American; and the extremely trifling advantages accruing to the merely educated German—such are the chief reasons, possibly, why the German nation in America has hitherto shown so little zeal in the item of self-advancement, preferring the gains from moderate labor

---

* 'Move the house' signifies to lay before the Assembly a question for decision by a majority of votes; the vote is taken either by a raising of the hands for 'Aye,' or by those in the affirmative going to one side and those in the negative to the other, where they are counted by the Speaker.

and trade (certain and uncomplicated) to any difficult pestering with books.

The language which our German people make use of is a miserable, broken, fustian salmagundy of English and German, with respect both to the words and their syntaxis. Grown people come over from Germany forget their mother-tongue in part, while seeking in vain to learn the new speech, and those born in the country hardly ever learn their own language in an orderly way. The children of Germans, particularly in the towns, grow accustomed to English in the streets ; their parents speak to them in one language and they answer in the other. The near kinship of the English and the German helps to make the confusion worse. If the necessary German word does not occur to the memory, the next best English one is at once substituted, and many English words are so currently used as to be taken for good German. In all legal and public business English is used solely. Thus English becomes indispensable to the Germans, and by contact and imitation grows so habitual that even among themselves they speak at times bad German, at times a worse English, for they have the advantage of people of other nationalities, in being masters of no one language. The only opportunity the Germans have of hearing a set discourse in their own language, (reading being out of the question) is at church. But even there, the minister preaching in German they talk among themselves their bastard jargon. There are a few isolated spots, for example in the mountains, where the people having less intercourse with the English understand nothing but German, but speak none the better. The purest German is heard in the Moravian colonies.—As proof I will give literally what a German farmer said to me, a German, in German: ✚

"Ich hab' wollen, said he, mit meinem Nachbar "tscheinen (join) und ein Stück geklaret (cleared) "Land purtchasen (purchase). Wir hätten, no doubt, "ein guten Barghen (bargain) gemacht, und hatten "können gut darauf ausmachen. Ich war aber net "capable so'ne Summe Geld aufzumachen, und konnt "nicht länger expekten. Das thät mein Nachbar net "gleichen, und fieng an mich übel zu yuhsen (use one "ill), so dacht ich, 's ist besser du thust mit aus (to "do without).— — Or thus: Mein Stallion ist über "die Fehns getcheupt, und hat dem Nachbar sein "Whiet abscheulich gedämätscht." That is, Mein Hengst ist über den Zaun gesprungen, und hat des Nachbars Weizen ziemlich beschädiget—But it is not enough, that English words are used as German—e. g. **schmart** (smart, active, clever)—**serben**, geserbt haben (serve, &c); they go farther and translate literally, as **absezen**, instead of *abreisen, sich auf den Weg machen,* from the English 'set off'; **einen auf den Weg sezen,** *einen auf den rechten Weg bringen,* from the English 'put one in the road'; **abdrehen,** *sich vom Weg abwenden,* from the English 'turn off'; **aufkommen mit einem,** *jemanden auf den Weg einhohlen,* from the English 'come up with one.'—Often they make a German word of an English one, merely by the sound, when the sense of the two is quite different, as **das belangt zu mir,** *das gehört mir,* from the English 'this belongs to me,' although 'belangen' and 'belong' have entirely different meanings; or **ich thue das nicht gleichen,** from the English 'I do not like that,' instead of *das gefällt mir nicht.* It is not worth

the trouble to put down more of this sort of non-sense
which many of my countrymen still tickle the ears
with. And besides speaking scurvily, there is as bad
writing and printing. Melchior Steiner's German establishment (formerly Christoph Sauer's) prints a weekly
German newspaper which contains numerous sorrowful
examples of the miserably deformed speech of our
American fellow-countrymen. This newspaper is
chiefly made up of translations from English sheets,
but so stiffly done and so anglic as to be mawkish. The
two German ministers and Mr. Steiner himself oversee the sheet. If I mistake not, Mr. Kunze alone receives 100 Pd. Pens. Current for his work. 'If we
wrote in German,' say the compilers in excuse, ' our
American farmers would neither understand it nor
read it.'

It was hardly to be expected that the German language, even as worst degenerated, could ever have gone
to ruin and oblivion with quite such rapidity—public
worship, the Bible, and the estimable almanack * might,
so it seems, transmit a language for many generations,
even if fresh emigrants did not from time to time add
new strength. But probably the free and immediate
intercourse now begun between the mother-country and
America will involve a betterment of the language.
Since America, in the item of German literature, is 30-
40 years behind, it might possibly be a shrewd specula-

---

* Several Deutsche Amerikanisch Stadt-und Land-Calender
appear annually, published by Mr. Steiner and Mr. Carl Cist.
Plan and arrangement the same as with our praiseworthy
Almanack in quarto—articles on bleeding and lancing, how to
judge the blood, how to fell trees, edifying stories, home-spun
verse—nothing omitted.

tion to let loose from their book-stall prisons all our
unread and forgotten poets and prosaists and transport
them to America after the manner of the English (at
one time) and their jail-birds.

There has existed for some years a **Privileged German Society at Philadelphia Plan and Status of
which an Address before the Society by Joh. Christ.
Kunze, Professor of the Oriental and German Languages at the University of Philadelphia, and Member of the said Society. Philadelphia. Printed by
M. Steiner. 1782. 8vo. pp. 62, sets forth. ✚**

Mr. **Kunze**, who plainly sees the lack of good German schools (and the consequent decline of the language), and feels as a patriot the necessity for better
instruction generally, proposed to establish such
schools * with a view mainly to the education of young
people of the three religions. His enthusiasm greatly
meriting approbation has thus far received little practical support. Meetings of this society are regularly
held; its objects are not merely scientific, but include
assistance to be rendered in-coming Germans who
finding no one to take them in and meeting with no
friends are often the victims of greed or other wicked-
ness—the attention of the society is directed to everything which may redound to the honor, good treatment,
and encouragement of the German nation. Since this
is a matter which cannot well be of indifference to
many of my readers, I can do no better than devote a
few pages of the Appendix to the statements of the
founder himself.†

---

* With regard to his plans for a Latin school among the
Germans of Philadelphia, Vid. Schlözer's *Briefwechsel*. I,
4, 206.

† A German Society at New York, ✚ on the plan of the Pen-

The clergy of the German nation, it was to be expected, would scatter not only the seeds of the gospel but those of scientific enlightenment as well. However, among the few ministers in all America a few only can give their mind to these things and fewer yet will. With the exception of several worthy men, chiefly in the larger towns, the services of the clergy are very ambiguous. Their position is not an agreeable one. They depend absolutely on the caprice of their congregations who (to use their own expression) hire a pastor from year to year at 20-30 or more pounds.—And so the ministers are often obliged to take charge of several congregations if they are to earn a passable support. Many of them, after the manner of the Apostles, have to carry on another occupation for a living. Mr. Kunze recently paid a visit to a worthy colleague beyond the Schuylkill. When he came into the house the pastor's wife asked him, ' Do you wish to see the pastor or the cobbler? '—the pastoral office not bringing in enough to support the little family, the son added to the income by shoemaking, in which his father lent a hand. Congregations may dismiss their ministers so soon as they have the misfortune to displease. But before that pass, much must happen; the pastor preaching no strict morality, out of recompense and Christian love little faults on his part are overlooked.

To be sure, all the clergy in America (outside the English establishment) were without support from the civil authorities, which not inducting them left them to their congregations entirely. Each sect was per-

sylvania Society, held its first meeting Sept. 15, 1784,—the President is Colonel Lutterlobe.

mitted to dance as it would and manage the whistling as it could—for if the state interfered in church affairs in America there would be no end, and only evil could come of it.   The Presbyterians indeed are not exposed to the blind choice or dismission of a freakish congregation, their discipline depending on an assembly of all the ministers.   Only the ministers of the English establishment (because consecrated by some one of the English bishops and paid by the King) had under the old régime a closer connection with the state.   The German Lutheran ministers, however, meet together at times in Synods to discuss general questions; at such meetings the office of President passes from one to another, since they are all equally independent.

The Philadelphia market deserves a visit from every foreigner.   Astonishment is excited not only by the extraordinary store of provisions but also by the cleanliness and good order in which the stock is exposed for sale.   The Market-house proper consists of two open halls which extend from First to Third-street, and additional space, on both sides of Market-street and along adjoining streets, swarms with buyers and sellers.   On the evenings before the chief market days (these are Wednesdays and Saturdays) all the bells in the city are rung.   People from a distance, especially the Germans, come into Philadelphia in great covered wagons, loaded with all manner of provender, bringing with them rations for themselves and feed for their horses—for they sleep in their wagons.   Besides, numerous carts and horses bring in from all directions the rich surplus of the country; everything is full of life and action. Meats are supplied not only by the city butchers, but by the country people as well—for America is not yet

cursed with exclusive guild-rights and the police is not
bribed. The Americans on the whole, like the English,
consume more meat than vegetables and the market
furnishes them the choicest store, cut very neatly. Besides the customary sorts of meat, Europeans find in
season several dishes new to them, such as raccoons,
opossums, fish-otters, bear-bacon, and bear's foot &c, as
well as many indigenous birds and fishes. In products
of the garden the market although plentiful is not of
great variety, for divers of our better European cab-
bages and other vegetables are lacking ; on the other
hand all sorts of melons and many kinds of pumpions
are seen in great quantity, and fruits also. I have by
me no prices-current of the Philadelphia market, but
I remember that at the time the best butchers' meat
cost only four pence, in the same market where we had
paid 15 times as much in the year 1778, 3 shillings 9
pence Pensylv. Current , that is, to 4 shillings ; and notwithstanding that prices of provisions have in general
not fallen to the low level customary before the war,
for not more than a guinea a week a room could be had
in several of the public houses, with breakfast, plentiful
dinner, and supper, and in private boarding-houses for
less or more as one preferred.

The war has left no sign of want here ; now, as before, the same exuberant plenty prevails. The inhabitants are not only well clothed but well fed, and,
comparatively, better than their betters in Europe.
Few families can be found who do not enjoy daily their
fine wheat-bread, good meats and fowls, cyder, beer,
and rum. Want oppresses but few. Work is rewarded
and there is no need of catch-pole beadles.

While the war still lasted several institutions were

8

established at Philadelphia which are not commonly
thought of during a war, and if so, only because a
fortunate outcome is anticipated with certainty.   In
this category is a public **Bank** *, an establishment as
useful to trade in general as to the individual merchant,
furthering his convenience and security.   This bank is
adequately secured by the subscriptions of a great number of moneyed persons, under mortgage of their real
property.   It is at the same time a bank of exchange
and of loans.   As a sure guaranty of hard money deposited, there are issued bank-notes (the smallest
amount 10 Spanish dollars) which are unhesitatingly
received, both in the city and in the country, at their
specie valuation.   These bills are signed by the President, Director, and Company of the **Bank of North
America,** but there is no right to the title except in so
far as this was the first bank established in North
America; for certain other cities, Boston and Charleston, are about to open banks, seeing the great advantages of such institutions in the furtherance of an extensive trade.   The founding of the bank was made the
easier by the great quantity of Spanish dollars brought
into the country during the last years of the war for
American flour sold at the Havannah, and by the number of British guineas put in circulation by the army,
both prisoners and effectives.   The guineas have all
been carefully clipped, partly to make them more uniform with the other currency, partly to prevent their
desertion to the fatherland.   Against security given,

---

* " The bank established at Philadelphia for the facilitating
of commerce and the circulation of money has had no stability
and is entirely given over " *Hamb. Polit. Jour.*, Octob. 1786.

merchants may borrow cash from the bank. Interest
accruing in this way and other perquisites bring in a
considerable amount. The first plan of this bank, if I
am not mistaken, was sketched by the celebrated financier Bob Morris.

Instead of a Bourse they use the Coffee-house, where
most people engaged in business affairs meet together
at midday to get news of entering or clearing vessels,
and to inform themselves of the market.

Trade was still at this time in a very uncertain and
disordered state, and it was difficult to foresee what
turn it would take. On the one hand the hatred of
England, as yet pretty general and pretty warm,
seemed to be favorable to the French and other nations
competing for the American trade, and all the more
because their goods were offered cheaper than the English. But on the other hand, their manufactures are
found to be inferior to the English in intrinsic goodness, not executed according to the English mode, and
less substantially ; and instead of the general preference
for the English manufactures being done away with,
they have gained by comparison with the goods of
other nations. Besides, no one of the trading nations
is able or willing to give such long and heavy credits
as the Americans have been accustomed to from England. The peace proposals in the spring of 1783 at
once tempted to America a great number of European
vessels from various countries. Only a few came off
well in the speculation. Most of the undertakers were
acquainted neither with the goods current among the
Americans nor with the American taste, and the market being so overset it was a difficult matter to sell
either for cash money or for produce. Money began to

be tight shortly after the peace, and the Americans, accustomed to deal with England on long credit, were neither able nor inclined to pay cash for cargoes. Produce was not everywhere to be had in such quantity as to make up profitable return cargoes, and prices rose so high with the heavy demand that on returning to Europe it was found that such articles were almost as cheap there as in America. The American merchants (a peace seeming to be pretty certain) had forehandedly placed their orders in England; but when they found that so many Germans, Hollanders, and French were coming in with goods, they hurriedly and secretly countermanded their orders in England, but at the same time gave the foreigners to understand that they were hourly expecting from England the same sorts of goods as those offered, and for other reasons as well could make no use of their goods. And so these adventuring foreigners were obliged to let their cargoes go under the hammer at any price at all; the Americans in this way secured the goods below purchase-price and, the English orders being in great part written off, could sell at a great profit.—Thus they came by their ends and gained at the cost of inexperienced foreigners, their very obliging friends.

Philadelphia is the only sea-port of Pensylvania; therefore the whole trade of the province centres at Philadelphia, with the exception of certain regions beyond the Susquehannah to which Baltimore lies more convenient. To Philadelphia the countryman brings what he has to sell and there buys what he needs. The products of Pensylvania are in no way peculiar to itself, being the same as those found in the adjacent provinces of Jersey and New York; however, certain of them are preferred to those of other regions. The chief products are,—wheat, flour and biscuit, peas, beans, Indian corn, salted meats, bacon and hams, tongues, dried and smoked game, salted and dried fish (shad and herring), honey and wax, hides and skins, iron, masts, timber, boards, rafters, shingles, stoves, and ready-built ships. Of this domestic produce, the greater part was formerly sent to the British West Indies, whence was brought back sugar, brandy, cotton, coffee, cacao, mahogany, and silver—part for use in the country and part exported to other colonies and to Europe. There was formerly a trade in wheat to the south of Europe, to Spain and Portugal; and to England there was sent iron, hemp and flaxseed, leather, skins, ships, and ships' supplies, and profitably, because on certain of these articles the Americans were paid a premium by the English government; others, however, could be furnished cheaper than it was possible for England to find them elsewhere, because the Americans took back manufactured articles, indeed were obliged to. For Pensylvania and America at large had not then, nor have they now, considerable manufactures of their own, and for this reason will long be dependent on Europe. Several obstacles stand in the way of manufactures. Lack of the necessary workmen, able on the whole to do better at farming, and for that reason the English government was careful rather to keep back manufactures than to encourage them. So long as land is to be had there will be few persons willing to subject themselves to the heavy, tedious, and regular labor necessary for manufactures, when by farming they may earn their bread with more freedom and on the whole with less work. Another hindrance is the high wages which every class of laborers demands, and all the more stubbornly demands because they know the scarcity. A third hindrance is the want of money, and the uncommonly high interest paid for the use of capitals—in Pensylvania and New York 6-7 per centum, in South Carolina 8 and more; this with the other difficulties in the way would too much diminish any profit that might be hoped for. Besides, it has been sufficiently shown by experience that nothing can be made in America which cannot be had cheaper from Europe. To be sure, America has the crude material (or can get it) for all kinds of manufactures, but until all the land is occupied and so far settled that all hands cannot be employed in agriculture and a part must look for other ways of getting a living, that is to say, for many years yet, America must bring from Europe the most of what it needs for use or luxury. The countryman, indeed, makes from his wool a sort of rough cloth or contrives linen from his flax, but such things are not for the exigencies of the multitude. Hats are made in several parts of America, but especially at Philadelphia, of an excellent quality and from nothing but beaver-skins, and in the country these are preferred to any of European make. The best are sold for 6-8 Spanish dollars. Their fault is they are too thick and heavy and do not hold the color so well as the European. They make commoner sorts of racoon, mink, and hare-skins; woolen hats of an inferior sort can be imported cheaper than they can be made, and of the finer hats a great number are sold every year to the Americans by Europe, and because of the cheapness. Notwithstanding there is no lack of shoemakers in America, every year a great quantity of shoes are brought over, particularly to the southern provinces. But **women's shoes** find a good market everywhere. There is made in America almost as good **upper leather** as in England, but not in sufficient quantity. Their **sole leather** is inferior to the English. A sort of rough **paper** is made in America, but not enough of it to supply the printers of newspapers. There are sugar-refineries in New York, at Philadelphia and in New England— here and there the domestic maple-sugar is mixed in and boiled with the rest. Rum and brandy distilleries are everywhere. Several **glass-fabrics** have been set up but they have not all succeeded. One at Boston and one at New York went to nothing. At Frederick-town in Maryland, in Pensylvania, and if I am not mistaken, in Jersey, there are several fabrics but the product is only a bad sort of green glass. It is said that no suitable earth has yet been found in America for the glass smelting-furnaces, and hence the necessary materials have had to be brought from England; but the materials will certainly be found whenever a vigorous enough search is made for them.

A **porcelain fabrick** was about to be established at Philadelphia [August 1783] by a French regimental surgeon. The clay brought from Maryland for the purpose is fine and smooth, and some small specimens of porcelain had been fused out very successfully. However, many difficulties are yet to be overcome and the price of the finished porcelain must be greatly more than for European ware.

Someone at Philadelphia had made **steel** from American iron, which, by the account of trustworthy people is equal to the best European steel; but nothing was done beyond the experiment, and I suppose that there were no profits to be reckoned on.

At the beginning of the war **salpetre** was prepared in America, but, as it appeared, merely because it was necessary to find a substitute for the cheaper European article. For so soon as the alliance with France made importations freer, the preparation of the inland salt-petre, was given over, and so, in the mountains particularly, no end of material is on hands.

A similar fate met other attempts in several branches of manufactures. But all this is proof only that in its present situation America cannot undertake what, after a few generations,* will be less difficult. Of individual craftsmen America has, if not all that are needed, at least the most necessary.

---

* And until then they must contrive to do without dispensable articles and must give thought to the best possible way of augmenting their inland products, these being not sufficient to pay for necessary importations from foreign states. For it is only because America, on the whole, needs or imports more foreign articles than it can pay for in cash or in produce that there have arisen complaints recently over the decline of trade.

From Philadelphia

After a stay of 10 days I left Philadelphia the 6th of August, intending to visit Bethlehem and from there to proceed into the mountains.

In the neighborhood of Philadelphia, towards Germantown, many doleful reminders of the war were still to be met with, that is to say, burned and ruined houses. The road to Germantown is over a level sandy-loam, through a pleasant, open, well-cultivated region, of many houses. Here as well as along the exquisite Schuylkill are to be found sundry neat and tasteful country-houses, although of a plan neither extensive nor durable. There met us going to market many wagons, drawn by four or more splendid horses, driven without reins merely by the voice and the whip.

Germantown is distant only six English miles from Philadelphia; the place itself is two to three miles long. The houses all stand more or less apart, and about each are grounds with garden and outbuildings. Most of the houses are well and thickly built of stone, and some of them are really fine. Among the most conspicuous is the house at the north end of the town, where Colonel Musgrave with a company of British light infantry so stoutly defended himself in the fall of 1776 against a numerous corps of the American army. Germantown owes its name and foundation to a German colony which was brought to Pensylvania by Franz Daniel Pastorius of Weinsheim in the year 1685. The in-

habitants are still almost entirely German, with a few
Quakers who have settled among them. Their business is farming with somewhat of linen and woolen-
weaving and other trades ; in particular a good quantity
of common woolen stockings was at one time made
here, but by no means enough to supply a fourth part
of the country. It is asserted that America does not
yet produce wool enough to furnish each inhabitant
so much as one pair of stockings. Among the residents
of Germantown are many well-to-do people ; and many
Philadelphians own land and houses here, and use the
place as a resort for summer. By reason of its nearness also, excursions are often made hither ; on Sundays the whole street is filled with the carts and coaches
of pleasure-seeking Philadelphians. There are in the
place a Lutheran and a Reformed church and a Quaker
meeting-house. Also a few families of another sect,
called 'Tumblers,' live here ; they wear beards and a
simple dress but not after the manner of the Quakers.
They are similar to the Anabaptists, but I cannot say
how they are distinguished in creed or opinions, for it
is a difficult matter to come at the idiosyncrasies of the
many religious sects in America.

Beyond Germantown the country lies uneven and
hilly, but still shows the sandy clay which in spots resembles somewhat the **red Jersey soil**. Some loose
fragments of rock by the way were made up of a sandy
slate or splintery stone with much mica. The same sort
of rock * appears frequently throughout the Germantown region and towards the Schuylkill ; most of the
houses of Germantown are built of this stone.

---

* A sort of gneiss containing granite at times. Kalm mentions that he found lime in the splintery mica-rock.

Two miles beyond Germantown we came to **Chesnut-hill** and spent the night there.   **Chesnut-hill** is one of a range of hills, all dry and infertile, or at least, if anything is to be got of them requiring more labor and manure then is commonly given.   The lower land hereabouts brings three and four times as much as these meagre limestone hills.   But here and there a beautiful prospect may be had from them, over the lowland in the foreground and its jewel the city of Philadelphia.   As yet one looks in vain for such prospects in most parts of America.   A Quaker, Mr. Elm, was moved by the situation to build him a house in the form of an ancient, high watch-tower.   So extraordinary a building astonished the country-people who with one consent gave it the name of *Elm's Folly;* but they come assiduously to make the Folly useful, for a small donative delighting the eyes from the roof of the building. From there can be seen, some miles distant, the **White-marsh** region where General Washington safe on the heights, mocked at General Howe in the winter of 1778.

In the woods by the road no remarkable plants were to be found.   These dry hills seem as if designed for sheep walks.   Nowhere in America are many large flocks kept ; it is common for landowners to keep a few, according to the acreage of their possessions.   Community pastures are not the custom, but by means of them in many places larger herds could be kept with less trouble and oversight.   What with the lack everywhere of manure (they give no attention to the matter), it is astonishing that **pen-folds** have not been introduced here to a greater extent—they are very seldom seen.   A farmer in Jersey found pen-folding very profitable, since in that way he made a tract of poor land rich and at the same time got wealth by the sheep themselves. Sheep in America, it is said, are less subject to diseases than our European sheep, and seldom have the snivel, except now and then a similar disease shows itself on low swampy meadows. Dr. Bond says that this disease resembling the snivel is neither so contagious nor so severe as the disease in Europe, and the same is true of cattle diseases, which very seldom appear and in certain regions are unknown. The wool, notwithstanding the negligence with which the sheep are handled, is really very good and fine; but nobody thinks of increasing the supply and making it a branch of trade.* The country people make hats or articles of dress of the wool, doing the work themselves. Indeed they are often too negligent to shear at the proper time, and quite indifferent, see wool on every bush, left hanging by the sheep pasturing beneath.

The taverns in the country are recognizable, even at a distance, by a sort of gallows arrangement which stands out over the road and exhibits the patron of the house. So far we have observed many times the counterfeit presentment of Frederick the Second, King of Prussia, hung up in this way, that monarch having been a great favorite of the Americans ever since the war before the last. We still found a few **Georges**, let hang perhaps out of sympathy, but of Queens of England we saw a good many. We have as yet seen no

---

* As yet no province has a superfluity of wool for export. Only from Nantucket Island is any wool exported, but there the most considerable flocks are pastured on commons. A pound of wool in America costs about 1 shilling sterling or a little more.

King of France, but a number of Washingtons and
still more numerous Benjamin Franklins—the latter
makes a particularly alluring sign if everything else is
as well kept.

From Chesnut-hill we came through **Flower-town,**
a very small place, the few scattered houses of which
stand in a low situation, but the soil of the region is
better than that about Philadelphia, although still of
the sandy-reddish description. Iron seems to be everywhere abundantly scattered about America; the color
of the soil in this region and that of the sandstone is
due to iron or its constituents. As far as this we have
found many good solid stone houses, the roofs of which
hereabouts are made of shingles, for the most part
after the German manner—the shingles of one thickness throughout and laid touching each other merely
at the sides. The English custom is to make the
shingles thinner at one edge, so that the edge of one
overlaps that of the next. From the exterior appearance, especially the plan of the chimneys, it could be
pretty certainly guessed whether the house was that of
a German or of an English family—if of one chimney
only, placed in the middle, the house should be a German's and furnished with stoves, the smoke from each
led into one flue and so taken off; if of two chimneys,
one at each gable end there should be fire places, after
the English plan. Beyond the region of Whitemarsh
the true Jersey red soil appears again for the first time,
perceptible only here and there on the slopes of the
hills, but towards the ridges overlaid again with the
common sandy soil and rock fragments. It was to be
remarked, as we proceeded West, that this red soil
showed itself very generally on the east side of the hills

and was more obscured on the west slope. The road lay over many ridges of hills, all running very nearly northeast and southwest. And therefore it is all the more to be wondered at how most of the brooks and streams of any size go through and across these ridges, having forcibly broken a way towards the sea from West to East, not following the lay of the valleys. We saw only a few smaller books running along the valleys between the ridges.

Somewhere near Spring-house Tavern, ten miles from Germantown, we unwittingly got out of the straight road to Bethlehem and into a by-road through extensive woods. From time to time we saw farm-houses standing at some distance from the road, and inquiring after a tavern we were directed farther and farther on until at last we had come 19 miles, a hot day, having found no tavern on this unfrequented cross-road. We were obliged finally to turn in at the nearest farm so as to get our horses fed. The owner of the farm, where we alighted without much ceremony, was a German. Our arrival perturbed him no little. There had been very recently several robberies in that neighborhood, which there was every reason to believe had been committed by some Tories scattered about through that country; for the perpetrators, untimely zealous for the royal cause, had selected only tax-gatherers for their prey, exacting from them, as they said, in this unlawful manner what they had unlawfully exacted from the inhabitants—they harmed nobody else. This royalist band of robbers appeared only in disguise and well mounted, but one of them after a pursuit was caught. Nothing could move him to dis-cover his comrades, who by letters scattered about the

country were making threats of fearful vengeance if
the prisoner, who had been taken to Philadelphia, met
with any hurt. This was the occasion for arresting and
taking to prison several of the inhabitants of those
parts, believed to be associates of the man who had
been caught—well known Tories apprehended merely
on suspicion. Thus our host fancied nothing less than
that we had come to haul him into court, but we soon
reassured him; he let it be seen that he was a Tory
but of such an honorable character that we too absolved
him from any implication in these thefts committed in
the name of the king. However, after his first alarm
was over he was for some time mistrustful of us for
another reason, and would not believe that we were
simply neutrals on our travels. During the war the
Congress had adopted every conceivable means to spy
out the royalists, so as to keep them anxiously ineffect-
ive. Besides ordering frequent hangings, imprison-
ments, and outlawing of those persons who openly
and actively supported the British cause, the Congress
was at pains also to find out who were still on the side
of the old government, but not declared adherents.
Such people had an understanding among themselves,
and if they could do nothing else, were able to help
British prisoners regain their liberty. In this way
many British prisoners of war succeeded in escaping
from Maryland, Virginia, and elsewhere, traversing,
undiscovered, an enemy's country for many hundreds
of miles to New York—directed from house to house,
everywhere joyfully received by the royalists, cared
for and hidden away until they were out of danger.
In order to discover what houses were giving shelter
in this way the Congress sent its agents about who pre-

tending to be escaped prisoners, asked assistance on
their way to New York.   And whoever was induced
by such methods to show his principles was informed
against and sorely mishandled.   The Congress succeeded in arousing a general distrust among the people,
suspicious of each other and of strangers, and all this
was vastly useful in the furtherance of their designs.

Since the beginning of August the people in this tract
of country had been busy with their second hay-crop.
The first is got in generally about the middle or towards the end of June.   Nowhere is a third mowing
thought of, even on the best of meadows; whatever
grows after the second cutting is pastured by the cattle.
The hay is nowhere kept under cover, but after the
English fashion in stacks standing out.   The soil of
this region is of still less fertility than that about Philadelphia or Chesnut-hill.   But red earth lies everywhere at a small depth beneath the surface, and could
be turned up with little difficulty.   Although it is well
known from the experience of other regions that this
red earth exposed to the air makes good land, it is let
lie where it is undisturbed.   The value of land rose
here unwontedly during the war, from 5 Pd. Pensylv.
Current to 8 Pd. the acre.   The reason was that many
people thought to employ their money more safely,
whether already invested or not; and also because of the
increased price of living due to the war.   Our host, who
really is only a tenant, pays 25 Pd. Pensylv. Current
land-rent for 146 acres, and has the taxes to pay as
well, 15 Pd., in all 40 Pd. a year.   Before the war his
taxes were only some twenty-odd shillings.   Formerly
the usual basis of the land-tax was 6 pence to 1 or 1½
shillings for every pound of land-rent.   This farm

lying in Philadelphia county, both rent and tax are higher than in other counties. The nearness of the capital, that is, assures the farmer more profitable and quicker returns, and there are other advantages which are taken into the account. Moreover, those land-owners suspected of adherence to the old government are still assessed higher, and (as just now mentioned) many British sympathizers are supposed to live in this region, of whom only a few have so far condescended to swear allegiance to the United States. The Provincial Assembly determines the amount which each county shall contribute for the good of the country. The counties themselves then apportion the amount among the several places and farms within that territory, and in their estimates and equalizations are governed by the extent, goodness, situation, and use of the lands—in this way the taxes apparently fall out very unequally. This same afternoon we came to another farm (in another county, Bucks) in a stony, hilly region called Rocky Hill, where a young man had to pay only 10 shillings for 74 acres, but mostly woodland.

Among the several classes of taxes in Pensylvania there is a special one levied on bachelors and called the ' Batchelors' Tax.' Every male person 21 years old and still unprovided with a wife pays from that time on 12 shillings 6 pence Pensylv. Current a year. However inconsiderable this tax is in itself, it effects the desired purpose, because young men will not long expose themselves to mockery of this sort in a country where working hands can so easily find support for a family.

This tax has long been imposed, here as well as in Maryland ; and very recently the example has been fol-

9

lowed in South Carolina from the conviction that such a tax will be useful in the furtherance of salutary ends.

Hereabouts there is a seeding-plough in use and highly regarded, which is known as the Bucks county plough. Elsewhere the wheat is seeded on fallow broken but once, and then the seed ploughed in. The allowance is one half to one bushel of seed to an acre, according as the wheat is old or new, if new a half-bushel is sufficient. They commonly expect, from three fourths of a bushel seed on unmanured land, 10-15 bushels yield, but in other parts of Pensylvania, about Reading and in the Tulpehocken valley, the yield is 25-30 bushels. A four-horse wagon hauls 40-50 bushels of wheat to the city, the price at this time being one Spanish dollar a bushel, or 7 shillings 6 pence Pensylv. Current. What with the quantity of land many farmers own, they cannot work the whole of it properly, and therefore many acres lie fallow 5-6-7 years together. The usual practice is to plant maize the first year; the second year wheat is sown along with English grass-seeds, and after the wheat is off, the field is pastured for four or five years. At other times they sow buckwheat (½ bus. to the acre) after wheat, or it may be turnips.

Most of the lime used at Philadelphia comes from the region about Whitemarsh and Plymouth, some 15-17 miles' distance. Nearer than that no good limestone hills are found, and wood for the kilns is not to be had. And beyond the Whitemarsh country no usable limestone occurs until five miles this side Bethlehem. Formerly the price of a bushel of burnt lime delivered at Philadelphia was a shilling, but at present a shilling and a half. A four-horse wagon brings in (according to the goodness of the road) 40-50 bushels.

Orchards are a part of every farm; when the trees begin to show age, a new orchard is set on fresh land, for it is not regarded as good practice to put young trees where the old ones stood—because commonly there is plenty of land, and people prefer to avoid the trouble of ploughing up the old land and improving it by manure and stirring. Little care is taken in the choice of good sorts of fruit; apples and peaches are the commonest, but they might be greatly improved, especially the peaches.

From our host's mentioned above we came through almost unbroken forest to **Rocky-hill** township, in which we could find only a few scattered houses; the road deserved the name stony. A blue stone like trap, and a laminated sort of rock resembling gneiss covered the surface, and beneath there was often to be observed something of the red Jersey soil. We went through a devastated tract of woods, probably 2000 acres in extent; the trees had all been destroyed by an iron-foundry which fell to ruin when the owners had used up all their wood. The forests are in great part oak, with beech and birch. Beech-bark and birch-bark are in this region especially liked for tanning. On this dry barren soil the growth was nothing but small trees of all kinds, apparently of no great age. However, most of the forest-growth in the farther regions is likely very young, the first settlers having made it their chief business to burn off the wood from their lands—the fire generally spread, and the original growth was in great part wiped out.

Fences certainly are nowhere else to be found of so many different varieties as in America, where at any moment the traveller comes upon a new sort and can-

not but be astonished at the inventive genius of the inhabitants.   But in every case the device shows that
more care has been taken to avoid trouble than to save
wood and space or to build durably.   Commonly the
fences are but dead enclosures, either light poles or
split logs, bound together in one way and another, laid
the one over the other, or, it may be, upright stakes
worked in and across, and so forth.   The so-called
'worm-fences' are the commonest, and for this purpose chestnut wood, if to be had, is used because of its
lightness and because it lasts well, barked.   Kalm took
the trouble to give drawings of several sorts of worm-
fence, but they deserve imitation nowhere.

Live hedges are extremely rare, only to be seen near
certain towns; they find the planting and the attention
too troublesome.   However, in many regions a live
fence is very ingeniously managed.   In order to enclose
a piece of land they choose out the younger trees, and
if a sufficiency is not found in the line, they plant others
so as to fill up the row—the trees must all be soft and
and pliant and stand together as much as possible.
Then, a deep cut is made in the trunk, several feet
above the ground, and the sapling is bent until it lies
horizontal, making a right angle with the butt.   In this
way the row is gone through, one sapling bent over the
other; the cut heals, and this part of the trunk becomes a good knuckle for all manner of growth.   For
the rest, the trees thrive, the branches spread, inter-
cross, and together with the sprouts coming up from
the butt and the roots, form a pretty thick and lasting
enclosure.   This sort of fence is seen especially in certain parts of Long Island.

From **Rocky-hill** the road, ascending, leads into a

wide-lying plain, known by the name of the **Great
Swamp**, which covered the whole region once, but the
greatest part of it is now made into good meadow-
land.   However the low situation causes overflowings
in the fall and the spring, and the inhabitants therefore
find it more profitable to cultivate summer crops than
winter crops, winter seedings often being heaved out
of the soil and ruined.

Quaker-town; a small place, probably twelve houses
standing together which are inhabited for the most part
by English and German Quakers, like the whole neighborhood.   Here the host paid for tavern license, and
perhaps five acres of land, 12 Pd. taxes Pensylv. Current.
He had very little to give and so much the more to
ask.   We were not a moment free of his curiosity;
unceasingly busy he inquired now of us, now of our
servants, what our designs were in going this journey.
It so happened that from all the answers he received he
could make nothing whatever, and we were the less
inclined to satisfy his curiosity, since he himself from
ignorance let all our questions go unanswered which
we put regarding the state of affairs in his region.

From this Quaker colony we came again (August 8th)
into a rough, hilly country, full of fragments of the
hard, blue stone already mentioned, and rode for a good
many miles through untilled land and wild forest.
Here and there in the midst of woods (but very rarely)
we came upon little spots of ploughed ground, the
settlers mainly Germans.   Thus without knowing it we
passed through **Philipps-thal** and **Richards-town**,
there being no such places and these designations to be
referred either to districts or to cabins.   Six miles from
Quaker-town we arrived at a little village of 10-12

houses and a mill, named for the first settler, **Stoffel Wagner's**, and after we had driven through more lonesome woods and between more high hills, and had crossed Saucon creek, there opened up a splendid valley, its mellow, fat soil presenting everywhere a cheerful prospect; and soon after we came to the quiet, but magnificent **Leheigh.** The last hills between Quaker-town and this valley have the same name as the river, that is, are called the Leheigh * hills; so far as I could see they do not form one connected chain, but are broken ridges and heights, quite separate or meeting by their jutties, and in appearance ranged in sharp lines from East to West, but really they fall in with the other hills and are part of a broken chain running northeast to southwest. The surface of the higher hills was partly of the blueish stone mentioned and partly of a sort of laminated gneiss. But in the valley there appeared a grey limestone, quite without petrifactions. A mile perhaps across the valley, and one reaches the banks of the Leheigh, which with a magical beauty show united every charm of a delectable region. Almost all the finest North American shrubs and trees push forward to lend the scene heightened grace, their branches flung far over the river and shadows cast—the calamus, the rhododendron, cephalanthus, sassafras, azalea, tulip-tree, magnolia, and many others which we desire consumedly as guests in our gardens. The Leheigh river is not more than 100 yards wide, a soft, clear, pure stream flowing over a rocky bottom. Soon we caught sight of **Bethlehem** lying near, the first view of which, from its situation

---

* Leheigh is commonly pronounced Lecho [?]

and from the orderliness (for America) of its large
houses, made from a distance the best impression, and
all the more because to reach this excellently chosen site
so long a road through such wild regions must be
followed.

The whole way from Philadelphia we saw only a few
birds in the forests, chiefly woodpeckers and certain
birds of prey.* We had met with no wild beast nor
with any other indigenous quadruped. Moreover, very
few flowers appeared along the road, and no great
variety of plants. The woods are in large part composed of the several kinds of North American oaks,
the sassafras, tulip-tree, sour gum, chestnut, birch,
wild-ash, and others, which are commonly found along
the coast as well. Nor did we find many mature seeds
nor many seed-bearing plants, so that we became uneasy thinking that if we had no better fortune farther
on our journey would afford us little pleasure in these
respects. And especially, we had seen nothing thus far
which as a product of the country might be highly
recommended for adoption in other lands. In most
places the soil seemed to be only of a moderate goodness, in the valleys and flats a few conspicuously fertile
spots. The inhabitants of such a country might, to be
sure, call themselves happy under a mild government,
so long as they lived by the yield of their lands in
peace and satisfied with very inconsiderable returns,
extensive possessions balancing want of natural fertility
and unskilful cultivation. I do not yet observe any

---

* Among others *Picus principalis L.* which at this season is
returning from the north; I had never seen this bird about
New York—We saw also the *Picus varius, Picus villosus, Sitta
europaea?*, which likewise I had never before seen.

exclusive advantage of this country in itself, beyond
that arising from the sparseness of the population—
that is to say, the diminished difficulty that people of a
certain condition find in accumulating a landed estate
has been hitherto the especial allurement held out by
America, and this may be the case for a long time to
come, but not everywhere equally so.

No one met us on this road until we came to the
ferry opposite Bethlehem, where on this side the river
there stands a tavern. The ferryman and two others
who were put over with us gave the impression as if
the pleasantness of the region had had its influence;
they were more friendly, politer, and more obliging
than the run of the inhabitants thereabouts.

Bethlehem; a colony of the Moravian Brotherhood,
stands on the north side of the beautiful Leheigh, on a
commodious rising ground, in North-hampton county,
53 English miles north of Philadelphia, and under latitude 40° 37′ north. Approaching, the place shows to
great advantage, and after one has come the last half of
the way from Philadelphia through a tedious sameness of
bush and forest, relieved only here and there by cabins,
often mean cabins, it is certainly an astonishment to see
all at once rising up, one above another, lofty buildings
in this presumptive wilderness. The whole number of
the houses may be about 60. The first settlement was
made in the year 1741, Count Zinzendorf himself having chosen the site and regularly secured the land from
the Indians there established and claiming title. The
chief building of the place is of good appearance, large,
and furnished with two wings—in one of them the
Assembly-hall of the Brothers and the ministers'
quarters; in the middle the children's house; and in the

left wing the house of the Sisters. Opposite this building stands the house of the Widows, and farther on (descending the slope), the house of the Brothers. These and all the other buildings are of stone, the limestone of the region; the houses mentioned are 3-4 storeys in height. In the house of the Sisters the greatest neatness is the rule, with no ostentation. The unmarried Sisters employ their time in spinning, weaving, knitting, and skilfully embroidering. Likewise the Brothers in their house are occupied with several crafts. For the rest, the arrangement of these houses is the same as in other settlements of the Moravian Brethren in Germany, and so, as everywhere, shows the marks of order and of constant industry.

The community here numbers probably 600 souls, of which by far the greater part are Germans, and the remainder a few English. However, almost every member is familiar with the two languages, and on Sundays a sermon is preached in the English language by one or the other of the ministers. Since most of the Brethren, the ministers in particular, are sprung from Saxony, it is not surprising that here at Bethlehem and in the other colonies of the sect, the purest and best German is spoken of which America can anywhere boast.

Mr. Ettwein and Mr. Hübner are at present the ministers. The first was absent, but in Mr. Hübner I found an agreeable and amiable man, and a lover of botany for which his profession allows him no time. The health of the community is cared for by Mr. Otto, at once physician, surgeon, and apothecary.

There is but one tavern here, maintained at the charge of the community, and not inferior to the first

and best of American inns. Everything is good, and
so much the better because in so obscure and small a
place a comparison is not to be expected with other
taverns of the same size or even larger. This house is
seldom without guests. ✚ Besides those travelling on
business, Philadelphians often come to the place on
pleasure excursions, as well to admire the excellent
institutions and edifying methods and industry of the
Brethren as to find good entertainment at the tavern.
At this house I made the acquaintance of the Baron
Hermelin, ✚ a learned Swedish mineralogist, who had
come over to visit the mines of America and with
other business in view. He had spent some time in
the various mines and smelting-houses of Jersey, but
as a consequence of the incidental fatigue and the uncommonly hot season had contracted a serious illness,
which induced him to come to this place. He was now
restored through the efforts of the skilful Mr. Otto.
His observations, if it seems good to him to communicate them to the learned world, will be of very great
importance to all mineralogists, but especially to the
Americans, for no one before him has given the subject such attention or has been so equipped with the
requisite intelligence.

The Leheigh, at the time of the spring rains and
thaws, often rises suddenly to a considerable height;
according to a measuring pole set up at the brewery,
as much as 7-8 feet any year, and once 11 feet, perpendicular height. This fresh always lasts for some
time and helps the flat-boats, laden with grain and
other produce, to pass the rocks and shallows which at
other times obstruct the navigation of this stream; the
Leheigh flows into the Delaware and so affords (dur-

ing the spring freshes) a convenient passage to Philadelphia.   In the Leheigh and tributary creeks are
found Muscles (a thin-shelled *mytilus* a good deal like
that living in European ponds) which at times contain
pretty large and clear pearls.   Recently a man of this
region sold more than an ounce of them at Philadelphia.   To find a few good pearls many muscles must
be opened.   The muskrats lighten the labors of the
pearl hunters.   These beasts are great lovers of the
muscle.   They hold their feasts preferably at still reaches
of the stream, on the sand or on rocks jutting into the
water.   If they find pearls they spit them out.   Certain
people observed the circumstance and made use of it—
they examined the sand of such places and found without trouble many pearls ready shelled.

We visited the certainly remarkable farm and factory
buildings of this place.—A well constructed oil and
flour mill.   The oil mill is new-built, having been burnt
a few years ago, and in an incendiary way, it is supposed.   On the topmost floor of the mill a crane is so
fixed that by the mill machinery itself the heaviest
loads can be drawn up without further trouble.—A
lucrative tannery, with tan-mill attached.—A considerable dye-works, where they dye red and blue to
excellent effect.

Since Bethlehem stands on a height composed of
limestone, a single spring, but a strong and beautiful
one, must supply the whole place and all the houses
with water.   This spring lies far below at the foot of
the hill and near to the river.   An excellently contrived water-works, (suction and pressure), raises the
water through copper pipes to a water-tower, standing
some distance away on the hill near the larger buildings.

The *reservoir* to which the water is brought stands more than 80 ft. above the spring, reckoning in the natural elevation. Thence the water is taken through sundry pipes to special cisterns, and is carried to all parts of the place, even to parts lying higher than the tower, and so every house is supplied adequately with good water. This water-works has repeatedly had the disagreeable experience that the strongest pipes were burst by the air held in the water—until there was installed recently a large copper air-bubble, at the point where the distributing pipes leave the pump-pipe, and by that means the air developing was given a void. ✚

Hard by the river stands a new brewery, a profitable and excellently ordered establishment under the direction of Mr. Sigmund Leshinsky. The water for brewing is pumped from the river. The cauldron in which it is boiled is placed so high that the boiling water is easily run out over the **malt**, and is thence sent back to the cauldron, by a hand-pump, for the seething of the hops. Thence it is drawn through pipes to the cooling-tub, and passed on through other pipes to the casks in the cellar immediately beneath. By this method two or three men are sufficient for all the work. The malt is air-dried. The beer is excellent. The year before Mr. Leshinsky had brewed beer of oats, and he makes the assertion that of all the American grains oats give the best beer ; but the preparation is somewhat troublesome and requires stricter attention, oats sprouting rapidly when softened.—When the cellar for this brewery was dug, it was matter of inexplicable astonishment to find 10 ft. below the surface and at least 15-20 ft. away from the bed of the stream, **an iron nail** of the thickness of a little finger and three inches long. Nobody knew

of former diggings at this spot and no trace of digging
was found.   They dug down two feet through garden
mould, four feet through the common yellow earth, one
foot through fine sand, and the remainder of the depth
through coarse sand, and from this bed, never before
disturbed, the " nail " was taken.   It will be easily understood how this find excited attention and started
theories ; but this is neither the first nor the only instance in America where on a casual digging artificial
products have been found,* in all probability of European origin.   Hence it may be supposed, with every
show of reason, that long before the discovery by
Columbus of this part of the earth European ships
bound for other regions by wind and weather were
turned out of their course and wrecked on the shores
of America, and their crews deprived of the means of
return either died of starvation or were murdered by
the inhabitants.   From the wreckage of such ill-fated
ships the roving Indians may well have taken things
strange to them, as a nail must have been, and since
they everywhere had their settlements on streams and
creeks it is easily fancied how this nail came where it
was.   What space of time may have been required to

---

* Kalm mentions several, foreign to the Americas, and discovered deep in the earth—It is told at Bethlehem that in
Jersey not many years ago a board was taken out at a depth
of 36 ft.—Mr. du Sumitiere, at Philadelphia, makes the statement on the authority of responsible people that a spoon was
found on the ' Neck' four feet below the surface, and in
Front-street an old sword at a depth of 19 ft.   A large and
heavy iron hammer of peculiar make was dug up at a depth of
many feet, in Maryland, and an iron axe 20 ft. deep somewhere in Virginia.   Very probably there have been similar
finds ✚ not made known generally.

bury it in sand under ten feet of earth might possibly
be estimated if for any given place it was exactly
known how much sand and earth was deposited by the
yearly fresh and a like amount reckoned for each year
of a term.

Much good earthen-ware is burnt here and the neighborhood far around supplied. I should be tedious if
I undertook to mention all that is good and beautiful in
this little place and among its inhabitants, of whom
there are those plying most of the useful arts and
crafts. Their manufactures are not yet enough to
supply them with all they need, but they have among
themselves the most important and are obliged to bring
in very little, and so much the less because the uniformity and frugality of their way of life admit of few
wants. Unlike their sister colonies at Neuwied, Ebers-
dorf &c, they have not yet established the finer branches
of manufactures, the fewness of their numbers and the
circumstances of their situation not rendering these
feasible.

The good order and the comfortable prosperity,
which are so especially pleasing to every foreigner, are
the fruits of religion and piety, activity, and industry.
Everyone is occupied and whatever is made shows intrinsic goodness and the marks of judicious pains-tak-
ing. Here are seen the effects of the same causes
which I mentioned when speaking of the Quakers—
the time wasted by the greatest part of mankind in
idleness or unprofitable pleasures is here applied unceasingly in the best manner and for the common good.
What a land might not America already be if all the
inhabitants had fashioned themselves on the pattern of
the community at Bethlehem. Certainly they make

excellent citizens for any land—and in America, in a
shorter time than any other people, they have changed
numerous wildernesses to flourishing spots.

The hills about Bethlehem consist of the common,
coarse, grey limestone in which, as elsewhere, occur
hardly any traces of petrifactions. Beyond the Leheigh in a shaly rock, (presumably limestone also)
large cavities are often found, when the stone is split,
full of a fine yellowish meal which they use here for
blotting strew-sand; in the meal there always occurs a
spherical pyrites. On another declivity beyond the
river there are to be seen, I am told, remarkable stone-
falls, i. e. large flaws are found hollowed out of the
rock-wall and stuffed with little pieces of stone of the
same description as the solid rock—as if designedly
broken up and poured in. By reason of later changes it
could not be accurately determined what was the cause
of this local disturbance of a former time. Similar
stone-falls are not rare in other parts of America.
Also, **landslips** (as they are here called), tunnel-like
hollows 20-30 ft. and more in depth and section are
not infrequently found in these limestone hills and are
caused by the shifting and sinking of the rock-beds at
a depth. For the same reason caverns are almost always found under landslips, but they are not everywhere of easy access.

Some six miles from Bethlehem and two from **Durham** on the Delaware there is a rather large cave of
which people at Philadelphia already talk with respect
under the name of the **grotto of Durham.** Mr. Otto,
the younger, has several times visited the cave. It is
near the ferry, opens towards the north, is probably
150-160 ft. deep, has a sloping course, but is wide

enough and high enough to be traversed without stooping. This cave is likewise in a limestone hill, but is said to contain no stalactites.

The lime which is burned from the grey limestone common here must be used fresh, because otherwise it worsens very fast and loses its best binding qualities. I was told at Philadelphia that agates, carnelian-stones, and fine pebbly flint-stones (all these are called there moccas or mocca-stones) are found in great numbers in this region, but they knew nothing of such stones here; nearer to the mountains, they said, there are such stones found. Likewise there was much told me regarding a silver-ore from the Nazareth region, but I was unable to procure any of it.

All the European pot-herbs flourish exceedingly at Bethlehem, under the good care of exact and indefatigable gardeners. They have very fine collyflowers which will not do well in New York and Philadelphia gardens—the sea-air which is given as the reason of failure cannot be so contrary, for collyflowers are raised excellently well on the coasts of Holland and also in England. The explanation is rather to be sought in careless looking-after—Peach and pear trees, which elsewhere yield much good fruit, sicken here after a few years and die in numbers; it is Mr. Otto's opinion that insects are the cause. For sundry observations on the medicinal properties of certain indigenous plants I must thank the experienced Mr. Otto. It is not generally known that the European juniper-bush grows easily from twigs stuck in the earth, after the manner of most cuttings from leaf-trees. In Mr. Otto's garden are several shrubs grown from the planted twig.

Their love of peace and quiet cost the Moravian
Brethren dear during the last war. On the one hand
suspected of adherence to the royalist cause, and on
the other prevented by their principles from taking up
arms, they had to pay double taxes, (like the Quakers
and other religious sects similar to them in this matter),
and were grievously burdened with many charges
besides.

Bethlehem is the principal seat of the Moravian
Brethren in North America, and thence are managed
the affairs of their other and smaller communities, of
which already there are many. In the neighborhood
of Bethlehem are **Nazareth, Christiansbrunn, Schöneck, Gnadenthal,** and **Gnadenhütten.** In Jersey there
is a considerable community at **Hope,** and others
smaller elsewhere. In North Carolina **✚ Salem** is their
chief place, from which **Bethabara** is seven and **Beth-
ania** 17 miles distant. Besides, there are communities
and meeting-houses at Philadelphia, New York, Newport, and Lancaster.

Their activities are not restricted merely to those
regions settled by Europeans. Through tireless zeal
and wonderful patience they have succeeded in making a wholesome impression on several of the Indian
nations. Beyond the mountains, on the **Muskingum**
(a stream flowing from the north into the Ohio) they
formed a numerous and hopeful community, confessing
the Christian religion, from nations not easily to be
tamed in any other manner. In three of their colonies,
Schönbrunn, Gnadenhütten, and Salem,* many Indian

---

* Gnadenhütten and Salem—two Indian villages—are not to
be confused with the settlements of the same name in Pensylvania and North Carolina. These Indian villages lay 160-
170 English miles west of Pittsburg.

10

families * have already come to live, under the oversight of directors and pastors, dwelling together
quietly and peaceably in well-built wigwams, having
renounced war and the chase, accustoming themselves
gradually to the tillage of the land, and so laying the
first foundations of a civilized way of life. Similar
attempts have been made with success by the Jesuit
missionaries in Canada and in Florida, and by blame-
less, pious men † in the English colonies; and by these
it has been proved that the so-called American savages
under a milder and more intelligent treatment are not
so absolutely incapable of a moral life as had been
commonly imagined. It is very general in America

---

* "At the beginning of the year 1781 there were at Schönbrunn 143, at Gnadenhütten 135, and at Salem 105, of whom
315 baptized and 68 unbaptized (mostly children), in all 385
persons" The bringing together of this Christian Indian
colony was due to the efforts some 30 years ago of an Indian
named Papunhank. At first these Indians lived at Whihaloo-
sing on the Susquehannah, 200 miles from Philadelphia. But
when European colonists began to increase in their neighborhood and grew troublesome the Indians voluntarily removed
to the Muskingum. An especial cause of their removal was to
escape the danger of intoxicating drinks, which had been
brought among them by their new neighbors and were making
idle all their efforts at keeping the peace and living orderly.
Papunhank, on a visit to Philadelphia, had particularly re-
quested that nobody give his people strong drinks or send any
to them where they lived.

† Thomas Mayhew, John Elliot and others in Maryland who
have left accounts of the happy outcome of their labors. Later
accounts, with proofs of the Indian susceptibility of moral and
religious instruction, are contained in, David Brainard's Mira-
bilia Dei inter Indicos, or The Rise and progress of a remarkable Work of Grace amongst a number of Indians, in the
Provinces of New Jersey & Pensylvania &c.

to bring out the blackest and most hateful side of the
Indian character in order the more easily to justify and
excuse every unrighteous and grewsome act committed
against them, and gladly committed. In confirmation
there may be given in passing the following sad and
little known story, of the inhuman treatment which a
part of these christianized Indians suffered without
cause at the hands of their neighbors who call themselves more enlightened and more moral.

The three Indian settlements on the Muskingum
(known under the general name of the Moravian
Indians) found themselves at the beginning of the last
war in a very unpleasant situation. They were often
urged by the contesting parties to join in the war, but
they remained constant to their adopted principles,
kept quietly neutral, and regarded not the threats and
maltreatment to which they were subjected by other
Indian nations taking part in the war. As was necessary in their uncertain situation they bore themselves
patiently with roving parties of the one side and of the
other. For in their expeditions through the wild
woods between Canada and the farther regions of
Pensylvania and Virginia both sides were glad to turn
in for supplies at the Moravian villages. I have heard
American officers, sent out against hostile Indian tribes
far back on the Mississippi and the Ohio and on their
return visiting the settlements of these Christian Indians, speak of the great pleasure it was to find so unexpectedly evidences of good order and careful management—they and their men, after long marches through
a wild country, being in want of supplies, the good
Indians gave them everything they could spare and
were only rejoiced to be left undisturbed to the minis-

trations of their spiritual directors. With the same
amiable hospitality, they received those bands of Indians from Canada, allies of the English, who came
through their settlements going towards the back parts
of Pensylvania and Virginia. So far were they from
encouraging hostilities against the outlying settlers of
the American states, that on the contrary it is well
known how by their representations they at times
turned aside certain Indian warriors from murderous
designs against the settlers. However, they were unable to escape the suspicions of both sides, parties to
the war. The American frontiersmen conceived that
they suffered all the more from the massacring expeditions of the English Indians, especially the **San-
duskys,** so long as these were able to get supplies from
the Moravian villages, without which support they
could not long maintain themselves in those otherwise
desolate regions. On the other hand, those Indians
allied with the English harbored suspicion against the
Moravians on the ground that they gave the frontiersmen information of their movements and so enabled
the settlers to escape craftily contrived ambushments—
they laid it to the account of the Moravians if their
plans were balked by the flight of the settlers.

Therefore both sides undertook by cunning or force
to remove the Moravian Indians from their villages.
On the part of the Americans the proposal was that
they withdraw from the Muskingum to the neighborhood of Pittsburg. They rejected this offer because
they preferred to remain in their comfortable dwellings and on their lands, and because they were unwilling, against their known principles, to declare
themselves so openly for one of the parties at war.

More stringent measures, apparently, were adopted by
the Canadian Indians, allies of the English. During
the first days of August 1781 a message, with a wam-
pum-string, was sent the Moravian Indians by the
so-called half-king or chief of the Wyandots: " that
" a great number of warriors were coming, but they
" should have no fear for he was their friend and was
" coming himself." After a few days 200 warriors
appeared. The chiefs and all the heads of families
from the three villages were summoned and it was announced to them, " They had come to take them away,
" because the Brethren and their Indians were in their
" way, and a great hindrance to them in their expedi-
" tions of war." To this unexpected outgiving the
Moravian Indians made answer: " That they held it
" impossible at that season of the year to undertake
" such a journey, because they should have to leave
" behind their grain and so could look for nothing for
" their children but death from hunger in the wilder-
" ness." The leader of the Wyandots and his council
appeared disposed to grant the reasonableness of these
views. The warriors were already making preparations for the return journey but certain Englishmen
who were of the company egged them on to carry out
their first intention, and now towards the end of August or the first of September the Moravian Indians
were compelled to leave their three settlements, the
Wyandots having burned their fences, killed their
cattle, and done much other mischief so as to hasten
their going. After a tiresome journey of four weeks
through the wilderness all the inhabitants of the three
villages came to an arm of the Sandusky river which
flows into Lake Erie. Here they were to remain and

here were bidden take up their abode for the future.
Within a short space they had built for themselves a new
meeting-house and some sixty block-houses. Their
new dwelling-place was 100 miles from their former
settlements and a like distance from Detroit. The
chiefs and a few of the most regarded of the Indian
Brethren were summoned to Detroit by the English
Governor (Major Arent Schuyler de Peyster) who at
once set aside the charges brought against them and
told them that they were to remain at that place only
during the winter and, come spring, might go and
plant anywhere in the country they wished, but nearer
Pittsburg they could not go. As it turned out, this
forcible removal of the Moravian Indians from their
villages was undertaken with the consent of the Governor at Detroit and was brought about in the first
instance through motives of philanthropy. This was
the reason why the destruction which menaced the
whole of these Indian communities befel only a part
of them. There were good reasons to fear that these
harmless Indians, delaying on the Muskingum after
their refusal to transfer themselves to Pittsburg, would
be exposed to great maltreatment at the hands of the
frontiersmen of the farther regions of the American
states, suspicious of them and embittered. The result
confirmed these apprehensions.

In the spring of 1782 certain of the Moravian Indians asked permission to go to the Muskingum in
order to fetch back some of the grain which at the time
of their marching off they had left standing in the
fields. On the Sandusky they were in great want of
grain and every other necessity of life. Receiving permission for the journey, a number of them set out ac-

companied by sundry of their wives and widows with
their children. News soon reached the settlers along
the Monongahela that a number of Indians had appeared in the Moravian villages, and from there were
intending to fall upon the frontier settlements—this
was given out in palliation of the subsequent inhuman
proceedings. However, from other circumstances
demonstrable it is more than likely that it was known
perfectly well who these Indians were and what their
intentions were. Towards the end of February 1782
there assembled on the Monongahela probably 160
white Christians, citizens of the united free American
states, who set out on horses for the Muskingum to
forestall, so they gave out, the hostile plans of the
Indians there.* There came forward as the leader of
this party a certain Williamson, Colonel in the Virginia
militia, a monster whose name should hardly be mentioned. As they drew near the Moravian villages, in
and about them they observed industriously occupied
Indians who made not the least sign as if to run or to
offer resistance. Although at first this sudden visit
alarmed them, they assembled without delay at the call
of the white Christians, (who greeted them in pretended friendship), and quietly allowed themselves to
be made captive. The whole number was 53 grown
men and women and 42 children. It is never the

---

* No sooner was news of this undertaking received at Pittsburg than the American garrison there and all the right-
thinking men of the place became alarmed for the safety of
the Christian Indians. Colonel Gibson sent messengers to the
Muskingum to inform them, if there, of the danger threatening them and of his anxieties in consequence. These messengers came too late.

custom of the Indians to take with them children and
women when they are on the war path. When sur-
prised they were busy making sugar (from maple
sap) and gathering their spoiled corn. As Christian
Indians they gave themselves up to their supposed
friends, and they told them that a small store of wine
which was found among them was their communion
wine. They manifested the greatest pleasure when the
white Christians explained to them in reassurance that
for the safety of both parties they had come to take
them to Pittsburg. But after **Williamson** and his
party had further advised together what should in fact
be done with these peaceable, unarmed captives, men,
women, and children, the unanimous conclusion of the
white American Christians was that on the following
day without any exception they should all—be put to
death. And immediately this judgment was announced to the captives, with the addition that since
they were Christian Indians they might in a Christian
manner prepare themselves, for on the morrow they
must die. This sudden message of death prostrated
them indeed but they went about patiently and spent
the night singing and praying. The next morning
they were taken to two houses chosen for the purpose,
(and still expressively called the slaughter-houses),
led bound two and two, first the men and then the
women and children, and without mercy were murdered in cold blood and scalped. They met death with
extraordinary patience and resignation. After this
blood drenching, begun by Williamson, the two houses
were filled with the bodies of the slain, and the whole
was set on fire and destroyed. Their horses, blankets,
and other possessions, which they were allowed before-

hand carefully to collect, were taken as good booty and publicly sold at Pittsburg. All this befel the villages of Salem and Gnadenhütten. At Schönbrunn there were still some thirty Indians. But a boy who had been scalped at Gnadenhütten and left for dead in a house there, contriving to escape in the night brought news of what had happened, to Schönbrunn 10 miles away—the Indians there took flight and escaped the bloodthirsty murderers, who came thither the next morning to repeat the scene of the day before, but could only burn the empty village.

Unheard of as were these murderous proceedings,* abominated by every individual right-thinking man, the murderer who gave the orders was not called to account officially,—for he acted without any orders except the promptings of his own bloodthirsty soul. He boasted of his deeds and exhibited everywhere his bloodstained hatchet. Eternal shame to the states. But this was the maxim throughout the war, to wreak vengeance on the innocent and allow no man justice. Whole nations of Indians were aroused by this occurrence to a zealous prosecution of the war and they redoubled their attacks in order to avenge the death of their Moravian brethren.

We left **Bethlehem** (the evening of the 9th of August) and came 10 miles to **Nazareth,** through a

---

* No longer so unheard of! For a pendant to this story, Vid. *Hamb. Polit. Journal,* 1787, p. 474 "The war with the "Indians has been begun by the Americans in a rather Indian "fashion. They fell upon the Indian chiefs who according to "their custom had assembled in council. After this slaughter "some 1900 of the Shawanese Indians swore blood-vengeance" —which will be thought extremely unreasonable in America!

high-lying country but for half the way pretty level.
The region is not yet much settled, but here and there
a farm is seen. The road was straight, almost due
north, and with the dry weather extraordinarily good.
The forests consisted for the greater part of white,
red, and black oak, with very little undergrowth.
There appeared frequently a dwarf willow, not more
than 3-4 ft. high, with small leaves. All this high
land between Bethlehem and Nazareth, and off towards Easton, goes by the name of **the dry land**.
And it is indeed dry. This tract, chiefly limestone
soil, contains few springs, slow, and found only in certain lower spots; and often water is in vain dug for to
a great depth. None of the dug wells is less than 80
ft. deep, and in some places they have gone as deep as
136 ft. through the limestone and found only weak
veins of water going dry in summer. The inhabitants
who begin to be numerous are here in bad case. Their
grass crops are insignificant, and during the winter
they have to feed their cattle on turnips, or stubble and
other dry fodder. Most of the houses get their water
one, two, and three miles away, for which purpose
each establishment keeps a special wagon with a barrel.
One stream, the Monocacy, goes quite dry in summer; we passed it without knowing it. The pasturing
cattle wander far around looking for puddles. But
cattle easily grow accustomed to infrequent supplies
of water, can indeed quite dispense with water for a
long time, if there is green pasturage or (as the rule
is in America) if the stock remains out day and night
and can get refreshment from the falling dew. I
know certainly that on Long Island horses as well as
horned cattle were enclosed throughout a long, hot,

and dry summer in a thin fallow pasture where there was no water at all and the puddles were dry from long drouths, and yet kept healthy and fat. Sufficient moisture was supplied them, partly by plant juices and partly by the dews of the morning, but these were infrequent. It is known besides that in some of the West India islands, Antigua for example, where all the supply of water is from rains or must be fetched from other islands, cattle are never able to get a drink of water, but live solely by the moisture in the vegetation. Notwithstanding the dearth of water, much cattle is raised in this dry tract. For the rest, the land is fruitful in grain and there are a good many prosperous farms of which only a few are settled by Moravians, but the industrious example they give their neighbors has an influence which is not to be mistaken—for everywhere hereabouts one sees good buildings and good management.

Nazareth was settled later than Bethlehem; and so numbers only about 20 houses, but of a good and spacious design, among which there are a House of the Brothers, an Assembly-house, and a ware-house. The plan of the place is more regular than that of Bethlehem, where the ground does not allow of a regular plan. As yet there is only one street, short and straight, leading to a pretty large square, half surrounded by buildings. Here also there are no wells, but from the springs of a neighboring hill an abundant supply of excellent water is had which is brought through the little town in pipes along one side of the street and at certain distances is distributed through pumps. All of the inhabitants have their trades and do not concern themselves with agriculture. They

have their own minister who at present is Mr.
Laembner.

In Mr. William Henry, a rifle-maker, I got to know
a modest and sagacious man. He not only under-
stands his art thoroughly but occupies himself with other
branches of knowledge. From him I obtained some
Indian arrow-points such as they at one time worked
from the hardest carnelian and agate. Since the Indians exchanged their bows for fire-arms, the art has
been lost among them of making these and other
utensils, such as pottery, tobacco-bowls &c, from different sorts of stone. Arrow-points like these are now
found only by chance in fields or other places where
Indians on the hunt had lost them. In this region
several rifle-makers are occupied in the making and
repair of arms for the Indians as well as for other
people of the country. At Mr. Henry's I saw a little
piece of a fine, yellow sort of marl which had been
dug up not far away at a depth of 15 ft. Near Bethlehem, on the other side of the Leheigh, marl is frequently found at a less depth, but coarser and not of
a uniform color. The people of the back country
yearn for marl because they imagine it to be a universal manure and fancy it might save them the trouble
(which they do not like at all) of collecting other
manure—and should they find it there it would not be
suited to their lands which are more sand than clay.
Mr. Henry mentioned that he had several times found
about Nazareth sand-stones containing a core, apparently lime. Sand-stones are also found which are
hard enough to be squared, but there are too many
quartz-veins in them. The limestone hills which begin
about Easton continue between and around Nazareth

and Bethlehem, next the Leheigh, Flying, and Oley-
hills.

The upper strata of this region in many places appeared to consist chiefly of a fine black slate, which
should be found quite adequate for every common
use, but is not used because the preparation costs too
much.   Under this slate, wherever it appears, is the
grey limestone which also comes to the surface frequently; and near to the town, along the road, there
occurs a light grey schist from which good lime is
burned. All the fields are strewn with quartz, at times
white, at times reddish; and in many of these stones
are seen thin layers of black slate and quartz alter-
nating. The commoner soil, on the high places especially, is of the general yellow-red, clayey sand description; only the low spots are black and fertile.
Where the slate can be found somewhat deeper, its
lowest beds appear like a rather dense pit-coal; and
somewhere in the region it is claimed that coal has
been dug up.—In the off-hang of a wood we found
sundry beautiful plants in tolerable quantity, the
Canadian cypripedium, helonias, the blue lobelia, the
collinsonia, and many others. When in full bloom as
now, the collinsonia fills the air with a strong and
pleasant odor. Nazareth lies at a considerable height
above the sea, but I could not learn that anybody had
had the curiosity to determine in any way what the
height is. The weather however seemed to us quite as
hot as we had found it on the coast. Here also the
complaint was that cherry and pear trees for some
years had not done well, but no certain explanation
could be given. A gardener said that the reason was
the gum worked out too much and insects lodged in

it. Plum trees, planted in the ware-house garden, bloomed full every year and yielded abundant fruit. But at one time either the blooms dropped or the fruit was lost before ripe. They assured me that the evil was remedied by boring two holes in every tree, one near the ground and the other higher up, both going clear through the trunk, and in each of which a piece of iron was stuck. Certainly, since this operation blooms and fruit do not fall so much as before. In other parts of America there are very few pear trees; it is said that along the coast they will not stand the climate, but it might turn out differently if good experiments were tried.

I had heard of sundry ores, among others a silver-ore, to be found in the neighborhood of Nazareth, but wherever I enquired people knew only of similar stories told of places more distant. But there was everywhere the belief, so common in all mountain countries, that really many treasures lay buried in the dear earth, if only one had them or knew how to find them.

Nazareth has a very good and clean tavern. In peace times the road this way is much travelled, from Philadelphia to Canada, Albany, and New England. But the excursions of the Indians made this road during the war extremely unsafe. Before the war this was the customary route of Indians travelling to Philadelphia, but they were never pleasant guests at Nazareth. There was a strict regulation that no Indian should be given more than half a gill of rum, and then only on payment of the cash money, two laws that the Indians did not willingly conform to, and not to be set aside without danger, if the consequences of their

brutal drunkenness were to be avoided. The people of
Wyoming are now again beginning to travel this road
more frequently, after having, for a long time, dared
use it only at the peril of their lives. These people,
among whom we shall shortly be, are described by our
host as a lawless and rude populace.

From Nazareth we travelled (Aug. 10th) North
and North-west. At a little distance from the place
the Blue Mountains come in sight. A mile on is **Schöneck**, an incipient village of the Moravian Brethren.
There are only a few houses and families, but several
families of the neighborhood are counted as of the
community, and at Schöneck they have their meeting-
house.

A mile beyond we entered all at once what appeared
to be a tract of public and vacant land. All the hills
about, as far as the eye could reach, were grown up
with the bush oak (Quercus nana, Dwarf oak).*
Only here and there stood a chesnut quite alone, or
one of the other oaks. We overlooked in part and in
part passed through some thousands of acres of land
bearing nothing but this description of oak. Their

---

* This bush oak was similar to that growing on Long Island
and called *Qu. Ilicifolia* by von Wangenheim (Vid. his *Ameri-
kanische Holzarten*, p. 79). Marshall in his *American Grove*
calls it Dwarf black oak (*Quercus nigra pumila*)—But Marshall makes dwarf varieties of almost every kind of oak,
according as it is a growth of poor, thin soil. Thus he has a
Quercus alba minor, Barren White Oak. Quercus rubra nana,
Dwarf Barren Oak. Quercus prinus humilis, Dwarf Chesnut
or Chinquapin Oak—In this way there might be dwarf varieties of every sort of tree, wherever there is lack of nourishment in the soil—and the question may still be put, whether
this oak is an independent variety.

twisted and bushy stems seldom exceeded a height of
3-4 ft.; at times we observed trees of 10-12 ft. or even 15
ft., but very few of them. These oaks seem to take
possession of this dry and infertile hill country as if
by privilege. And there is found among them besides
scarcely any variety of other plants. We nòticed only
the *Actæa racemosa* (which we missed hardly anywhere along the whole road), the *Galega virginiana,
Sophora tinctoria, Gerardia,* and a few others, along
with a dry bristly grass. In the lower valleys between
these hills the other oaks occur, as also the Chesnut
Oak which is seldom seen elsewhere in this region.
The land grown up in this dwarf oak is of very little
value. The people living near by set fire to the bush
every spring, in order to give air to the grass beneath
and so furnish their cattle a little pasture. However,
the growth comes out again, although the bark is almost coaled. Fire seems to do them little hurt, whereas the chesnut and other tree-oaks stand among them
dry and scorched. Nobody cares to buy this land or
put it to use. For should the fire kill the dwarf oak,
it would mean more labor than elsewhere to dig up the
roots standing thick together. It is a rare prospect
over this extensive tract of low bush-growth, made all
the finer by the nearness of the Blue Mountains—but,
however agreeable, it is little inviting to the planter.
Everywhere these oaks are taken to be a symptom of
an unkind soil. Not a single dwelling is discovered
among them; everything is desolate and void. Even
wild beasts and birds dislike to live here, where they
find neither food nor shade nor shelter. The whole
way from Nazareth to **Heller's House,** eight miles,
we came upon only three houses, standing in the hol-

lows, of which the best was at Bushkill. But the road
was for the most part good, and the grades gently
sloping. However, these hills and foothills are very
broken, cut irregularly by valleys in divers directions.

Our quarters for the night were at Heller's, a lonesome tavern at the foot of the **Blue** or **Kittatinny
Mountain**. Already a good many settlers, especially
Germans, have come to live here, in a narrow but
pleasant valley, and scattered as they are in the bush
one hardly knows they are there. It was a Sunday
and we found assembled at the tap-house, (according
to the traditional German custom), a numerous company of German farmers of the neighborhood, who
were making good cheer with their cyder and **cyder-
oil**. Cyder-oil is a pretty strong drink; it consists of
the combustible spirits of cyder, mixed again, in divers
proportions, with cyder of the best grade.

The farmers were not very well content with their
lands. The nearness of the mountains brings them in
winter unpleasant visits from wolves and now and
then bears. And there is no lack of other sorts of
game; deer and foxes are numerous; elks * wander
hither at times. The turkey-cock is seen more frequently here than nearer towards the coast. The
passage-dove (*Columba migratoria*) which appears
along the coast only in the spring and autumn, moving

---

* From several descriptions furnished by people hereabouts,
it seems that they give the name Elk to the Moose as well as
to the Canadian Stag, **+** and so give rise to errors. Both animals come down from the North where the one is known as
Moose, Black Moose, or Original, and the other (the Canadian stag) as Grey Moose, to distinguish it from the first.

11

to warmer climates or coming thence, is found here
now in pairs.

The celebrated Blue Mountains appear from here
not so high and praiseworthy as, from descriptions, I
had been led to expect. What gives them a particular
face, at a certain distance, is their lying so straight the
one after the other. Thus the first range (at the foot
of which we are here) seen from Heller's house extends south as it were a steep wall; the little foot-hills
and offsets and other irregularities disappear in the
view of the great and uniform whole with its covering of forest. Measured from its foot, the height of this
first range, called particularly the **Blue** or **Kittatiny
Mountain** (and under this name extending from
Jersey through Virginia) is by no means considerable.
Beyond Heller's house, a mile to the north, is a natural
pass, from three-quarters of a mile to a mile wide, the
so-called Wind Gap which vastly lightens the labor
of crossing the mountain, the cut being at least half
the height of the mountain and only a moderate climb
remaining. It is not easily guessed what was the
cause of this section through the otherwise pretty uniform ridge. No water flows through this gap. Perhaps ten miles to the north-east there is another opening through the mountain where the Delaware crosses
and hence called Delaware Gap; a third, and the nar-
rowest, is to the south-west, also at no great distance;
the Leheigh comes through this and its name is the
Water Gap. There is a very fine view at this gap, it
is said.

In the Kittatiny the rock-species is a hard, fine-
grained Cos, either grey, whitish, or verging on red.
Fragments lay along the road in vast quantities and

of every size but with no indications of a water-polishing. This sort of stone, that is, appears at the surface and covers the backs of the mountain. But near the Delaware Gap, about Easton, mill-stones are quarried, of a rough and sharp-grained quartzose sort of stone, which with other circumstances inclines me to think that this or a similar stone lies beneath the first. On the north-western slope of the mountain the red soil appears again; and beneath it patches of a fine brown earth very like umber, in every case surrounded by a paler earth. This would certainly make a good dye-earth.

The Kittatiny is crossed without especial difficulty and in the next valley one comes to **Eckard's** house, 3-4 miles from **Heller's.** The man who lived there had the place for a third of the nett income from all produce; but there is the stipulation that every year six acres of land shall be cleared of wood and made ploughable—that is to say, four acres of upland and two of bottoms. These are hard conditions.

Beyond this house the next mountain (much lower than the Blue Mountain, but running in the same direction) contains a blue limestone; the darker the color the better it is held to be. Along the road over this hill no limestone comes to the surface, only sandstone; with it is a horn-stone or agate which in color and exterior appearance resembles the limestone but strikes fire on steel.

Leaving Eckardt's we got out of the straight road which we should have followed to **Brinker's Mill,** and bore to the right, in this way passing by several plantations which we should not have looked for here. These lie scattered in the forest-valleys and are settled

mostly by Germans, who are well satisfied in such remote regions where they can have land at a trifling
cost. We passed a little wooden meeting-house which
serves alternately as a place of worship for a Lutheran
and a Reformed congregation. Pastor **Weber** lately
had charge of these congregations, but he mispleased
because he preached too much of the war; they asked
him to leave and he was under the necessity of with-
drawing to Pittsburg. The first settlers of these
wastes came a few years after the last peace and before their numbers grew somewhat, had many hardships to bear. The neighborhood of Indians, at that
time still numerous there, was not the most agreeable.
They had to fetch in all their necessities and seed-
grain a distance of 50 miles, and if they wanted bread
were obliged to go 30 miles and more to the nearest
mill. For fear of the Indians, during the recent disturbances, many left their cabins, which now stand
deserted and gone to ruin.

We reached **Brinker's Mill** not before midday
(three and a half miles from Eckardt's) and found
the family over a repast customary here but which in
Germany the farmer permits himself only on festive
occasions: young chickens and rice.—Three more miles
to Dieter's who settled here just ten years ago. He
was at that time quite alone and had many Indians
around him who at first caused him great uneasiness
but later showed themselves placable. But when he
began to bring more and more land into cultivation
and found it necessary to take up for meadow a field
planted by the Indians in **wild red plums**, that dis-
gusted them and they went away. They are very fond
of this insipid fruit, which grows wild in the woods,

and plant the seeds wherever they stay for any time.
And so these plums, not much bigger or better than
sloes, are called Indian Plums.*

The land in this wilderness shows good spots only
here and there, in low places. The high land is dry
and owes its green appearance merely to the thick bush
growth; there is no good grass and little pasture for
cattle, and were bush and forest once taken off, the soil
would grow thinner and thirstier. The woods still
showed all sorts of oaks, black and white walnuts,
elms, elders, sassafras, maples &c., but few pines. All
the dwellings are block-houses, so-called (houses of
squared timber) and stand mostly near streams or
brooks. The farms, unlike those less remote, are un-
fenced—living far apart and the cattle keeping mostly
in the woods, people do not take the trouble to fence.
The first and most important crop of these mountain
people is corn, and then potatoes; these supply the
necessary food for themselves and their cattle. What
else they need comes from hunting and the sale of
skins. These farmers, as they express it in their Eng-
lish-German **machen es just so aus**, make out pretty
well, which is to say, they do not get rich, have a
plenty to eat and drink, do little work, and pay no
taxes.

We staid the night at Sebitz's, whose house is the

---

* These Indian Plums thrive in low rich spots, where they
grow to a height of 5-6 ft. The leaves are spear-shaped, twice
as long as broad, sharply dented, and pointed. The fruit
grows single, is round like an egg, and at maturity reddish.
There are, however, several varieties of this native wild plum
—Prunus sylvestris, fructu majori rubente—Gron. *fl. virg.*,
and Prunus americana, Marshall's *Amer. Grove*, p. 112.

last, absolutely, on the road to Wyoming, a distance
reckoned at 37 and one half miles from here. Therefore Sebitz regards the 'Great Swamp' as his best
friend—because all travellers, coming or going, are
compelled to stop with him, and in consequence his
house, however sorry and draughty, is well supported
as a tavern. The entertainment in woods-hotels of this
stamp, in lonesome and remote spots throughout
America, consists generally of bacon, ham and eggs,
fresh or dried venison, coffee, tea, butter, milk, cheese,
rum, corn-whiskey or brandy, and cyder. And everything clean.

Sebitz, a German Anabaptist, settled here some nine
years ago, and two or three neighbors about the same
time. He paid for the land 1 Pd. Pensylv. Current the
acre. For fear of the Indians all his neighbors left
him during the war; he alone had the courage to stay,
notwithstanding a whole family was murdered a mile
from his house. Often he was surrounded by Indians
who simply lurked about waiting for somebody to
open the door or come outside (for it is not their way
to enter a house forcibly); and they shot down his
horses and cattle. To be sure, he had with him a
militia guard because this place was looked upon as
an outpost; but they lived all together behind closed
doors and barricaded, in continual fear of death; they
opened to nobody without a close examination as to
whether who knocked was friend or foe. Such is the
doleful case of the frontiersman in times of an Indian
war.

We met a troop of carpenters here who were likewise on the way to Wyoming, to re-build a mill burned
down by the Indians. We were very glad of their

company, because we had 37 and a half miles to go,
through wilderness, the road bad and several streams
to cross—and must drive the distance if we were to
avoid spending the night in the woods. We got early
upon the road (Aug. 12th) but reached our destination
not until after sunset. That part of the mountains
beyond the **Kittatiny** and between the Delaware and
the Eastern arm of the Susquehannah is called in several maps **St. Anthony's Wilderness.** I could not
learn how St. Anthonius, who is not much known elsewhere in America, received this honor. The region is
better known by the name, above-mentioned, of the
Great Swamp, which designation applies in strictness
only to a part. The entrance to this unpeopled waste
is, at one point, through the gap in the **Pokono
Mountain,** pretty high but not steep. Then the Pokono
creek is passed and the road lies up that stream six
miles to White-oak Run, a frightful and narrow path
over stump and stone. Then follows upland, with a few
smaller hills. The whole way the road is grown up
on both sides in bush, notwithstanding that fire has
often passed over and left standing great numbers of
fine trunks half-burnt. These fires in the woods spread
at times accidentally from the camp-fires of travellers,
and again the woods are purposely burned by hunters
who post themselves behind the wind and wait for
game frightened out by the fire and smoke. Farther
on, we got into the veritable **Great Swamp,** so-called,
which extends only 15 miles across but no one knows
how far it lies to the north and south. Really, the
whole of this region is not what is commonly called
swamp, several mountains and valleys being included
under the name. I do not trust myself to give a pic-

ture of this region. The road cut through is nowhere more than six foot wide, and full of everything which can make trouble for the passenger. On both sides the forest so thick that the trees almost touch, by their height and their matted branches making a dimness, cold and fearful even at noon of the clearest day. All beneath is grown up in green and impenetrable bush. Everywhere lie fallen trees, or those half-fallen, despite of their weight not reaching the ground.—Thousands of rotten and rotting trunks cover the ground, and make every step uncertain; and between lies a fat bed of the richest mould that sucks up like a sponge all the moisture and so becomes swampy almost everywhere. One can with difficulty penetrate this growth even a little way and not without danger of coming too near this or that sort of snake lying hidden from the sharpest eye in the waste of stones, leaves, and roots. Nature shows itself here quite in its original wildness. The trees were still of the same sorts as in the country behind. A particularly deep and narrow valley in this great swamp is **The Shades of Death**; its steep mountain sides are distinguished by a great number of the tallest and slimmest pines, with white and hemlock spruce, and these are mixed below with a profuse and beautiful growth of rhododendron and calamus, their roots waxing lustily in deep beds of the richest mould. One must imagine for himself the effect of a very narrow, steep, stony, marshy, melancholy, dark road which on both sides is shadowed thickly by pines more than 80-100 ft. high.

Our fellow-travellers were of the opinion that all these hills and valleys would never be used for anything, because they thought cultivation would be im-

possible or certainly too troublesome. If there was
ore here, they said, there was wood enough for the
working of it; for all this immeasurable quantity of
wood grows and rots at this time quite unused. Certainly, the numerous streams which traverse the region,
and in the spring and fall become greatly swelled, will
later, (particularly when the woods to the east have
been more ravaged), offer a profitable trade in timber
and masts—for these trees would make ship and other
timber. Many spots would then be available for as
fine plantations as are to be seen in any other mountain
country where men find an easy and rich support.
But the people here, already, are all the time dreaming
of mines and sudden wealth, and many of our German countrymen still help to keep strange hopes alive.
The farmers about Heller's, mostly Germans, have
brought with them their stories of kobolds and mountain sprites and treasures lit; still hear the hill homun-
culus working and knocking, see the tell-tale flames,
but unluckily can never find the spot.

Without wasting time on the road, now near being
swamped and again almost breaking our necks, we
hastened forward as fast as our horses could go, and
all the more because we were threatened by storm
clouds. We stayed half an hour at Locust-hill and in
the evening half an hour at Bullock's-place, our
friends sharing with us their store of provisions without which we and our horses should have had a hungry
day's journey, for besides grass and water there was
nothing to eat; we were pretty thoroughly wetted in
the swamp, and coming over the last hill were obliged
to stop in black darkness on account of a thunder-
storm; reaching Wyoming after eight o'clock, tired,

wet, and hungry. This road was formerly nothing but
an Indian foot-path and was made as usable as it is
not until Sullivan's expedition which was sent out
from Wyoming against the Indians in 1779.

Wyoming, the settlement of this name, (the chief
place of which is really **Wilksbury**), lies in an extraordinarily fertile valley west of the Blue Mountains
and on the Eastern branch of the Susquehannah,
leisurely winding through. Some 20 years ago a few
New Englanders came hither, followed shortly after
by people from anywhere, so that in a brief space 90
families had come in who would or could not live elsewhere. Fear of the law drove some of them and the
goodness of the land tempted others to settle in this
remote wilderness, cut off from the inhabited parts by
rugged and pathless mountains, but their numbers
rapidly increasing the country was soon changed to a
region of beautiful open fields. Then, the colony having begun to take on importance disputes arose over
land-titles between the states of Connecticut and Pensylvania. Connecticut claimed that this tract of land
was included in its charter, by the terms of which
(about the middle of the last century), the state was
granted a region bounded to the south by a line pro-
ceeding from the Atlantic ocean continually west to
the Pacific sea. At that time there was little known
of the geography of the interior, and some other
charters were given in England to the states of New
York, Jersey, and Pensylvania, by which was apportioned a large part of the territory falling to Connecticut, the boundary lines following given streams the
course of which was very uncertain as well. Connecticut begins its old line at the **Byram** river, carries it

through Phillips' Manor, across the Hudson, across the
Delaware at East-town, and in this way divides Jersey
and the Moravian establishments in Pensylvania into
two districts. By such claims as these a great part of
the state of Pensylvania was made disputable territory
and Connecticut asserted title to lands it had never
possessed. Connecticut admits that the debateable
tract in the state of New York was set off from itself
by grants to New York made later, but claims that it
does not therefore follow that its right has been withdrawn to lands falling on its line beyond New York.
Thus it has happened that the first settlements in Wyoming were made by New England and these have
kept their hold there in matters of government. Pensylvania, on the other hand, shows by its grant that
the Wyoming region, with other districts in dispute,
lies in the midst of its original territory as fixed by
England. These claims and assertions on the one side
and the other have been the cause of many difficulties.
Pensylvania as well as Connecticut sold and made
over lands there, so that of the land-owners of Wyoming one held his land under the one state and another
under the other. With such dispositions, animosities
were inevitable, and thus even before the outbreak
of the Revolution there was a continual private war
between the Pensylvania and New England parties
in Wyoming. People fought over the right to the
land. If a Pensylvanian came with a deed to so much
land, he must first see if it was already taken up by a
New Englander. If so, he must attempt to gain possession by force: failing, he reserved his right for the
time and chose an unsettled place in the neighborhood,
from which after a few years, and improvements be-

gun, he might very probably be dispossessed by another New Englander coming with a Connecticut deed.
The New Englanders were always the strongest
party. ✙ In the early seventies bloody fights took place
between the colonists, when several lives were lost.
However this was only private war and the war with
England coming on suppressed the quarrels beyond the
mountains, the matter at issue having not yet been decided.   But since the peace these dissensions have been
again renewed, and both states recently laid their
claims before the tribunal of the Congress.   A commit-
tee decided for Pensylvania.   The New England party
is altogether dissatisfied with this judgment, because in
this case they must lose their gains, Pensylvania having long since granted to its own subjects much of the
land in dispute.   To be sure, Pensylvania has offered
the New Englanders reimbursement in lands elsewhere, but they prefer if they can to stay where they
are, and threaten to do so by force of their fists ; for
orders of the Congress are not regarded here if not
pleasing or unsupported by force.   So far the outbreak
of further hostilities has been controlled by the little
garrison which the state of Pensylvania maintains here
against the Indians until a treaty with these nations
is drawn up.*

Wyoming, according to the New England claim,

---

* According to sundry items of a public nature, there have
been of late other bloody proceedings in Wyoming, and the
disquiets among the colonists of both states have only very
recently been brought to a peaceable conclusion—Extract from
a communication from Philadelphia, 1787.   "The tedious
"territorial quarrel between Pensylvania and Connecticut has
"at last been happily ended without bloodshed.   The Connecti-

lies in **Westmoreland County**; but in Pensylvania it
forms a part of Northumberland County. The colony
consists of **Wilksbury**, the chief place, and a few
smaller beginning villages, as **Nanticook, Hannover,
Abraham's, Jacob's Plains**, and **Shavannah**, in all of
which there are probably 400 families. Wilksbury had
a court-house once where the laws were administered
after the manner of Connecticut whence the Justices
were sent. But during the disturbances of the war
they lived some years in complete anarchy, without
law, magistrates, taxes, or priests. " We act on our
" sense of honor, and depend pretty much on that,
" said the miller of the place ; nothing can be gained
" by law and nobody punished,—our only rule is trust
" or distrust." Since a garrison was placed here, however, the commanding officer has at the same time
acted as Justice, without any recourse to military law.
The inhabitants hear his opinion and adjust their dealings thereby, if that seems good to them. But the
people of Wyoming, with all their freedom and living
on the most productive lands, are pauper-poor. The
war was something of a back-set, but their sloth still
more. They live in miserable block-houses, are badly
clothed, farm carelessly, and love easeful days. Last
winter most of them sent all their corn and wheat over
the mountains, turned it into cyder and brandy, (for
they have not yet planted orchards themselves), so as

" cut party has peaceably submitted to the government of Pen-
" slyvania. This happy outcome is an effect of the magnanimity
" with which the government of Pensylvania has forgiven and
" forgotten past injuries and deeds of violence, by an especial
" mildness suddenly converting old enemies to friends and
" brothers."

to drink and dance away the tedium. And so in the
spring they had neither seed-corn nor bread; lived
meanwhile on milk and blackberries, or by hunting,
(and many of them on less), in expectation of the
harvest which has turned out well, and now they are
preparing for fresh quickenings. With all their negligence, they had before the war fine store of cattle,
hogs, hemp, flax &c., of which the superfluity sold
brought them what they needed. Of their mills one
was burnt by the Indians, and there was no water for
the other; they must therefore send their corn 50 miles
over the mountains, or whoever could not do this was
obliged to pound it in wooden troughs after the fashion
of the Indians. Of what faith they are, no man
knows. An old Anabaptist lives among them and
preaches to whomsoever has a mind to hear. We came
a day too late to see the solemn baptism of a young
girl 20 years old, who was baptized in the Susquehannah.

The especial fertility of this splendid valley is owing
chiefly to a thick clay-bed which lies just beneath the
fat and strong black mould. They dig through 2-4-8
inches of good garden earth, then 4-5 ft. of rich white
clay, then several feet of rough sand, and below a bed
of sand holding large smooth pebbles. At this depth of
12-14 ft. they find their wells of water, having struck
no hard rock. There are places where the soil is
greatly richer. The Shavannah bottoms, four miles
down the river on the west side, are 14-15 ft. deep in
mould, with little clay or sand intermixed. This spot
of perhaps 1000 acres of the choicest, inexhaustible
land is like a garden. But this fatness of the soil gives
the water an unpleasant taste.

The mountains which border the Wyoming Valley are not without traces of ore and fossils. The high steep water-side a mile above Wyoming contains, beneath the surface covering of sand and clay, a heavy bed of coarse slate which becomes finer on going down. Along the open wall of the mill-race there, many traces of ferns and perhaps other plants can be seen impressed on the slate fragments. But after hours of search in the exposed and mostly half-weathered strata, I could find no fair specimen of any size; the incomplete specimens which I took back with me to Philadelphia were the first of the sort which they had seen there. Going down, the slate gradually changes to a bed (not deep) of fine, light, lustrous coal which rubbed leaves no smut on the hand and burns without any bad smell. This coal is to be had for the taking, and a smith who has set up his shop hard by praises it much. Although this coal is good, that found on the western branch of the Susquehannah and on the Ohio is regarded as better still. Beneath the coal is a red splintery sand-stone with much mica; then, a course of rough slate; and next the water-line a reddish white sand-stone occurs again in layers. The transition from slate, (with plant-impressions), to coal explains the origin of the coal, and is warrant for an antiquity of this part of the world greater than that assigned it by certain investigators. The same alternation of slate and coal is observed at other places in this valley, on both sides the river, and one cannot but suppose that at some time the whole valley was filled with piled layers of plant-earth, from which slate and coal developed, and afterwards the river cut through.

Higher up the river the banks consist solely of a

laminated sand-stone, with mica in varying quantities, and the layers of divers degrees of hardness. At one place in this region, near the river, there comes to the surface a vein of ore thick as a man's leg, blackish, and micaceous, which from its look might be **lead-ore.*** For a long time this was thought to be silver, until experiments were made at Philadelphia showing that there was no ground for the belief but not determining what the ore was. Beyond the river there are said to be ores at one or two places which have been found on experiment really to contain silver. These spots, I am told, were once pointed out to certain persons by the Indians, and are at present known to a few who speak of them mysteriously. It appears also that a long time ago Europeans may have worked there; at least, the first New Englanders who came hither said that they found remains there of horse-trappings and smelting tools.

On the rocky banks of the west side, and at other places there is seen after dry weather a deposit of natural copperas and alum, both of which are often collected in pounds by the country-people. According to accounts they use this copperas for dyeing, and in the following strange way: For each pound of the yarn to be dyed, a pound of the purest copperas is taken. The yarn is dipped first in a clear, warm lye, and then into the copperas solution, the dippings repeated 6-8 times; but each time the yarn should be a little while hung up to air; in this way, it is said, a deep straw color is given the yarn.—I saw nothing of this cop-

---

* I had specimens of this and other minerals and rocks of the region, but lost them.

peras. But several miles down the river I had myself taken to a place where an outcrop of saltpetre is scraped from the cliffs, which with the addition of lye is made into good saltpetre. At the beginning of the war many hundred-weight of saltpetre was prepared here and farther up the river. I shall have further opportunity to mention the natural saltpetre of America.

At Jacob's Plains, a few miles from Wyoming, there is a spring on which floats a fat, viscous scum depositing a yellow sediment. The water is said to have an unpleasant bitter taste; probably contains petroleum; the neighborhood of the coal-beds makes it likely.

Down the river towards **Sunbury** cubical lead ore has been found; and on the western branch of the Susquehannah lead occurs in still greater quantity, as also alum and marcasite.

Taking a turn to Nanticook we passed by the ruins of a beginning iron-foundry. Much swamp-ore is found thereabouts, which is probably what was used; besides, there is iron-stone in the neighboring mountain. The reopening of this works will mean a considerable gain to the region, since the distance and the bad roads over which the iron needed must be fetched vastly heightens the cost to the farmer. One obstacle in the way of further attempts at getting out ore in this region was the territorial quarrels; hence anybody who thinks he knows where there is a good spot is very mysterious about it. About Wyoming there has been discovered so far no lime or marble, but 15-20 miles down the river, especially about Sunbury, several hills are said to show lime and marble; and likewise higher up the river.

12

On the west side of the Susquehannah several
mountain-ridges, belonging to the principal chain, are
little known because only hunters and Indians go
through them. The first of these ridges (bordering
this valley) is remarkable for its singular slope, which
gives a dented appearance to the whole. Whatever
the thrust of the mountains, it is invariably the case
that their southern slope, reckoned from the highest
line, falls away more precipitously; the northern slope
is longer and gentler.

The Susquehannah on its way to the sea has to pass
more than one line of rocks and as often makes what
are called falls. Not far above this place is the so-
called Upper Fall where there is heard merely the
rushing of the water between rocks that hardly show
above the surface. Several miles below Wyoming
there is a more considerable fall. But the stream finds
its greatest impediment farther down towards the
Chesapeak Bay at several places not impassable for
boats but extremely difficult. The stream has been
proved to be navigable down by a few bravos who
made the voyage in two boats from here to Baltimore
and back. This was only out of vanity, for the difficulties and dangers have kept them and others from
any further attempt. But if in future the passage can
be made easier by blowing up the rocks, this region
will be the gainer in the more convenient sale of its
produce. From here up the river there are few obstacles or none. Single batteaux have already as-
cended from Wyoming 360 miles to the small lakes
west of Albany where the Susquehannah rises, and so
have come within 18 miles of the Mohawk river
which flows into the Hudson.

At the beginning of the war a stockade was built against the roving Indians and later a little fort, in Wyoming on the river. Thence went out that great expedition against the Indians which was undertaken by the Americans in the autumn of 1779. The inactivity at that time of the English army in New York gave the Americans all the more leisure to carry through a work of vengeance upon the Indians for the many grewsome and inhuman acts they had long been committing in the frontier regions. A small corps, with artillery, was chosen for the purpose, under the lead of General Sullivan assisted by several other well-known officers, among whom was General Irwin. At the same time other smaller corps proceeded from Pittsburg and Albany, to support the main body and also to divert the attention of the enemy. The real objective was the famous five or six nations (as they are diversly called) who in the remotest wilds of America exhibit a sort of republican union. The Five Nations inhabit a wide region at the back of the Northern and middle colonies, among the great Canadian lakes, rivers, and impenetrable woods. They have been long known for their courage and for the especial fidelity with which they have supported the English crown against the French and even against their own people. At the beginning of the war they had an agreement with the Americans to observe a strict neutrality during the contest between the colonies and the mother-country. It is pretended on the side of the Americans that these nations offered at that time to wield the war-axe against the English, which proposal was rejected, with the well-known American large-mindedness and humanity, and merely neutrality

was stipulated. Presumably, the Americans did not
seal the bargain with largess. So it came about that
the preponderant English generosity, and the influence which Sir William Johnson and several others
had over these Indians, brought them easily to the
point of letting go their peaceful sentiments and promises and indulging their inborn and quickly aroused
propensities to war and ferocity. They were soon taking a most active part in a very bloody war, and they
brought desolation to all the frontier settlements (those
on the western side of the mountains) of the United
States. The Oneida Indians, it is said, were the only
nation which remained true to their promise of neutrality, or at least no hostilities against the Americans
were laid to their charge. Therefore these were to be
excepted from the universal destruction which had
been determined on for the others. For nothing less
than an entire extirpation and rooting-out of those
nations was the proud purpose of this expedition, so
far indeed as this might be possible against an enemy
who rarely lets itself be found or placed, and is tempted
to show itself only by the appearance of an especial
advantage. There was the conviction beforehand that
these Indians must be forced quite to relinquish their
haunts if the numerous but helpless settlers of the
frontier were to be given any hope of lasting peace and
security.

The troops composing General Sullivan's command
assembled in Wyoming. Already they had had to
make their way through the wilderness so far, bringing hither the necessary provisions and military supplies which were to be sent on up the river in boats,
and as opportunity presented were to follow the troops

by pack-horse. In order to bring up these stores the Congress had summoned all its strength and had been at great expense. The Indians, who were thoroughly informed of these fear-striking preparations, assembled numerously and in good heart on the borders of their country. They had as leaders Butler, Brant, and Guy Johnson, and all their related and united tribes were further strengthened by several hundred Refugees, or Tories as the Americans called them. They took position advantageously in a pass, in the woods between Chemung and Newtown, not far from the Teaoga river; here they threw up a breast-work, or rather abattis, more than half a mile long. Posted thus, Sullivan attacked them in August 1779, and they defended themselves so obstinately and stoutly that only after a warm fight of two hours could Sullivan bring them to yield, and then not without the very active support of his rude artillery. He boasted, however, of his complete and stupefying victory over the allied Indians, so much so that during the subsequent devastation of their country they would not let themselves be drawn into a second stand-up fight. This battle merely opened the way for the beginning of Sullivan's real enterprise, and there remained a number of other difficulties to be overcome which offered the greatest obstacles to the undertaking. If any impression was to be made it was necessary that this corps should stay at least a month in the field, in an entirely unfamiliar country moreover, where nothing was to be hoped for in the item of any of the necessary supplies. But notwithstanding all the care taken, on account of the distance, the bad roads, and other circumstances, Sullivan found it possible to secure provisions requisite for

hardly the half of a month; and had there been the
desired amount on hands there was a lack of pack-
horses to get it forward,* although in order to have
less to carry, the cattle intended for meat-rations was
driven along with the army, for of salted meat they
had none. The burning desire of the troops to be
avenged on the Indians, the enthusiasm of the officers,
and an animating speech of the General removed all
obstacles; the proposal to diminish the daily rations
was universally approved, and without protest the
ration was fixed at half a pound of meal and half a
pound of fresh meat.

I should not have given so much space to this expedition had it not been a doubly remarkable one, on
account of the fact that on this occasion there was discovered among these nations more of a polity and a
higher degree of civilization than even those had
guessed who had long lived in their neighborhood, indeed had lived almost among them. Sullivan found
with astonishment that no guides familiar with the
country were to be had, and there was no way for
him to find out where the Indian villages were except
by following up their tracks as if they had been wild
beasts. But since it is their custom to march one behind the other, the last always covering with leaves
his own track and his companions', it is a difficult
business to trace them, requiring much practice, much
patience, and a sharp eye.

By Sullivan's account (which I have made use of)
the degree of civilization remarked in these Indian vil-

---

* However the statement was that some 1200 horses were
either worn out on this expedition or lost in the woods.

lages was superior to anything which could have been
expected from former observations or from the general
opinion regarding the morals and way of life of these
nations. The beautiful situation of their villages, often
plainly the result of choice ; the size, construction, and
arrangement of their dwellings, these were the things
first to strike the beholder in this new and unknown
country. Sullivan reported, (and I had later General
Irwin's personal confirmation), that their wigwams or
houses were not only spacious but even cleanly, and
he several times mentions that they were regularly
framed. The size of their corn-fields excited astonishment no less than the industry with which they were
cultivated. As to both facts an indication is to be had
from the statement that the troops destroyed corn in
the field to the amount of 160,000 bushels. Still more
striking was the number of fruit-trees found and destroyed, and also the size and apparent age of several
of their orchards. Sullivan mentions that at one place
they cut down 1500 fruit-trees, many of which seemed
to be very old. To be sure, he does not say of what
varieties these were ; the greatest part of them were
very likely the above-mentioned Indian Plum-trees.

Such circumstances are proof that these nations have
long practiced agriculture, and are not to be charged
with an incapacity of providing for the future or with
an absolute carelessness of their posterity. No doubt
the case with man in his uncivilized state is the same
as that observed among beavers and other animals,
that is to say, they become more careless, wilder, and
less regardful of the future when they find their works
disturbed by the approach of man and their peace and
quiet interrupted. It is well known that the natives of

America have quite forgotten most of the devices and arts of their ancestors in the fabrication of utensils, now that the coming of the Europeans has supplied their needs and spared them the trouble of manufacture.

This business of devastation was concluded within the time fixed, and really there was not an hour to lose. Forty Indian villages were burnt, among which Chinesee was the largest, numbering 128 houses. From Sullivan's report, as well as from oral accounts, it appears that this region, until then unknown and unvisited, was beheld with no indifferent eyes; descriptions show it to be an especially beautiful and fertile country. Several days' march from Wyoming, northwest, the troops found themselves in a fine, level country extending as far as the Canadian lakes and covered with an excellent grass extraordinarily tall.

But the expedition, extremely tedious, costly, and bloody as it was had not the desired effect, had none except that of destruction carried almost too far. The Indians fled everywhere before their pursuers, offering no resistance after the first battle, but they followed on the track of the enemy and all stragglers, sick and wounded, or those cut off in any way from the corps became their victims.

When one hears of the trouble the Indians have made for the settlers in this frontier region, the backwoodsmen must be in a measure pardoned if they speak of these nations in the bitterest way, swear eternal enmity against them, and are dissatisfied that the Congress should be making preparations to conclude a peace with them; for they are at this time kept from further hostilities only by the peace negotiated between

England and the United States. But although the
usual peace-ceremonies have not yet been observed
between the American states and the several Indian
nations, many people have ventured up the Susquehannah, exposing themselves to the danger of falling
in with Indians still perhaps in a vexed state of mind.
I have, however, heard of no instance in which the
Indians have misused the good faith reposed in them
or have broken the peace of the English, their allies.
The journeys to their country were undertaken by
people searching for new lands and what was found
suitable they wished in part to measure off. Several
land-surveyors were already come here with commissions. In America speculations in land form the
trade of a certain class of people, who either singly
or in companies take up great tracts of land from the
Indians, disposing of them later at a great profit. To
that end, skilled judges of lands are sent out in advance so as to pick out the best spots which are then
bargained for. In one way and another the Indians
are often scandalously overreached.

We collected in this region several varieties of
mature seeds; but I must confess that considering the
place and the season we found little that was new.
Rattlesnake-root (*Polygala Senega*) grows here in
quantity; also *Chenopodium anthelminthicum;* and
Cleome dodecandra, which is praised as a vermifuge.
A new species of the *Parnassia,* which I discovered
about New York, grows here plentifully in swampy
meadows. Among trees there was conspicuous a
group of beautiful larches, called Tamarac; they use
here a drink made from the bark, for swollen feet after
fevers.

After a stay of five days, delayed by the weather, we left this country the 18th of August in the afternoon, and made seven miles to Long Meadow where we spent the night in a half-ruined cabin and on the bare earth. We found a small boy there, whose parents were intending to settle here, but they had been several days absent looking for provisions and had quite carelessly left the youngster by himself in the woods. He was extremely happy when we gave him some bread and meat.

Very early we left our dreary quarters but were several hours delayed when we came to Bear Creek. Since our passage that way a family had appeared, even here, and within the few days had made their block-house nearly ready. Of the logs meant for that purpose one had fallen across the narrow road, and it was in no way possible to get our horses through the very thick and swampy bush at either side; we had therefore to wait patiently until the log was sawed through and got out of the way. Farther on, in that half of the road lying through this wilderness, we happened on still a third family which likewise had just come to settle there. These people expect to make a temporary support by selling brandy to travellers, until they have gradually brought enough land into cultivation to supply their needs. This will indeed require some time, but meanwhile through them a beginning is made of the future settlement of this waste. All these poor families chose the region because here they can at no outlay have the use of land taken up by nobody else, until some one acquires it by purchase and obliges them to leave, in which case however they have the right of pre-emption. Going back we followed the

road we had come as the only passable one through
this comfortless region, and about sunset reached
White-oak Run. The last eight miles we had to go
a-foot, for there was now thick darkness among the
high, close-standing trees, obscuring the friendly light
of the moon which shone clear, but not for us, and it
would have been neck-breaking work to keep on horse-
back. We could find our way only by knocking from
time to time into the trees and stumps on both sides,
and thus being put back into the narrow path. The
dull light from the many rotting trunks was pleasant
to be sure but of no use. Finally we had 2 or 3 times
to wade through the circuitous Pokonoke Creek, and
at nine o'clock arrived at Sebitz's house, tired and
wet. It is indeed thoroughly tiresome to drag along
throughout a whole day in such a wilderness where,
besides the plants growing just by the way there is
very little to entertain. The restricted outlook is always the same; after the highest summits of the
mountains are past, there is nothing more to delight
the eye except, in the deepest valleys, the environment
of trees. On this return journey I counted ten different ranges of hills and mountains which have to be
crossed between Wyoming and Sebitz's.*

These particularly distinct chains of mountains and
hills are all parallel and extend northeast to southwest.
Their divisions are reckoned merely by the larger
brooks and streams running through them; for all
together they may be aptly regarded as one mountain,
of which the several ridges are set apart by these

---

* Vid. *Beyträge zur mineralogischen Kenntniss des östlichen
Theils von Nordamerika*, p. 118 &c.

streams. Such streams taking their rise on one or the other side of a range, the number of them must in some measure modify the plan of the whole, although the breadth of the entire range is not affected. What is called the Great Swamp of the region is in itself an extensive and high-lying tract observable especially from the last long slope. One has no opportunity to examine the different rocks except in so far as these appear along the road, only six feet wide; everything else being covered with stumps, roots, trees, leaves, grass, and swamp. What most commonly appears at the surface is the often mentioned laminated sandstone, which is everywhere of a very fine grain but pretty hard; the eye seldom discovers micaceous constituents; the smell shows the clay content. The color is of many sorts: white, grey, blueish, reddish, reddish-brown &c. Each particular fragment, solid as it may appear at the first glance, is made up of divers and diversly thick plates, close bound together; such is the appearance on breaking. All these hills are superficially overlaid with this sort of stone. Not only along the roads, but in the few open and level spots there are seen millions of fragments or scales of this stone; it is rarely found at the surface in a dense stratified formation. What was the cause of this general shattering of the uppermost layers? Frost and weather may have done somewhat; but the explanation of the people hereabouts is not entirely from the purpose. They liken this burst upper shell of the mountains to the bark of a tree split by its growth, and a few form the erroneous conclusion that their mountains grow.—But that by some ancient convulsion of these mountains their shell may have been so cracked to fragments, this may be indeed supposed.

The deeper, less shaken, and older bed of this range appears to be of the unpolished, quartz-grained stone elsewhere mentioned. For this is seen on the east side of the mountains, at Easton, and to the west in the hills towards Wyoming; is therefore probably the underlying bed, and is throughout overlaid with the laminated sand-stone, which quite as probably is to be regarded as a deposit from water standing above these mountains. Not here indeed, but later, and on the continuation of this range, I have found in similar sand-stone impressions of muscles and animalcules of the sea. But it is surprising to find in this part of the range no appearance of limestone. On the road followed by us today I saw none, and I could on inquiry hear of none. The greatest part of this road, the land seemed too stony or too poor to be used for cultivation; but in the Swamp especially and in most of the lower spots, there are tracts affording deep layers of the finest black earth. In such places are to be found many beautiful plants and shrubs, but to be come at only with the greatest difficulty. Here the American botanist has much in reserve for him, and it is to be hoped that his zeal will soon be aroused.

From Sebitz's to Heller's the road is for the most part down-grade, through a multitude of sand-stones. The Pokonoke Creek is again crossed several times; it winds through very pleasing low-grounds. In the mountains as well as here it is plainly to be seen that most of the higher trees, especially those standing apart, lean sharply from northwest to southeast, the course, that is, of the strongest and most frequent winds. Near Brinker's Mill there is a rarity—a beautiful prospect, of the Delaware Gap to the left and in

front, (over a lower ridge of hills), the range of the
Blue or Kittatiny Mountain running straight away.
The smaller hills in the foreground are adorned now
with a beautiful green covering, and at a distance give
the look of a fertile landscape, but it is only a green of
leaf-bearing trees or of plants growing in their shade.
For where the bush is taken off, the soil is burnt up
by the sun and the air, and all the meadow and pasture
land looks brown and yellow.

Some iron-stone appears in the hills between Sebitz's
and the Mill, and traces of copper have been discovered. Quite at the top of a hill, between the Mill
and Eckhardt's we came upon a little lake, in which
there should be fish. There is also such a clear little
separate lake to be found on a higher hill near Sebitz's,
and another on Locust-hill.

In order to rest our horses and to pack the plants,
seeds, and stones we had collected on the road to Wyoming and thereabouts, we were obliged to spend a
warm day at Heller's; in the cool of the evening we
returned to Nazareth. Just out of Nazareth there
stands a roomy stone house, with a few outbuildings,
which is at present called Old Nazareth. The famous
Methodist preacher, Whitfield, who with such an ad-
venturous zeal preached through all the American
provinces, and either established or sketched several
praiseworthy institutions, built this house, intending
it as a school-house for Indian youth. The Moravian
Brethren afterwards came into possession of it. There
is nothing remarkable about the house; but the report
that the steps before the entrance were of alabaster induced me to visit it, since I had as yet heard nothing
of alabaster in this part of America. The stone is

largely white, showing broad flecks reddish and yellowish, and scraped comes off very white. Wanting a mineral acid I could not determine whether it was really alabaster; I could not knock off a specimen and take it away with me. It was not exactly known whence these steps had been brought; it was believed they came from near Easton, 6-8 miles from Bethlehem, where it was known that several sorts of marble occur, but as yet no alabaster has been found there within the memory of the inhabitants. From Nazareth we saw at the distance of a mile the beautiful farm, **Christiansbrunn**, belonging to the Brethren, which lies in a pleasant and fertile spot. The farm contains about 500 acres of land, of which only 100 is good clean meadow. Some 300 head of black cattle are kept there; several yoke of draught oxen which they showed us exceeded in size and beauty all others I have observed in America. All the buildings and arrangements here have the conspicuously pleasing neatness, decency, and carefully ordered plan which are nowhere missed in the settlements of this Society. There is a water-wheel mill there of the over-thrust description, a sort rare in America. The water is conducted in underground pipes, and has sufficient fall to ascend 20 ft. and turn the wheels. There is also a large brewery, and a large dairy where much butter and good cheese are made. Of craftsmen there is none here except a gun-smith, an indispensable man among the mountain poachers. The place takes its name from an excellent spring in a beautiful stone casing, whence the region for 5-6 miles around is supplied with water.

From Nazareth, by Reading and Lebanon, to Carlisle

From Christiansbrunn to **Allen-town,** 11 miles, we passed over a new road, for the most part through woods ; we saw only a few insignificant houses. The dead trees still standing numerously in the corn fields was proof besides that these were new settlements mostly. It would be impossible for the new settler to bring a piece of woods-land thoroughly into cultivation the first year, felling all the trees, getting them out of the way, and rooting up the stumps. And so at the first they have to be content with ' girdling.' This operation consists in cutting a ring out of the bark, in the lower part of the tree, one or two spans wide. In this way the sap taken up through the roots is checked in its ascent through the veins found particularly in the bark, and the upper part of the tree gradually dies. Death follows quickest with the pine ; leaf-trees appear to be somewhat more tenacious of life. We observed, in these and other fields, oaks girdled last year and a few as much as two years ago which notwithstanding have put out new leaves this year, although few and small.*

---

* Therefore it must be that the veins carrying up the sap lie not only in the bark but in the outer spongy wood-rings as well—or, the suction-veins in the bark may for a certain time supply nourishment to the upper parts of the tree—or the little sap still remaining in the sap-tubes after girdling may be expended entirely in forcing the leaves—I saw on Long Island

The Blue Mountains were now to our right. Nearer towards Allen-town, Leheigh Gap appeared in the distant view, and a mile from it we passed the river at a ford. The land of this region seemed to be of middling strength and less stony; we noticed sand-stone scattered about here and there, but everywhere limestone jutted from the soil, for the most part a reddish sandy-clay.—The landscape, of low hills following the river, offered a pleasant change to the eye, weary of monotonous and gloomy woods. But not so the inhabitants of the region; all who met us looked so defiant and independent that it was easily seen they were not of the Moravian Brethren whose softer and more pleasing manners were still fresh in our remembrance.

Allen-town, of which the official name is Northampton, numbers 40-50 houses; the first name was that of a fort which in the war before the last stood several miles away towards the mountains, as defence against the Indians, called Fort Allen and now in ruins.

The road from here to Reading leads over the ridges of connected hills which are counted a part of the afore-mentioned Dry Land. Perhaps three miles from Allen-town is the famous curiosity of the region, the

---

a sour gum cut down the fall before, putting out leaves and blooms in the spring. Single branches of certain trees may continue alive regardless of the fact that rings have been cut in them down to the wood, and the connection thus broken between the veins taking up the sap through the bark; of this I saw a remarkable instance in a pear-tree at Hampton Court in England—one branch had been widely girdled for many years and nevertheless bore more heavily than any of the others.

13

so-called ' Big Spring,' which breaks out of the earth
in a vein large as a man's leg and within the first
hundred rods of its course sets three mills going.   It
appears that in this hilly and dry country the water is
assembled at only a few places, gushing out thence in
greater volume and force.   This range of hills is too
low to furnish such supplies of water, but running as
they do with the Blue Mountains it may be supposed
that the few (and therefore more considerable) springs
of the **Dry Land** come from the mountains, and are
here raised through subterranean canals, as by an el-
bowed pipe.

Ten miles from Allen-town is **Maguntchy,** a village
of few houses; its name is Indian.   Not far off is
Cedar Creek which also rises in a very large spring.
The Leheigh hills are now to the left and pretty near;
they appear to make a continuous parallel course with
the Blue Mountains, which are constantly in sight at
a distance of 8-10-12 miles running uniformly; whereas the summits of the Leheigh hills are more cut into
and of a wave formation.   The land hereabouts is
fairly good; fields and meadows of a fertile appearance, the latter conspicuously green at this time.   The
farm management seems pretty orderly.   One gets a
glimpse of many good stone houses, many of them
very neat, and everything about the premises shows
order and attention.   The people are mainly Germans,
who speak bad English and distressing German.   The
buck-wheat, greatly seeded here after wheat for the
second harvest, stood in full bloom and with the penny-
royal (*Cunila pulegioides*), so common on all the
roads, made a strong and pleasant evening odor.

America is indeed the land of the oak.   All the

forests are largely oak,* but the trees are nowhere either large or strong. What we have seen yesterday and today would be counted young wood, but this is hardly probable, because we observed no old stumps. Besides, the thin trunks do not stand very close together; the dry soil of these hills does not give any superfluous nourishment. And this was confirmed by the accounts of the inhabitants who say they rarely find an oak more than six inches through. Hence they are obliged to fetch their fence-rails 4-6 miles, split chestnut-rails being used for this purpose, the oak rotting faster, especially if the bark is left on.

After sunset we came to **Kutz-town** (19 miles from Allen-town and 31 from Nazareth). A well to-do German, in order to cut something of a figure with his name in his ears, gave the land for this place, which is only some three years old, and the houses but few and not large.

From Kutz-town to Reading, 19 miles, through a similar landscape, over limestone hills.—Nearer the town the land grows better and is better farmed; and the houses are more numerous and finer. We did not cross a brook until six miles from Reading; on the road there appeared many kinds of soft clayey-slate, grey, white, reddish; at times we saw the red earth, but the common surface covering continued the reddish-loam.

Along all these limestone hills, and only on them, are

---

* The soil of these forests is not a very good grass-soil and furnishes but meagre pasturage for cattle. It was long ago remarked that the European oak was a hindrance to the growth of grass and other plants within its influence. Is this true here also?

to be found numerous black horn-stones often in large fragments.   Hence where these stones occur else-where, it may be guessed with considerable certainty that there is limestone soil near by.   The limestone of this region is also frequently covered with sand-stone.

At the first glance, on account of its especial dryness the soil on these hills seems not to be very fertile.   Be-sides, it promises little by reason of the common goose-grass (*Verbascum Thapsus*) which so often takes pos-session, and other plants fond of dry and poor soils. But this land is praised as very good wheat-land.   The wheat sown in the fall grows through the temperate and commonly moist spring until by June, when the greatest heats begin, it has reached so much of its growth as rather to be helped than hurt by the summer heats; whereas later field crops, such as maize, buck-wheat, turnips &c depend more on seasonable rains and therefore oftener fail.   The lighter soil of this region is moreover not disagreeable to the farmer because it requires no great labor in the working.   They flatter themselves here that they can increase the fertility of the soil by lime and plaister,* but this method is by no means adapted for this soil.

From the last hill, a mile from Reading, there is an agreeable prospect over sundry ranges of larger and smaller hills that with apparent regularity rise one be-hind the other.   The Blue Mountains are hardly to be

---

* About Philadelphia and Germantown, Whitemarsh, Lan-caster, and York the use of plaister for grass and plow-land has recently become a favorite practice, because there is less trouble involved than in the collecting, lading, hauling, and spreading of the common dung of cattle—trouble which the farmer here does not willingly submit to.

discovered in the back-ground.   To the left are the
Oley hills, a continuation of the Leheigh hills.   In the
fore-ground, on the lowest of all the hills, by the
Schuylkill river, one is pleased to find a neat town,
(and not a small one), where only 36 years ago there
was mere wilderness—for older Reading is not.   The
town has four principal streets which stand exactly
with the compass-points, and where these cross is a
fine Court-house.   The inhabitants are chiefly Germans, almost all of them in good circumstances.   And
the farmers living around are all well clad and well
fed, few of them owning less than 200 acres of land.

Mr. Daniel Udree's iron-works lie 10 miles from
Reading, in a narrow valley among the Oley hills.
The mine which supplies the ore is five miles beyond,
and has a depth of not more than 6-7 fathom.   Recently ore has been discovered still nearer, which in
several respects is better than the first, and in future
this will be used in mixture; hitherto they have not
known how to apply the advantage to be gained from a
mixture of several ores.   Nearly at the top of the hill
and immediately behind the high-furnace, a mine was
formerly worked which is rich in the best and most
compact ore.   The rock of this hill is a coarse-grained
wacke, lying in thick beds running almost north and
south.   The ore is found at a depth of only 12-20 ft.
below the surface mould and in places along the hill
even shallower.   A gallery-stoll had been driven in the
hill, some 12 ft. high, 15 ft. broad, and about 300 ft.
long, and then a 60 ft. shaft was sunk, and a beautiful,
compact, quartz-ore, shimmering green and blue, was
taken out which was the richest and most easily fluxed
of any ore in that whole region.   But water broke in

strongly and drowned out the work. And besides, the
ore having to be blasted, at the beginning of the war
powder was too dear and work-people scarce ; and so
they were compelled to give over this mine, but will
now take it up again.

A reddish fine-grained sand-stone which stands the
fire excellently is brought to the high-furnace from
beyond the Schuylkill, and is called merely Schuylkill
stone. Formerly they tried at a loss the wacke found
on the nearest hills ; this split and burst in the fire.
The cost of setting up the interior of the furnace, including the expence of breaking and hauling the stone,
amounts always to about 100 Pd. Pensylv. Current ;
but the furnace often bears two smeltings. Some
10,000 acres of forest are attached to this high-furnace.
The oaks on these dry hills are small, to be sure, but
there are among them many chesnuts which make the
best coals. The furnace consumes 840 bushels of coals
in 24 hours, for which 21-22 cords of wood are necessary. It is estimated that 400 bushels of coals are used
in getting out one ton of bar-iron. A turn of coals,
about 100 bushels, costs about 20 shillings, Pensylv.
Current. (The guinea at 35 shillings.) Wages for
wood-cutting are two shillings three pence the cord.
A man chops two and a half to four cords a day, and
so can earn 6-9 shillings. At present only six men
work at the mine ; but they supply more than the
furnace can consume. If the work was uninterrupted
there could be turned out yearly between 2-300 tons
of iron. A hundredweight of the ore worked at this
time yields 75 pounds of cold iron. A miner receives
40 shillings a month and rations. The furnace men,
founders and hammer men, are paid by the ton. For a

ton of pig—5 shillings; for a ton of furnace iron or other ware—40 shillings. In this way, if much is worked, the first founder stands to receive several pounds in the week.

Nowhere among the sundry mines and forges of America had wages become fixed as yet, the custom being to treat with each man conformably and according to his abilities. Miners by profession worked commonly by the fathom; in Jersey they asked 5-6 pounds current a month, with lights and tools. Common laborers there received always 2-3 pounds a month. But then they asked more during hay-making and harvest, when with lighter work they could easily earn for some weeks together 16-20 shillings a day. Coalers and founders were likewise well paid in Jersey. A foreman or head-founder 9 pounds a month; a coaler 5-6 pounds. Hammer men were paid in Jersey by the ton also.

The price of a ton of pig-iron (which on account of the easier transport is cheaper in America) is 10 pounds current. A ton of furnace iron, kettles or other utensils, 20-25 pounds. Bar-iron, in the good times before the war, cost the iron-masters 22-23 pounds a ton; they sold it at 25 pounds cash money or 30 pounds at six months credit. But at present they cannot deliver a ton for less than 32-37 pounds.

If the furnace is not properly managed the slag is pale green and coarse, but otherwise a fine sky-blue. There lay at the furnace more than 200 tons of such slag, which Mr. Udree had turned over to a man who was to give him 15 tons of iron for the privilege of breaking it up, washing it, and getting it worked over at a bloomery; his estimate is that it will take him two years to clear out this slag.

Mahogany wood is used for mould-forms at furnaces, because it is the least subject to warping and splitting.

Formerly Mr. Udree dealt with his workmen as is customary in Germany; that is, he furnished them with all necessaries on account. They made use of the opportunity to run up their accounts, and not being trammeled with families got out of the way; and so he changed his method.

America throughout its mountainous parts is richly supplied with iron, and the ore besides is easily to be got out; but with all that, (and the superfluity of wood notwithstanding), the high price of labor at present makes it possible to bring iron from Europe cheaper than it can be furnished by the high-furnaces and forges in America. The owners of iron-works in several provinces, in Jersey and Pensylvania particularly, attempted without result to bring their governments to forbid the import of foreign iron or by high duties to make it difficult. But this proposal being against the immediate interests of the Assembly-men as well as of their constituencies it was hardly to be expected that they should agree to raise the price of their domestic iron and iron-ware. Therefore several of the richer furnace and forge-masters proposed to hinder the further import of foreign iron by coming to an agreement among themselves that whenever iron came in from Europe they would offer their own at a certain loss under the price of the European merchants, so as to frighten them off from any further imports. But they all would not come in, and the few who made the proposal were unwilling to sacrifice themselves for the profit of the rest. However, the Americans were formerly in a position to send their pig and bar-iron to England at a profit; that is to say, they were exempt from the heavy imposts which Russian and Swedish iron had to pay in England. This was the case chiefly in the middle colonies, and during the years 1768-70 the export to England amounted to some 2592 tons bar-iron, and 4624 tons pig, with which they paid for at least a part of their return cargoes from England. And besides they took back axes, hoes, mattocks, shovels, nails, scythes and other fabricated ware; for although several of these articles could be as conveniently made in America as in Europe it could only be done at a price three times as high. Thus there has been no especial profit hitherto in America in anything except cast-iron. There was even a time when crude American iron might be sent to England cheaper than it could be supplied there. The English owners of iron-works were in this way inconvenienced and there was much debate in Parliament over the permissibility of letting in this article from America duty-free. However, under the pretext it was a worse product, every ton of American iron was paid for at an off-set amounting to the duty on Swedish and Russian iron. The advantages which this export to England of American iron formerly enjoyed are, naturally, now removed; and for the first time attention will now be given in America to the preparation and sale of the cheaper domestic product, so as to hinder the import of foreign iron. Steel was formerly made to some little extent in New York, Jersey, and Pensylvania; but during and since the war greatly more has been done in that regard, and it is asserted that at Philadelphia steel has been prepared quite as good as the

Styrian steel; so much at least is proved, that there is no lack of iron suitable for the purpose.

The following forges and high-furnaces are to be found merely in Berks County in Pensylvania:

Mr. Udree's forge, Glasgow-forge, Pine-forge, Spring-forge, and Oley-forge.

Furnaces: 1) Mr. Udree's, already mentioned. 2) Mr. Bird's, whose iron-mines are said to yield lead also. Two men supply as much as the furnace uses. 3) John Patten's, ten miles above Reading, near Heidelberg; the ore from the mines is not sufficient and more is fetched from Schefferstown and Grubb's mine, 10-15 miles off. 4) Warwick-Furnace, 19 miles from Reading, near to Pottsgrove, makes the most iron; often 40 tons a week; the ore lies only 10 ft. below the surface. 5) Reading-furnace, not far from the preceding; is at present gone to ruin; at one time there was often smelting here for 12-18 months together. The story is that a negro who had been foreman at this furnace discovered silver in the region and made an excellent thing of it; but being at outs with his master could not be induced to disclose the spot; he broke his neck accidentally and they still look in vain for his silver.

The Oley hills run pretty well northeast to southwest; but not quite regularly, making a few turns. The hills between them are smaller, broken, and lie in sundry directions.

They told us of the Ringing-hill, or as the Germans call it the **Klingelberg** which lies on the road from Philadelphia to Reading, some 36 miles from Philadelphia, near Falkner's Swamp or Pottsgrove. On this hill there is a quantity of large, loose rock-frag-

ments, one over another so that people ascribe the
disturbance to an earth-quake. These stones struck
together give out divers clear and ringing tones; the
largest fragments, and those not lying on the earth but
upon a bed of other pieces, give the clearest and
sharpest sounds, like a bell. The stone is of a blue
tint, and by reason of the sound is thought to contain
iron, especially since in the springs near-by there is
found a considerable ochre-like deposit; so this appears to be similar to the bell-stone mentioned by
Linnæus in the *Westgothische Reise.** The last two or
three days the weather among these hills was uncommonly hot.—On the road from Reading to Lebanon,
at Red-house Tavern, a new well had been dug. They
found no water until at a depth of 40 ft. The upper
stratum was several feet of the common sandy-clay
soil; then, coarse sand and gravel for 18 feet, intermixed with iron-bearing stones. Next was limestone
in fragments, and farther down limestone in beds.

We crossed Tulpehacken Creek, and passed through
a part of the Tulpehacken valley, an especially fine and
fertile landscape along that small stream. The inhabitants are well to-do and almost all of them Germans; for long since the Germans have been looking
out for the best and most fertile lands. Everywhere
here the limestone protruded from the ground, showing in bulky lines from northwest to southeast, also

---

* *Saxum clangosum;* Saxum tinnitans; Bell-stone. " Set up
" it sounded like a metal. It was blackish-grey, showed a little
" iron, consisted of mica so finely flecked with quartz as hardly
" to be seen with the naked eye; these stones contained besides
" many opaque granates." Linnæus, *Westgoth. Reise,* under
June 28.

from north to south.—We met this morning the first travellers since we had left Nazareth. They were taking wheat to Philadelphia in wagons. Hauling is done to better advantage in Pensylvania than in most of the other provinces. During the war Pensylvania alone supplied almost the whole of the American army with wagons and horses; and in the British army there were many Pensylvania horses and teamsters. The Pensylvanians regard size and strength of breed more than beauty, and their wagons are the strongest and best in America; they cover them with sail-cloth stretched over hoops, and always have four good horses hitched in front.—We reached **Myerstown** at midday, a small village; a German to whom the land belonged gave it his name. He was shot thirteen years ago in his own house at supper, and the murderer has not been found to this day. His son, the present landlord, came to the tavern in a beggarly rig; he did not know how many houses there were in the place; 'all I know,' said he, 'is that I have about 600 Pds. rent to collect.' The lots * are 50 ft. by 100, and pay 16 shillings Pensylv. ground-rent a year.—Keeping on over similar roads, limestone hills and dry, thin, monotonous oak woods we came to

Lebanon, a not inconsiderable country town; which like Reading is laid off in straight streets; and contains many good houses. And this town also is not over thirty years old. The town-lots are 40 ft. by 60, and pay 6 shillings a year ground-rent. The inhabitants are for the most part Germans. There is a

---

* The portion of land measured off in a new-settled place for house, yard, and garden.

Lutheran and a Reformed church here, but no Court-
house as yet. I made the acquaintance of the Lutheran
minister, Dr. Stoy, who, after he had been many years
settled as pastor of the congregation, left them for a
few years to go to Leyden and study the art of medicine. At his house I saw several large and beautiful
pearls which came from a near-by stream, in which
region also traces of excellent pit-coals were found.
Hornblende and several other trifling minerals were
shown me with a mysterious confidence by a German
goldsmith who is hunting for silver. Large specimens
of quartz, brown on the outside and white within,
showing blunted crystals at the surface are often
ploughed up hereabouts.—A dense reddish sand-stone
(freestone) comes to the surface a few miles from here
towards the South Mountain, and is fetched hither for
chimneys &c; but for house-walls they use the common
grey limestone. A lump of gold, according to Dr.
Stoy (and he named witnesses who had heard it from
other witnesses) was out of gratitude given last spring
by an Indian to a Pensylvania farmer who had furnished him supplies through the winter; he got it from
the neighboring mountains, and the silly farmer was
too skittish to follow the Indian, who was willing to
show him where his gold-pocket was. There are always Germans who bother themselves with such fairy
tales. If the Indians knew where there was gold they
would oftener make it manifest, for they know very
well the value of the yellow metal. Dr. Stoy maintained that the descendants of the Germans originally
settled here are less strong and healthy than their
fathers and do not live to be so old, because their
better circumstances make them less industrious and

more given to extravagances and excesses. He may
be right; but one must take into consideration that it
was impossible for those to be weaklings who came out
from Germany and got as far as Tulpehacken, over-
coming all manner of difficulties so as to establish
themselves in the wilderness. It is true that the physical constitutions of the Americans, taken in the average, are certainly not particularly strong or stable. It
may be that the great contrast between the hot season
and the cold, and the frequent sudden changes of the
weather gradually weaken the bodily strength; it may
be that the minor degree of physical labor to which the
country people are subjected fails to build them up
sufficiently. However, they are healthy, and there is
no lack of instances where people have lived to a great
age. On the other hand, they have in general several
striking advantages. Throughout America one sees
few mis-shapen people. The generality is slender, tall,
and well formed. So will be found the Virginians in
especial, and among them may be observed again the
happy influence of a warm climate, characteristics
which in the old world distinguished the Georgians,
Circassians, Persians, and Greeks. A number of physical deformities very common in Europe are much more
rarely seen in America.

A letter which I had brought to him gave me the
opportunity of knowing another Doctor; and only
with difficulty was I able to rid myself of him. Quite
against our will he insisted on taking us the next
morning to a marvellous cave, the like of which according to him was not to be seen elsewhere in the
world. It was a rainy day, and for several hours we
were led about aimlessly through the woods; finally,

having crossed the Quitupahilla, we came to a limestone quarry in which there was a natural opening,
narrow and low, pointing towards the southeast. We
went up a few steps to a milk cellar which had been
installed at the entrance of the cave, for the convenience of the houses near-by. Thence the hole
wound away about 150 ft. towards the southwest; there
was no going farther, because the cave continually
got narrower. The greatest height and breadth was
some 6 feet, and a few smaller cavities gave off at the
sides. The cave contains a quantity of stalactites, in
which our Doctor has discovered a new and powerful
antidote, news of which he has sent to Philadelphia.
He calcined, that is to say, these stalactites, and found
—that the powder was as efficacious as *Mercurius
praecipitatus* in extreme cases; and he told us repeatedly that he would not have disclosed this treasure to
merely anybody. Mr. Grubb's iron-works are known
throughout Pensylvania. We directed our way thither
but found neither the Colonel nor the Captain (father
and son) at home. They had gone to salt-water, that
is, to the sea coast; a journey which the well to-do
living inland often make during the hot season, for
their pleasure and for the healthfulness of the baths.
In the absence of the owners, to whom I had letters, I
could find nobody who would take the trouble to give
us any information. These iron-works lie near to the
South Mountain and not far from Lebanon. Several
short and broken hills running in promiscuous directions are made up almost wholly of good rich ore
which lies shallow beneath the surface. To get out
this ore nothing whatever need be known of mining.
The ore is dug out of the hills quite as elsewhere pav-

ing-stones are got out. They make a distinction here between a red and a black iron-stone, these differing in magnitude and the layers breaking out differently. Grubb possesses such a store of iron in these hills that he supplies other establishments at a price. The wooded hills adjacent, for 6-8 miles around, belong to him. An Irishman, just recently come out from Europe, was the only one polite enough to show us the place where the ore was dug and roasted. He seemed very dissatisfied, deceived in his expectations of America; 50 shillings a month and keep hardly seemed to him worth the trouble of exchanging dear Ireland for America.—There lay about numbers of 12 and 24 pounders, and a quantity of iron ovens. At times there is a lack of water, and the works are often long interrupted on that account. Very near is to be found also the red foundation-stone, as about Reading. —Another iron mine, ✚ on one of the hills near-by, contains copper besides, which is often a great hindrance in smelting, unless every care be taken, spoiling the iron. Many other of the American iron-mines contain copper, it is said, and several of them lead.

Three miles from here, at Orth's Tavern, we found quarters for the night. The whole family and neighbors willing to help, all of them Germans, were occupied in peeling and cutting the fallen apples, (mostly green), so as to dry them; the English country-people have not so generally adopted this means of using their superfluous fruit. For the entertainment of the numerous company a humorous old Irishman was retailing his jests. He was 65 years old, drank every day his allowance, and more, of brandy, and worked emulously along with any young man. His trade was

stump-grubbing, and since he dug more stumps and more skilfully than others he called himself the King of the Grubbers. This business, always difficult, is not so much so in America as in Europe; because almost everywhere here the roots take no great hold in the earth. A stump-grubber receives 20-24 shillings Pensylv. Current and victuals, for every acre of land he clears; clearing up an acre in 3-4 days.

This evening the extraordinary number of locusts, (apparently more numerous here than elsewhere), were making an unspeakable uproar in the near-by garden, woods, and bush. The history of this insect is not yet thoroughly known. They are called locusts and again grass-hoppers.—They are said to appear only once in 16 or 17 years in the extraordinary numbers they show almost everywhere this year. In the year 1766, and thus 17 years ago, they appeared in similar quantities. They deposit their eggs on the young branches of most trees. When, after a few weeks, the sun's warmth has hatched them out, the young descend to the ground, get into holes and remain until after some time they come out in force, chiefly to carry on their breeding. It is claimed that they have been found 30 ft. deep in the ground; trustworthy people have assured me that they have seen them 8-9 ft. deep. Regarding the time they spend in the ground there is uncertainty; some people hold that they stay in the ground many years, and point to the following circumstance. It is universally the case that these locusts keep in and about woods and nowhere else, and the young creep into the ground immediately where they are. And often they have been observed coming out of the ground in places where for several years

14

the wood had been cleared off, and hence it is believed they were all that time in the ground at those places. But this is not proof that they have passed 16-17 years in the earth. When they come out, they bring a thin, transparent coat of exactly their shape. In this coat they crawl to the nearest bush, tree, or other fixed body, stick themselves fast, and extract themselves from their shell through an opening from the shoulder to the fore-part of the head. Of these empty hulls there are found numbers fixed to trees, fences, and strong grass-stalks. These locusts furnish many animals with a gluttonous fare; hogs and chickens especially fatten on them; and the Indians, it is said, eat them at times as delicacies. During their breeding season, throughout the summer almost, they make from morning until evening a loud, incessant noise, so that wherever they are numerous in the woods hardly anything else can be heard. (*Cicada septemdecim. Linn.*)—Another insect, of the cricket species, makes nearly as much noise; they call them about New York 'Katy did's' ✚ and 'Katy did's not,' from the similarity of their shrill note to those words. They come every year and are heard throughout the summer until late in the fall.

The road to Hummelstown was mostly level; through nothing but woods, and we saw few houses. A skunk ran straight across the road; our dog gave chase, but sure of his defence the skunk by no means doubled his pace, trotted quietly on, and all at once gave the worrisome dog his entire stinking cargo. The dog was close behind; at the opportunity the skunk raised his tail, turned it over his back, but made no use of it, as is elsewhere stated, in squirting the

dose. He kept on his way quite calmly, but the dog
jumped back with a distressing howl, and was chased
off by us as precipitately. For both he and the atmosphere stank unspeakably at the moment; he rubbed
his muzzle incessantly in the sand, and wallowed in
every puddle, but the unbearable smell stayed by him
4-5 days, and he had to submit to be run out of houses
everywhere.

Hummelstown—a place of perhaps 50 houses, built
along the road, and only 20 years begun. The first
land-lord, Hummel, a German, has been dead some
years. The town lots are 60 ft. by 80 and pay 15
shillings yearly Pensylv. Current.—A mile from the
place, behind Valentin Hummel's house, there is a
cavern which reaches quite through a limestone hill.
The cavern is 4-500 ft. long, and from 12 to 30 ft.
high. The larger entrance curves considerably to the
southwest, towards the Swatara; the smaller opening
gives to the northwest. The rock is the grey, scaly
limestone, which is the same as far as Nazareth. Large
pieces of rock lie fallen in the cave, which has nothing
remarkable to show beyond many variously shaped
stalactites. Bats live there. Petrifactions are looked
for in vain, as throughout this limestone tract. Without doubt there are similar caves in this and other
regions where the rock is stratified; far above this
cave may be seen sunken spots due to the rock giving
beneath; sinks like these appear frequently where no
caves are known to exist below. Valentin Hummel,
who took us to the place, was of the opinion that the
land of this region is too good for dunging because it
still brings good hemp; indeed the hemp stood hereabouts six to eight feet high, but is raised only for do-

mestic use.   Such over-confident opinions regarding
the inexhaustible goodness of his soil gradually puts
the farmer's industry to sleep, and when, finally, betterment is necessary many of them had rather move on
to take up fresh land than be at the trouble of improving the old.

A few miles from Hummelstown flows the Susquehannah.   Here at Harris's Ferry it is three quarters
of a mile wide, but in the summer months so shallow
that only canoes can cross; horses and wagons ford
over.   In the middle are a few small islands, called
Harris's and also Turkey Islands.   These, with the
steep limestone banks on the farther side, the mountains running left and right, and the fine breadth of the
stream make all together a beautiful landscape.   A
shallow ford being at this place, it comes about that
most travellers, particularly the Virginia cattle-dealers
(and others farther on), bringing up their herds,
choose this ford while the water is low, so as to avoid
the expense of the ferries above and below, where the
river remains deep even in summer.

On the farther bank an extraordinary ' stag-horn '
sumac (*Rhus typhinum*) excited our astonishment; its
trunk was over 12 ft. high and near a foot in diameter.
In the more northern parts they grow smaller and
bushier.   There is a spring of the finest water near
the edge of the river; it is thought remarkable that this
spring is governed by the rise and fall of the river,
and stands at a constant level above the surface of the
river-water; there is nothing wonderful in this when
it is considered that the spring and the river communicate through a bent pipe as it were.   This side the
Susquehannah the Conedogwynet Creek flows in
through a beautiful and deep valley.

At White's Tavern, seven miles from the river by
the road, we met a herd of black cattle **+** which had
come about 500 miles from the frontiers of North
Carolina, and was destined for Philadelphia.   The
handlers do not always find their account in this long-
distance traffic.   Shortly before, a herd had been driven
by this place which could be sold at Philadelphia for
only 9 Spanish dollars the head, 3-4 years old and
weighing some 500 pounds.   Not only do the cattle
in so long a journey become thinner and worse-look-
ing, but the Pensylvania farmer squints at the business because he himself raises enough cattle to over-
stock the market.   But the people from the back parts
of Carolina and Virginia, having no large populous
towns near them, must make this long and tedious
journey if they are to get any use of their numerous
cattle.   But situated as they are they themselves gain
next to nothing.

Almost the entire family at White's Tavern **+** was
smitten with an intermittent fever.   Nothing of this
sickness was known in this hitherto dry region until a
few years ago a mill and dam were established here.
Afterwards I heard the same complaint at many places
in the mountains and everywhere a similar reason was
given.

The forests this side the river had a better look, although still consisting largely of oak.   We saw only
a few good houses along the road from the river to
this place, and little cultivated land.   Coming nearer
to Carlisle, after riding through so many miles of
woods, one is agreeably startled to find suddenly spread
before him a beautiful, open, high-lying plain, quite
without trees.   In the eternal woods it is impossible to

keep off a particularly unpleasant, anxious feeling, which is excited irresistibly by the continuing shadow and the confined outlook. One breathes freer and everything seems to take on a brighter, more gladsome look, so soon as the eye feels the limits of the view extended, although really this bald prospect anywhere else would have precisely a contrary effect.

Carlisle. This pretty little town is the chief place of Cumberland county, and very nearly midway between the South and North Mountain, here about 10-12 miles apart. Carlisle is 17 miles from the Susquehannah and 120 from Philadelphia, whence by this place is the customary road to the Ohio, as well as from and to the outlying regions of the southern provinces. The town is therefore well situated for the inland trade, and drives a considerable trade of that sort; formerly it had also the greatest part of the trade with the Indians, who brought hither and exchanged their furs. This traffic came to a stand during the war, and it is not yet known whether in future the Indians will consent to come back to this place. The consuming hate which the citizens of the new states have for them and will not at once cast off, makes it probable that in the future the Indians will seek markets for the exchange of their furs either to the north along the Canadian lakes and the river Lawrence or to the west on the Mississippi, and they will find plenty of encouragement to do so. But even with the loss of this traffic, Carlisle has still a great deal of trade, because all the people living in the mountains fetch hence what they need. It is already noticeable in the place that trade is carried on there, which has an influence on the manners of the inhabitants. The

streets of the town are straight and there are many
genteel houses, with a German Lutheran church, a
Presbyterian Meeting-house, a Town-hall, and a gaol.
Outside the town there is a long, new-built, four-file
barracks where during the war a number of workmen
made muskets, locks, sabres, and the like. Here also
cannons were forged from iron gads and hoops sol-
dered together, which in strength and beauty were
little inferior to metal ordnance. Not far from here
are Mr. Eger's iron-works. To the north, and not far
away, is a cave through the opening of which a loaded
wagon may pass, very spacious within and said to contain smaller chambers and a fine spring. All that was
said of it did not tempt me to a visit, because nothing
more remarkable was probably to be expected than I
had already seen in other caves afore-mentioned. The
ladies of Carlisle are accustomed to resort thither to
drink tea.

The bat common on the coast, without front-teeth,
(or the North American bat *) is seen also farther
inland. From the snout it is commonly four inches
long; breadth of the wings 10 inches, the face of a
light brown color, but the ears and wings black—I have
also seen them with two front-teeth in the upper jaw,
straight and sharp, but with none in the under-jaw; I
saw one here like this; it may be asked whether these
are merely sports? It is more probable that the description given by Mr. Pennant of his New York bat
was made from an immature specimen.

In a musk-rat † which we saw along this road I ob-

---

* Schreber's *Saügthiere*, I, 176.
† *Ondathra*. Schreber's *Saügthiere*, IV, 638. Kalm, III, 25.

served that the skin of the roof of the mouth is built up in terrace fashion, as it were, and that at both corners of the mouth long bristles are pointed in towards the mouth. The eyes appeared to me smaller than I had before observed, and there were no hairs on the lids. The upper front-teeth were not covered by the lip. The female of this animal has not the strong musk-like odor of the male. The testicles are placed in the abdomen.

From Carlisle to the Ohio

Coming from Nazareth we had the Blue or Kittatiny Mountain always in sight except for a little while near Reading. It seemed always as if the road was leading straight to the mountain, and one never got nearer; the reason being that in these parts the range makes a bend to the west without altering its chief course from northeast to southwest. Towards Carlisle the ridge does not lie so unbroken as before, but shows more and deeper cuts, and falls away more precipitously to the South. At any point where there is an outlook over a tract of this range, the view is indeed august, of its high and seemingly straight wall extending away. From Carlisle to Shippensburg it is 21 miles through tiresome woods, still over the same dry limestone soil and between the North, or Kittatiny, and the South Mountain. At M'Gregan's, 14 miles from Carlisle I saw for the first time a variation in the marble and limestone hitherto observed by me. The house was built of a very beautiful grey and liver-colored marble, of a hard and fine grain. The quarry was not far off. Since I had before seen everywhere nothing but rough, grey limestone and marble, I had been very much inclined to believe that several persons were right whom I had heard say that America stands far behind the old world in the variety and the beauty of coloring of its marble. Those observations were grounded merely on the species occuring in the nether regions, among which, to be sure, there is little variety.

As yet, too little is known of the fossils of the new world to warrant any invidious statements.—Marl, building-stone, and iron-ore are found in this region; but we saw very few and insignificant block-houses and plantations.

Shippensburg has a good number of houses, but mostly of wood. There are really two distinct places. each standing on the side of a little hill. We paid here uncommonly dear for very sorry entertainment. From here the great road to the frontiers of Virginia and Carolina keeps on along the valley between the North and South Mountain; but our road now lay to the right towards the mountain itself, and from now on began to grow worse, for miles together full of loose limestone rocks. **Wild turkeys** we had hitherto seen only here and there, and singly, in the remoter parts; but today we came upon sundry large flocks. They were running on the road in the woods, and with the utmost speed got into the bush; a few were roosting on trees. They are distinguished from the tame sort only in being more uniformly black, brown, or dirty white; for the rest they are quite like them and belong to the same species. Here and there the statement is made that they mix and breed with the tame sort, but this is also denied. Their flesh is well-tasting, and they are found of good weights.

Seven miles from Shippensburg a well was digging where a new house was going up. The first 15 feet there was the common yellow sandy clay; then 20 ft. through limestone rock; the limestone growing darker, verging on black, farther down, and showing holes and nests of clear white spath-crystals which in the air soon softened and grew darker. At 35 ft. no water had been found.

The man here owned 300 acres of land in part
ploughable. A few years ago he bought it at 5 Pd.
Pensylv. Current the acre, and paid for it in paper-
money at a time when this was worth about 50 for one
in hard dollars; so that the small estate cost him only
60 Pds. hard money. He was one of the few who were
wise enough during the war to exchange their paper-
money for land ✝ at the right time. In order to get free
of the linen-money, high prices were offered for land,
and thus many land-owners, willing to put faith in the
solemn promises of the Congress, were tempted to let
go their holdings, in the expectation of putting out the
paper capital at usury, for they flattered themselves
they would be able to exchange it very soon for like
amounts in silver. But unfortunately all these speculators found themselves vastly deceived in the result.—
On his 300 acres this man pays 12 Pd. Pensylv. Current, and praises it as good land.

Just in this region both the North and the South
Mountain appear all at once very high, steep, and
crested, but the latter soon falls away and seems to
disappear. The road to Fort Loudon now proceeds
over hills alternately of yellow flint-stone and rough,
black, broken, slaty soil through the whole of Hamilton Township; and no more limestone is to be seen on
these hills. It is said that on digging down gravel is
reached after 10-15 ft. of this sort of slate. Most
of the foot-hills seemed to be of this structure. Limestone very probably lies beneath, for the other road
through Chambers-town to Loudon is through limestone the whole way, and it appears again on descending the other side of these hills towards Fort Loudon.
This almost forgotten and certainly ruined fort was

built for protection against the Indians during the war
before the last.   Now nothing is there but a few miserable cabins.   For the site of the fort a wide opening
was chosen, several miles broad, which occurs here in
the wall of the **Blue Mountain** or its continuation.
Keeping on by a narrow road cut out of the great
woods and, as the case was today with cloudy weather
besides, one finds himself suddenly, (and apparently
without having climbed any especial ascent) in the
rear of the mountain which shortly before had lain in
front ; for the road which hitherto has run southwest
turns gradually through the gap and continues north
and northwest around sundry high and noble eleva-
tions.   Among them Bernard's Knob is the steepest
and highest, of a truncated crest.   Every 1-2 miles a
sorry block-house is seen in the woods, until (a few
miles from Fort Loudon) the somewhat better house
of a Mr. Harris is reached.   It was late, and it was
raining ; the wife had first to be consulted, she agreed,
and we were taken in ; having set behind us 27 miles
from Shippensburg.

Our agreeable host was a native Englishman and,
for such a mountain country, well to-do.   Besides his
farming and cattle-raising he makes a trade of tanning ; pays out nothing for bark and little for hides,
but sells his leather as dear as that brought from elsewhere.   For tanning he prefers especially the bark of
the chesnut-oak, because it gives the leather a higher
and clearer color than the bark of other oaks.   Besides,
this bark is distinguished for a particularly pleasant
odor, which it imparts to the water.   The bark of the
black-oak makes good leather also, but gives it an ugly
dark color.   Most of the country-people in America

know how to tan and themselves prepare, in little pits, the greatest part of the leather they need. They have even learned from the Indians an easy and rapid method of making leather from the skins of both wild and domestic animals. They call it *Hirn-garmachen,* i. e. brain-tanning. The skins are scraped; the brain of the animal, perhaps a bear, is broiled with the fat, and then the soup is thinned with water; the skins are several times rubbed smartly with this brew, and afterwards smoked. It is not a very cleanly process, but the leather is supple, good for all manner of use, and durable.—Our host had also set up a saw-mill, and makes a profit on the boards, getting the logs for the mere trouble of taking them. For these remote forests are at this time almost nobody's property. With all the rest of the unsurveyed, unsold, or unleased land, they were formerly held by the Penn family; but now belong to the state of Pensylvania which has not the time to worry over such a trifle as a few thousand tree-trunks. The former proprietors were glad if anybody in the more unsettled parts cut off the wood and made use of it, because it was then the easier to bring in people and sell them the land at a good price.— However, these desolate-seeming woods are not altogether without inhabitants. They are about in spots, where one hardly expects to find them, at the foot of hills and by brooks. There is even a plantation on the top of a high mountain to the right of us. Not until after the war before the last did people begin to settle here and spread about.

The basis of these mountains is a quartz-grained rock, from which good mill-stones are taken. Rough grind-stones are also found, but not many. The valley here extending north, like most of the valleys from this point on, contains limestone. Iron-ore is found here and there, and there are traces of copper. To the left there runs a little chain of hills towards Fort Littleton and Sideling-hill, with other hills enclosing fertile valleys, already thickly settled and known as ' the great and little Cove.'

The next morning, a mile beyond Harris's house, we came to the so-called tavern which we had been unable to reach the day before; and had no cause for regret, finding a lamentable cabin, and shop at the same time. For the convenience of the people living scattered about, shops of this sort (under the very engaging name of ' stores ') keep everything that may be needed; as, sugar, coffee, tea, wine, spirits, linen, woolen stuffs, hats, stockings, paper, books, spices, iron-ware, and the like. The country-people have not always cash money for purchases, but then the storekeepers or merchants take any sort of produce in exchange. In the mountains and other remote regions hides and skins are the especial money. This or a similar adjustment is the case almost everywhere in America. Other travelling merchants (pedlars) go about the country in little wagons, selling and swapping; fetch their freight from and return with it to the larger and smaller towns where, as yet, there is no great variety of handicraftsmen, but at least the most necessary, such as tailors, cobblers, dyers, smiths, locksmiths, hatters &c, and then, merchants, lawyers, surgeons, and others, who supply the wants of the far-scattered settlers.

After seven miles through a stony valley the foot of the Tuscarora is reached, which from its situation appears to correspond to the Pekono, mentioned in the journey to Wyoming. In the woods we saw a few cabins and only a little ploughed land. The soil of this valley was for the most part gravelly and slaty, with fragments of a reddish sand-stone showing quartz-veins. The Tuscarora, which is pretty high and steep, was of the same sort of rock. There appeared also a reddish quartz, the surface quite covered with little clear-glistening crystals. The mass of the mountain seemed to be partly fine, partly coarse-grained quartz, overlaid with grey sand-stone not so regularly laminated as elsewhere. At the top of the mountain was a tap-house built of wood, where, as commonly in these parts, nothing but bad whiskey is to be had. The Cove-hills were to the left and Path Valley to the right. From the ridge of the Tuscarora to Fort Littleton it is 10 miles. We saw several deserted cabins, so they call the smaller block-houses, built of unhewn logs placed one above another. Passed the Burnt Cabins, a region still so called from a few cabins burnt during the war before the last. Arrived at a negative inn. The host answered everything with No; one might ask for whiskey, cyder, milk, food, anything; he had in return for every question two others to put—Where bound? Where from? How far? Frenchmen? Prisoners? Looking for land? Trafficking? &c &c., all which, in retaliation, we answered with No. Three miles further, over gentle hills of sand and clay brought us to

Fort Littleton. It is merely one house that bears this name; but a considerable extent of land around is cleared of wood, and this of itself gives the place a cheerful aspect. Behind the house are the remains of a fort, set up against the Indians in the war before the last war—from which the house has inherited the name.

The valleys around are pretty well settled, but, for the trees one cannot see the houses, of which there must be a number, if one is found every mile or two. Path Valley and Aughwick Valley show a good and fertile soil and excellent grass. These people were greatly embarrassed over the long drouth this summer. They must always get their winter wheat into the ground before the end of August, because otherwise the following year it will not be large and strong enough to be safe against the mildew. But while the farmer, here as elsewhere, is expecting the rain necessary for seeding, he often loses valuable time and finds himself in the end mistaken, or his harvest not so good. In such cases it would be an advantage, with a little more trouble, if the device was adopted which Hasselquist mentions as in use among the Egyptians, where the ploughman, by means of a water-skin slung over his shoulder, supplies the furrow with enough moisture for the development of the seed which is dropped immediately behind him.—Iron and lime are found in these valleys. In these mountain regions, as throughout Pensylvania, much spelt is raised; which is used more as feed for horses than in any other way. There are nowhere set up mills of a fashion to grind the fine meal from it. Horses like it and thrive on it. —From here to the foot of the Sideling-hills, nine and a half miles, we found the road better than we had expected, for the most part level, and red clay soil, which promises good wheat-land. Saw only two cabins the whole way, the only ones in these parts.

Sideling-hill is, together with the Alleghany and

Laurel-hill, one of the most considerable ranges of these mountains. We had been given a fearful description of it, and therefore probably found it the more endurable. The road up and down is somewhat steep and stony, but along the ridge there are many wide, level, sandy stretches. The range is in fact two ranges, (running parallel and joined by hills between), of which that to the east is called Sideling and that to the west Rayshill. Both show quartz-grained rock, coarse and again clear, and scaly sand-stones. The range is in height by no means above the limits of vegetation, but like all these mountains is covered with forest and bush in which, along our road, we found nothing especially remarkable. The same trees prevail as in the lower country. On the sandy flats of the ridge there grew many twi-bladed firs, or 'Jersey pines.'

It is seven miles from the woful tavern on the one side to the first house on the other. Half way over the mountain we came upon one of the encamping-grounds very many of which are seen along lonesome mountain roads and in other sparsely settled regions. These are grazing spots and little places cleared of wood, near a good spring or a clear-flowing stream, some of them having been selected by the Indians. The farmers, teamsters, and pack-horse men in America do not commonly lodge or feed at the rare and necessitous taverns; they take with them provisions for themselves and their horses, make fires, go to bed in the forest and turn their horses out to graze—and these sometimes wander off or are set upon by wolves and eaten.

The western slope of the mountain is very much the steeper. In a house standing at its foot a poor

15

family, with their cattle, were murdered the last year
of the war, probably by the Indians. The dog belonging to the family came to a neighbor's house and in his
whimpering dog-language bewailed the sad event. He
was chased off, but continued coming back to repeat
his story, and by flatteries and courteously running before seemed to be asking the neighbor to follow him,
until finally some one went with him back to the house
and there found the slain.

Farther on we came over Crossing-hill down to
Juniata Creek, its crooked banks shaded by calamus,
cephalanthus, rhododendron, Weymouth fir, chesnut
and beech. The Juniata falls into the Susquehannah;
it was not deep at this time, but in the spring and
autumn swells to the inconvenience of the traveller.
The slopes of Crossing-hill showed a red, micaceous,
compact sand-stone (cos), iron-bearing, and splitting
in half-inch slabs. Towards the summit there appeared a fine grey grind-stone which is used for the
purpose to good advantage. Beyond the stream there
lives a Colonel in a wooden hut.——We kept on over
hills not so high, in which there is found greyish or
reddish whet-stone (cos) splitting in slabs an inch
thick; in these were to be seen dendrites roughly
sketched across. At midday, seven miles this side
Bedford, we arrived at Captain Paxton's house. The
bread was baking in the pan. The meat had a smell.
There was no whiskey. Coffee and tea had just given
out.——However, the country between these hills is at
times beautiful and there is much good land, especially
up the Juniata along which runs the road to Bedford,
a narrow valley between high steep mountains where
warmth and moisture assure a livelier green and the

trees luxuriating in a fat soil cast wider shadows. Before reaching Bedford, the Juniata has to be crossed five times; the last crossing is over a neat wooden bridge. We passed several houses and a mill.

The blue magnolia or mountain magnolia (*Magnolia acuminata Linn.*) was one of the more conspicuous trees peculiar to this mountain region. They call it here the cucumber tree, because its long cones, before they ripen and open, are in shape somewhat like that fruit. The seeds, seed-receptacles, and in less degree the bark and twigs have in common with other magnolias a very pleasant bitterness of taste, and the seeds are often used in bitter spirituous infusions. This tree is distinguished from its relatives by its habitat; it is found only in dry spots in the mountains, and bears more cold than other magnolias. The ripe seed-vessels have a pleasant odor and taste something like the calamus. The unripe fruit blackens the fingers and stains the knife.

Bedford is a little town, but a little town in a great wilderness may easily please without beauty. Here one has come 96 miles, or not quite half the way from Carlisle to Pittsburg. The place is regularly planned, has a court-house, and is the county-seat of the extensive Bedford county, its namesake and as yet very little peopled. There are two houses of worship, for Lutherans and Presbyterians; these cannot be called churches, being only wooden huts. In the war before the last a fort was built here, partly to control the invading Indians and partly to aid the operations directed towards the Ohio; this fort was in connection with the old Fort Cumberland on the Potomack, 20 miles south of here, and Fort Shirley on the Juniata.

After the capture and abandonment of Fort du Quesne (now Fort Pitt) on the Ohio, these defences were given over. But the establishment of this town was seen to be necessary in order to the easier maintenance of communication with the new conquered frontiers, and particularly as an encouragement and convenience to the people settled in these mountains. The place is quite surrounded with hills and mountains. The elevation of its site makes the weather often somewhat cool, although the latitude is almost the same as that of Philadelphia. The 2nd of September, the day after our arrival, it was so cold that fires could not be dispensed with. In the morning the thermometer stood at 42 degrees Fahrenheit. Heavy hoar-frost these mornings covered all low and shaded spots, and people claimed to have seen ice and even snow on the mountains. All cucumbers and melons were frozen in the gardens. And yet the week before, the heat was so excessive that clothes were burdensome. But the country is healthy and supports no Doctor, because the people are not often sick; and they are sick less because they have no Doctor. Just now there prevails an uneasy wonderment in the neighborhood. Two young girls at a mill, in a spot made swampy by the new mill-dam, were attacked with the cold fever or ague, a malady hitherto unheard-of here. People came from a distance to see this wonder.

The town of Bedford and the country around do not yet produce what is necessary to pay for their wants. Hunting must supply the rest; skins and furs, which their guns bring in, are all they have to send to market. And on account of the distance and the badness of the roads the people are kept from taking up more land than they themselves can use in a small way. The Juniata may contribute somewhat to a better trade in future. Boats of 12-15 tons can almost nine months in the year come up to within a mile or two of Bedford. Four men can with no great trouble push such a boat against the stream.

There was mentioned to me a man who had smelted silver from stone found on Stoney Creek. He lived in the woods a mile from the town in a miserable smoky cabin, quite alone, with neither human nor animal society. It so happened, but not without the persuasions of my landlord who accompanied me, that be brought out a small piece of his silver, which he pretended had been melted out at a forge, and showed me a large sack full of roasted and powdered ore, but no crude ore. Like all people of this stamp he was very mysterious, and notwithstanding his find extremely poor. The next morning he came and offered to sell me his sack of powdered stone. The owner of the land, whence he fetches his supposed wealth, does not hinder him from taking all he wants. This same man told me of a blue stone, full of muscles, which he had seen three miles from here at a certain Henry White's mill, but that was several years ago. I promised to reward him for his trouble if he brought me some of it; he went away and came back with the excuse that he could not find the place now. In the sand-stone of the mountain near-by I knew from my own observations that impressions of muscles are to be found, but I should have been curious to know whether those mentioned by this man occur likewise in the limestone common hereabouts—for I have never observed even the slightest trace of petrifaction in the limestone.

The mountains, in the midst of which we are, consist of several ranges running pretty nearly parallel. At one time they are called all together the Blue Mountains and again the Alleghany Mountains, but these designations belong more exactly to individual ranges; for each of the sundry ranges has its own name. The easternmost of all is the often mentioned North or Kittatinny Mountain which is often preferably called the Blue Mountain merely. Between it and the South Mountain lying parallel and farther east, runs the broad, beautiful, and rich limestone valley which we followed a distance of 140 miles from Nazareth to Shippensburg; this extends much farther towards the south, into Carolina and perhaps Georgia. Behind the Kittatinny, to the west, lie several indefinite ranges following the same direction. Among these are the ranges observed on the road from Fort Loudon to this place, the Tuscarora, Shade Mountain, Blacklog, Sideling-hill, Rayshill, Aleguippy, and Evits Mountain; and before us now, between Bedford and Pittsburg, are Willis's Mountain, Alleghany, Laurel-hill, Chesnut-hill, and others. But the continuations of these mountains have most of them other names farther north (as will be recalled from the journey to Wyoming), and others again farther south; but they all belong together and form a principal chain of mountains. This chain begins really near the Hudson river in New York, and thence runs through almost all the more southern provinces, in a direction from northeast to southwest, and in consequence pretty nearly on a parallel with the eastern coasts washed by the Atlantic ocean, from which these mountains keep a distance of 100-150 miles, and farther south 200 miles.

From New York into Virginia they have the name
Alleghany Mountains; through Carolina and Georgia
and until, gradually diminishing, they lose themselves
in Florida, they are called the Apalachian Mountains.
To the north and east of the Hudson river, they have
very probably a connection with the New England and
Canadian mountains. Northwest of these mountains,
towards the Canadian lakes, the country is indeed less
mountainous, but its level is higher than that of these
mountains themselves, and so there is ground for regarding the region about the Canadian lakes and beyond them as the highest platforms of North America.
But considered as mountain-chains and ridges, the
Alleghany and Apalachian Mountains are the highest
within the territory of the United States, and probably
in all North America (the more western parts of which
we still know very little of) ; however they lose on
comparison with the mountains of South America as
well as with the chief systems of Europe.

Between the principal ranges of these mountains
there lie smaller hills, cut-offs and jutties, which for
divers reasons show different directions. The great
and principal ranges are distinguished by their more
parallel course, their greater height, and the species of
their rock. This appears to be in basis a grained,
quartzose rock, invariably overlaid with laminated
sand-stone or whet-stone species, in which appear
pretty often traces of sea-organisms. The lower hills,
frequently parallel with the mountains, and the valleys
contain limestone, in which I at least have discovered
no traces of organic remains. The chief ranges such
as the Kittatinny, Tuscarora, Sideling, and others,
present on the whole very regular, uniform slopes, but

their continuity is here and there broken by great openings or gaps. Between their highest ranges there are
long, broad, and fertile high-lying valleys. These
mountains as a whole, but especially the Alleghany,
(more distinct throughout its course), form the water-
shed of the country to the east and the west, the
streams flowing off to the one side or the other. These
mountains, in regard to their ranges and branches, are
very differently traced in the several maps, and it can
hardly be otherwise since no examination of them has
been made for the purpose. Governor Pownall's and
Captain Hutchins's maps ✚ in this respect seem to be
the most reliable.

Although there are said to be many farms about
Bedford, some of them already good, we did not pass
a house until we had gone four miles on our road, and
it was three miles farther to another house. The
owner of this one had recently, for 200 Pd. Pensylv.
Current, bought no less than 300 acres of land, was
satisfied with his purchase, and called it good land.
From here on we had 12 miles through a thin forest
of little, spindling oaks, which had to find a meagre
living on a dry and narrow ridge, and there was among
them almost no undergrowth or bush. This long
drawn-out hill, 'the dry ridge' is a jutty, what they
call here a 'spur' of the Alleghany, and a good many
like it leave the main ridge. It is covered with broken
slabs of a reddish, micaceous sand-stone, from half an
inch to an inch thick; it is noticeable that most of the
fragments along this road and everywhere hereabouts
have more or less a four-cornered shape. We found a
dearth of plants here and little variety among them.
In the afternoon at four o'clock we arrived at a large

tavern where, if one brings meat and drink along with
him he finds room enough to dispose of them. Two
young fellows kept house but had nothing except
whiskey and cheese; bread and meat are accidental
articles. We were obliged to push on over the Alleghany and as far as its foot had a swampy and stony
road.

The Alleghany, one of the longest and most conspicuous ranges, does not appear so high as might be
expected from its giving its name to the rest. But it
must be remembered that the road has been continually
over higher and higher ranges, and in consequence the
base of the Alleghany must be very elevated. On the
other hand the eye is again pleased with a steep wall
of a mountain running almost straight from northeast
to southwest. The sun was just going down when we
reached the foot of the mountain, and the tall thick
woods soon hid from us completely the dull twilight
and we found ourselves in darkness. A few other
travellers had joined us at the last house; they were as
much strangers here as we, and were as little pleased
at stumbling from stones to slough, and from slough to
stones. We were not prepared to stay in the woods;
we could neither make a fire nor care for our horses.
Everything was dead, still, and dark about us; nothing
could be heard from the four-footed or feathered inhabitants of these wastes. After four miles, which in
our situation seemed to us endless, we reached the
cabin of a smith on the other side of the mountain who
on occasion plays the innkeeper. Unfortunately his
house was no inn this evening; he had nothing, and
we must grope for two heavy miles more, to the farm
of an Anabaptist by the name of Spiker whose milk-

white countenance stood out of a raven-black beard. We arrived after 10 o'clock; he kept no tavern and we were glad of it, for we were taken in willingly and given milk, butter, and bread, and straw for a couch.

The **Glades** or 'Glade-Settlements' begin here. This is the name given the great broad valley, which lies between the Alleghany and the next-following Laurel-hill, and is here 10-12 miles in breadth. The level of the valley is naturally high, for from the ridge of the Alleghany, as well as of the Laurel-hill, down into this valley the way is by no means so long and abrupt as that up the other slopes of both these mountains. Really the word Glade denotes a meadow, pasture, or other open tract in the woods, naturally free of timber, commonly not of great extent and lying about large springs or along brooks. There is always much high, thick grass in such places, which are unfavorable to the growth of trees, because the seeds are either swept away or rot faster than they can find lodgment in the ground. Similar glades occur even more frequently in the southern provinces and are tempting spots. Ten or twelve years ago several families began to take up land here, and now there are many settlers, so that this part of the mountains is already as well peopled as many tracts of the lower country. The land is good and well watered. An acre at this time costs 35-45 shillings Pensylv. Current. It produces good wheat and other crops, and on account of the continual passing-through there is no difficulty in the sale of them. Besides, they have near them the Potowmack on the one side and the Ohio on the other. Several times during the war, and even this spring, all the wheat of the region that could be spared was sold and

sent down the Ohio to New Orleans in Louisiana and
to Mexico.

From our Anabaptist's we continued five miles
through a fine fertile country, of excellent meadow-
lands, and then seven miles partly good land, partly
dry or ridge woods. Last night there was ice, and yet
only ten days ago there was burning heat in this valley.
The road to the Ohio cuts across this valley and hence
there can be seen only a few of the plantations scattered
up and down.

Over **Laurel-hill** it is 12 miles from the last house
in the Glades to the first on the other side. A desolate
and wild mountain it is, its ridge and western slope
exhausting for horse and man; not so much because
of steepness, as on account of the abominable rock-
fragments lying in the greatest confusion one over
another and over which the road proceeds. On this
mountain we fell in with two heavily loaded wagons,
carrying the baggage, women, and children of several
families travelling together. They lived far below on
the Ohio, at the Wabash; during the war they were
taken captive by the Indians to Detroit, where they
passed several years until the peace. From Detroit
the road to their former settlement would have been
not more than 3-400 miles; but because the English
thought it unsafe to allow these people to go among
the still unpacified Indian nations, they were obliged
to come from Detroit to Montreal by way of the
Ontario and the St. Lawrence, thence over Lake
Champlain and down the Hudson to Albany and New
York, and so to Philadelphia. This road, with that
still remaining, might be counted at least 3000 English miles. With them was a Captain Dalton, at one

time a hunter in the woods and later Governor and
Commandant of the post of St. Vincent on the Wabash. It was distressing to hear what these people,
(living in the immeasurable forest so far removed from
the actual seat and source of all the hostilities), had
to tell of the frights and dangers they had passed
through; and yet, returning thither, they were more
fortunate than many of their neighbors who had been
tomahawked on the spot. They travelled slowly and
camped every night in the woods. In the evening we
reached the first cabin on the western side of Laurel-
hill. This was the residence of Doctor Peter, a German, who was absent looking for his pigs gone astray
in the woods. His wife, a good little old woman, and
energetic, gave our horses oats for their refreshment
and set before us mountain-tea and maple-sugar, which
as well as her bacon, whiskey, and cakes were the
products of her own land and industry.

We had been long coming down the mountain, and
from this place there still remained a few miles to go
until we reached the foot of the Laurel-hill. Here we
saw particularly extensive tracts of forest killed out
by fire. Barked and stripped of branches the high,
white, trunks stood naked, and among them there was
springing up an indescribably thick bush, not to be
found among the living, tall trees of the same region.
A man met us who was taking to Philadelphia some
500 pounds of ginseng-roots (*Panax quinquefolium L.*)
on two horses. He hoped to make a great profit because throughout the war little of this article was
gathered, and it was now demanded in quantity by certain Frenchmen. The hunters collect it incidentally in
their wanderings; in these mountains the plant is still

common, but in the lower parts it has pretty well disappeared.   It grows in not too rich woods-earth in
mountain regions from Canada down to North and
South Carolina.   Much is brought in to Fort Pitt.   Industrious people who went out for the purpose have
gathered as much as 60 pounds in one day.   Three
pounds of the freshly gathered make only one pound
of the well dried; which is sold by the gatherers for
one, one and a half, to two shillings Pensylv. Current,
commonly about a shilling sterling.   The physicians in
America make no use of this root; and it is an article
of trade only with China, where the price is not so high
as it was, on account of the great adulteration.   All
manner of similar roots were mixed in.   The English
take very little of it.   The taste of the fresh root is
very similar to that of our sweet-wood, or liquorice,
but is somewhat more aromatic.—In these mountains
also are gathered many pounds of the Senega (*Polygala Senega, L.*) and of the Virginia snake-root (*Aristolochia Serpent. L.*) ; the pound, dried, sells for two,
two and a half, and three shillings Pensylv. Current.

We breakfasted at a Captain's whither we had been
directed; for along this road, and others like it in
America, one must not be deceived by the bare name
of taverns.   The people keep tavern if they have anything over and above what they need; if not, the
traveller must look about for himself.   The Captain
was not at all pleased that the neighborhood was beginning to be so thickly settled.   ' It spoils the hunting,' he said, ' makes quarrels ; and then they come and
want to collect taxes; it is time some of us were leaving and getting deeper into the country.'   Hence we
supposed we should find a thickly settled region, but

had to go not less than seven miles before we came to
the next neighbor.   Like most of the inhabitants of
these frontiers, he was of those whose chief occupation
is hunting, who from a preference for doing nothing,
and an old indifference to many conveniences, neglect
and dread the quieter and more certain pursuits of
agriculture.   These hunters or ' backwoodmen ' live
very like the Indians and acquire similar ways of
thinking.   They shun everything which appears to demand of them law and order, dread anything which
breathes constraint.   They hate the name of a Justice,
and yet they are not transgressors.   Their object is
merely wild, altogether natural freedom, and hunting is
what pleases them.   An insignificant cabin of unhewn
logs ; corn and a little wheat, a few cows and pigs, this
is all their riches but they need no more.   They get
game from the woods ; skins bring them in whiskey and
clothes, which they do not care for of a costly sort.
Their habitual costume is a ' rifle-shirt,' or shirt of
fringed linen ; instead of stockings they wear Indian
leggings ; their shoes they make themselves for the
most part.   When they go out to hunt they take with
them a blanket, some salt, and a few pounds of meal
of which they bake rough cakes in the ashes ; for the
rest they live on the game they kill.   Thus they pass
10-20 days in the woods ; wander far around ; shoot
whatever appears ; take only the skins, the tongues,
and some venison back with them on their horses to
their cabins, where the meat is smoked and dried ; the
rest is left lying in the woods.   They look upon the
wilderness as their home and the wild as their possession ; and so by this wandering, uncertain way of
life, of which they are vastly fond, they become in-

different to all social ties, and do not like many neighbors about them, who by scaring off the game are a
nuisance besides.   They are often lucky on the hunt
and bring back great freight of furs, the proceeds of
which are very handsome.   Uncompanionable and
truculent as this sort of men appear to be, and however they seem half-savage and, by their manner of
life, proof against the finer feelings, one is quite safe
among them and well treated; they have their own
way of being courteous and agreeable which not everybody would take to be what it is.   Their little house-
keeping is, for their situation, neat; and their wives
and children are content in their solitudes where for
the most part they spend the time in idleness.*

Chesnut-ridge was still before us, which is tedious
not for its height but for the stoniness of the road.   This
ridge appears to be scarcely more than the continued
declivity of the Laurel-hill range, its height from the
east being very inconsiderable.   Indeed there would be
no great error in regarding the Alleghany and Laurel-
hill (with the Dry Ridge to the east of the first, and
Chesnut-hill to the west of the second) as forming
together in basis one and the same great range of
mountains, near 60 English miles in breadth from east
to west.   The rock of all these mountains, on their
west side, is still the laminated sand-stone; but here
commonly more of a greyish tint.   On the roads
through these immense forests the many fallen trees
are every moment a disagreeable hindrance, for nobody removes them out of the way, and one must go

---

* For more in this regard, read St. John's Letters; the 3rd
letter.

over or around as well as one can. Those inhabitants more familiar with the country trouble themselves very little about beaten roads. Through the woods, for the most part clear of undergrowth; guided by the sun, the course of the streams, the appearance of the trees, they travel straight to the place they are going and seldom lose their way. In the less travelled regions and along roads leading to remote dwellings or other places, the way is marked by long, broad cuts in the trees; the white wood is even to be discerned at night. This method was originally adopted from fear of getting lost in the forest. Roads thus marked are called ' blazed paths.'

In the afternoon we arrived at the house and mill of a Colonel Berry. A few miles farther on, at a Captain's, we asked quarters for the night, but he having nothing for man or beast directed us a mile beyond to Salisbury or Millerstown. This town of the future consists at this time of one house only, where we had the good fortune to be taken in, the owner first protesting at length that the Captain had called his house a tavern when he had no provisions. The region has been settled only 8-10 years; was it older most of the people would not have been frightened off by the last war. Several persons are living in the neighborhood who have been scalped by the Indians; when these make hasty attacks or are in dread of resistance, they often do not take the time to see whether the scalped is actually dead, caring only for the sign of victory, snatched hurriedly. We were shown a girl whose scalp-marks after six years were not completely cured; doubtless from lack of good treatment.

From Millerstown it is still 32 miles to the Ohio—

Many deserted cabins stand by the way, the people not yet returned, having fled from the Indians. The country continues hilly and rough, but the hills are but low and wavy; the landscape somewhat more open and not at all unpleasing; the soil almost everywhere very good. The Laurel-hill passed, everything takes on a better and more fertile aspect, in comparison with the land on the east side of the mountains. An observation which strikes everyone coming thence.

We took breakfast at a house where several children lay very ill of a malignant pox; this year the disease has raged in these parts and carried off many young people. Thence 10 miles along the ridge of a barren hill, without seeing a cabin; but there are several in the valleys. On account of the dryness the road has been carried along the ridges, and here, as often elsewhere, is very tedious for being so dry and monotonous; scarcely a flower even is to be seen. Descending a steep mountain we came to

Turkey Creek Settlement, in a fine but narrow valley. Our host here, as often happens in the mountains, gave our horses unthreshed oats in bundles; in this way there is a saving of trouble, the horses indeed losing a little but not the host.—There are a good many houses here. Again up a steep mountain, and seven miles through nothing but woods. The last three miles the country was a little more settled. Sundry brooks are to be crossed, named according to their distance from Fort Pitt, as Six-Mile, Four-Mile, and Two-Mile Branch. From the last the road lay along the Alleghany river. It was already dusk, but the sky was clear, and the landscape open and charming; to which contributed no little the prospect of a beautiful stream,

16

the freedom from incessantly troublesome woods, and
the pleasure of having reached the end proposed. In
Pittsburg we were directed to the best inn, a small
wooden cabin set askew by the Monongahela, its exterior promising little; but seeing several well dressed
men and ladies adorned we were not discouraged.
Not we but our vehicle had the honor of being the first
object of their curiosity, for we had come the whole
way in a two-wheeled chaise, ✛ what hitherto had been
regarded as next to impossible. Thus we did not think
it at all strange if, on passing a house in the mountains,
the mother called her children together in consterna-
tion to show them what they had never before seen in
their lives—a chaise.

In this mountain-journey one misses what might be
probably expected, finding no extraordinary works of
nature, cataracts, rock-peaks, or abysses. And so I
was disappointed with what I had seen, because from
what I had been told by the Americans I looked for
great things. Only those who have seen no others speak
of the Blue Mountains as a *non plus ultra*. From
Carlisle it is not only continual forest, but a very
monotonous forest, there being little variety among
the trees. For plants, the best season was over, but
along the dry roads we found not so many as we
could wish, and we could not explore all the swamps.
Indeed, there are very few birds to be seen, and all
wild animals are frightened off by the noise of the
passenger. We saw but one young bear which quite
without warning climbed down a tree on to the road
like a clown, and hurriedly made off. We heard here
and there of rattlesnakes, ' copper-bellies,' and moc-
assins (which being smaller and making no noise are

more dangerous) but saw not one.—The commonest wild animal is the Virginia deer; the Grey Moose, very similar to the European stag, has also been seen in these woods, but is more numerous in Canada. The black moose, or elk, is seen here but very rarely.

Fort Pitt, formerly Fort du Quesne, lies in latitude 40° 31′ 44″, about five degrees west of Philadelphia, on a point of land where the Monongahela and the Alleghany unite, both of them considerable streams, and thence under the name of the Ohio proceed through the western country to the Mississippi. After this place was transferred in the war before the last to England, and with it the whole immense tract lying between the mountains and the Mississippi, in the year 1760 there was first settled near the Fort a little town, called Pittsburg in honor of the then minister. Before that time, under the French, only a few hunters and Indian traders lived there. In the year 1763 the Indians began a bloody war against the British colonies, and attacked this region among others; the inhabitants, still few in number, had to leave their houses and take refuge in the fort, and the new town was given over to the enemy by whom it was entirely destroyed. Two years afterwards the place Pittsburg was re-established, and more regularly than before, on the eastern bank of the Monongahela some 300 yards from the Fort; and numbers at this time perhaps 60 wooden houses and cabins, in which live something more than 100 families, for by the outbreak of the last war the growth of the place, beginning to be rapid, was hindered. The first stone house was built this summer, but soon many good buildings may be seen, because the place reasonably expects to grow large and con-

siderable with the passage of time—Of public houses
of worship or of justice there are none as yet. However a German preacher lives there, who ministers to
all of the faith; and the state of Pensylvania, as is
customary in this country, sends hither a Judge once
or twice a year to administer the law—The inhabitants
are still poor, as circumstances are at present; but also
extremely inactive and idle; so much so that they are
recalcitrant when given work and opportunity to earn
money, for which, however, they hanker. There was
general complaint in this respect and we also found it
the case that every trifling thing made here is dearer
than at Philadelphia even; that the people here do not
grow rich by industry and fair prices but prefer rather
to deal extortionately with strangers and travellers;
and shunning work charge the more for it, their comfortable sloth being interrupted. They gained their
living hitherto by farming and trafficking in skins and
furs. But now that considerable settlements are beginning farther down the Ohio which continually increase by the great number of people daily going
thither, they find trade very profitable and what is to
be gained by catering to those passing through. However little to be regarded the place is now, from its
advantageous site it must be that Pittsburg will in the
future become an important depot for the inland trade.
The Ohio, (la belle rivière) is the only great river in
the whole extensive western country between the
northern lakes, the mountains, and the Mississippi,
receiving all other rivers into itself and flowing into
the Mississippi (at 36° 43') after a course, reckoned
from this place, of 1188 English miles. Of its two
chief branches the Alleghany comes from high up

towards the Canadian country, and through it (by
Venango and through sundry small streams) there is
opened up a good connection with the Canadian lakes.
Almost every season, very dry ones alone excepted,
boats of 2-3 ft. draught can go up the Alleghany and
into French Creek, and from thence there is but a
short portage to Lake Erie.* Down the Alleghany
such boats can make 50-60-100 miles a day. It has
even been estimated that goods and wares may be
brought hither (and expedited further) by the river
Lawrence and the Canadian lakes as profitably as by
the land road from Pensylvania or Maryland. The
Monongahela comes up from the South along the
frontier mountains of Virginia, and thus makes here,
where the Alleghany joins it, the most convenient
place for a staples-depot. ✠

The mountains perfectly well admit of very convenient land routes being established in time for the
furtherance of the trade with Philadelphia and Baltimore, but the road may be very much shortened by
streams † on both sides the mountains. At present
there is paid 40-50 shillings Pensylv. freightage the
hundredweight from Philadelphia to Pittsburg, a distance of 320 English miles; but this is diminished if
the waggoners find a return freight. The number of
considerable streams which net the extensive country

---

* Only a mile of land-passage, or portage, separates the
Cayahoga river, (which flows into Lake Erie and through it
into the St. Lawrence) from the Muskingum which falls into
the Ohio; and so, but for that inconsiderable space, the Gulf
of Mexico is joined with the Gulf of St. Lawrence.

† From where the Potomack ceases to be navigable to the
nearest navigable arm of the Ohio it is only 60 miles.

from the great Canadian lakes as far as the western
regions of both the Carolinas, (the most of them bearing ladings of 50 tons and more), almost without exception fall into the Ohio, and so facilitate communication between the remotest limits of that country.
This wealth of navigable waters inland will indeed
prevent Pittsburg from drawing to itself exclusively
the trade of the western country, as many are apt to
think, but it will always have the greater part of that
trade among other favorable conditions. In a country
of so many rivers no one place can expect to have the
exclusive trade, particularly if the people of these
frontier regions are themselves to become engaged in
trade, setting up their own little warehouses; as is the
case in Virginia, which province has no especially
large commercial town for the reason that nearly all
the planters living as they do close by navigable streams
have built their own wharves and store-houses; which
however is to be explained by other circumstances and
cannot be so generally imitated here.

A part of the northern fur-trade cannot escape this
place, (if the friendship of the Indians can be assured) although New York has greater hopes in that
regard, and may secure the heaviest part of the trade
through the most convenient channel of the rivers
Oneyda, Mohawk, and Hudson.—From Pittsburg
down the Ohio and the Mississippi the way is long,
but the journey is often made in 14 days from here to
New Orleans at the mouth of the Mississippi. The
current of the Ohio is swift and supports great
burthens in the spring and in the fall. And this will
be the easiest, indeed the only road for the future export of the produce of these mountain parts.

The first French fort, which was only a stockade
and stood directly in the angle between the rivers, has
long since fallen to ruin. Under the English government a spacious work of five bastions, with wall and
moat, was begun, but was not yet finished when the
last British garrison came away in the year 1774. At
that time peace had long prevailed with all the Indian
nations; hence this and other fortified places, on the
Ohio, the Wabash, the Illinois, and the Mississippi,
were regarded as useless and the garrisons withdrawn.
The Americans, to whom this fort was very opportune
in the last war, have been at no further cost in its
equipment, but on account of the Indians have always
kept a garrison there, which just at this time is on the
point of being taken away. From its situation the fort
can be serviceable only against the Indians; for it can
be quite commanded from several neighboring hills,
but especially from a high hill standing above the fort
on the other side of the Monongahela, at this point only
some 1200 ft. wide; and it is even said that the Indians
have shot their arrows from this hill quite into the fort.

Another, smaller fort stood 30 miles below at Mac-
Intosh, and still another at Wheeling. The garrisons
maintained there helped to support this place and even
enlivened it, for during the war there were balls, plays,
concerts, and comedies here, 400 miles west of the
ocean. Therefore the Pittsburg ladies cannot but be-
hold with troubled hearts the withdrawal of so many
fine gentlemen, and the cessation of so many diversions.

The Alleghany and Monongahela come together almost at a right angle. The point of land between them
is a sand-hill built up by their alluvion, and containing
polished pebbles, with the same reddish sand as that

of the mountains hereabout. The banks are 20-30 ft. high above the water ; but this deep channel fills in the spring and autumn, and at times the river overflows. At such times, it is said, a frigate of 20 guns can pass clear of all obstacles down the river, which then has a depth of nearly 25 ft. throughout ; the swiftness of the current is such that boats can descend about 100 miles in a day. There are so far but two wells, 35 ft. in depth, at this place, and they are often short of water. The bed of both rivers at one time lay much higher, over what is now dry and cultivated land. Two or three points of land may be observed rising one above the other, of precisely the shape and direction of the point at this time washed by the rivers. Of these, Grant's-hill is the hindmost, half a mile off from the river. And so there may be distinguished very clearly the gradations of the originally higher-lying channels.—Both streams were at this time so shallow that at many places one could ride through them.

The lowness of the water and our brief stay prevented me from seeing anything of the fishes of the region. It is said, and with great probability, that the streams rising on the west side of the mountains, and through the Mississippi associated with the Gulf of Mexico, have but few species of fishes in common with the rivers which flow from the east side into the ocean. They have a sort of sturgeons or horn-fish which is described as different from that seen in the Delaware and the Hudson.* I was told of large trouts and pikes which are similar to others of that kind. The yellow perch is said to be found here. A sort of cat-fish, very

---

* See Carver's Travels.

like the common cat-fish of the Delaware, (*Silurus catus L.*), is caught weighing 30-50 pounds; some people even pretend to have seen them lower down the river weighing as much as 80-100 pounds.*

A peculiar turtle, which I could not get a sight of, keeps in the Ohio and its tributaries. It is called **the softshell'd**, and again the green turtle. The higher and middle part of the shell is hard, but the edges are said to be soft and pliable; and the whole shell may be cooked to a jelly.† The hind-feet are described as webbed, as with the sea-turtle, the fore-feet being supplied with digitals, and the flesh very good to eat. Also the snapping-turtle is found in the waters of the Ohio. This variety of turtle, little known in Europe, is very common on the eastern coast of America, particularly in the middle provinces. It lives in swamps, and on the banks of little streams as well salt as fresh; swims, but also goes on land; I myself found one near New York on a dry hill in the woods. It is distinguished from all others of its kind by the sharp indentations on the hinder edge of its dirty black shell; by the breast-bone which does not, as with other turtles, form a shield wholly covering the under part, but has the shape of a broad cross; and finally by its uncommonly long tail.‡ The feet are 4-5 inches in

---

* Carver mentions the cat-fish in the Mississippi, but of a weight only of five or six pounds.

† So probably the same indeterminate species as that found by Catesby on the Savannah river, which sodden over and over is said to become soft and edible, although the shell before cooking appears as hard as that of other kinds. See, Schneider's *Naturgeschichte der Schildkröten*, p. 347.

‡ With regard to the indented hinder shell and the long tail

length; the long neck can be shortened at will or extended with great rapidity. It snaps impatiently at whatever is held before it, at the same time supporting itself on its hind-feet, as if to venture a leap; and from this singularity it gets its name. What it has once got hold of with its sharp nib it does not easily let go, so long as it has any strength. It is eaten, as are almost all the varieties of turtle; and found weighing 2-3-4 pounds.——Still other sorts of the American land and swamp turtles are to be seen here.*

---

this snapping-turtle appears to be most like the *Testudo serpentina L.;* but the singularly formed breast-shield makes it a species apart. A more exact description of the dry specimen will be given elsewhere. Its method of defence it appears to have in common with the *Test. ferox.* See, Schneider's *Naturgeschichte der Schildkröten,* 333.

* Besides the soft-shelled and snapping-turtles mentioned, the middle colonies of America (and probably the others) have three other sorts of turtles, all of which are found frequently about New York and Philadelphia. The first is that described by Dr. Bloch as a new species, under the name of Box-Turtle, Dosen-Schildkröte, (in *Beobacht. der Gesellsch. Naturf. Freunde zu Berlin,* Bd. 1, 1stes Stück), which is particularly distinguished by the movable breast-shield, divided in the middle, and adapted for the complete closing of the upper shell—The two others have immovable breast-shields closely attached to the upper armor by bony continuations of the middle side-shell; but in several ways are distinct from each other—to mention only the most striking differences, (there will be better opportunity elsewhere for an exact and circumstantial comparison), in the second species the evenly arched upper shell is quite smooth, brown along the back, and at the fore-edges marked with a narrow black and a broader yellow border, likewise smooth, from which three yellow streaks run over the back. The side-shell is blackish brown, the breast-shield white. This I believe to be a new species.

The whole region about Fort Pitt is hilly, but these
are fertile hills, of good soil, excellent meadows, and

Its habitat is in swamps. The third sort is in coloring similar to the first, the upper armor flecked brown and yellow, a
keel-shaped elevation along the middle of the back; but all
three varieties are lozenge-streaked, with shading at the middle of the figure. The breast-shield of the third is white; but
the seams of the different parts of the shell are arranged unlike those of the second. Its habitat is preferably the creeks
and streams near the coast; this is probably the *Test. Carolina L.?*—These three distinct species are often confused
under the name Terrapins, but especially the two first—The
coloring and distinctive marks of the young of these turtles
seem to me to be very variable, and likely this is often the
cause of many errors in determining the species where so
little is accurately known of the several characteristics.
Hence it would redound to the credit of the North American
naturalists if they gave attention to the history of these animals of which, in the southern provinces alone, they have
examples continually before them. I am convinced that still
other new species may be found in the more southern provinces of North America or at least corrections of former observations might be made. In addition, as material for a de-
sirable contribution to the history of the turtle, there appear
every summer in America the three West Indian sea-turtles,
the Green, the Hawk's-bill and the Loggerhead. And finally,
there is seen on the American coast the Trunk-turtle (*Test.
coriacea L.*). In August 1779 one of this sort was taken in
the harbor of Rhode Island; it was already cut up when I
got news of it. It weighed almost 600 pounds, and from the
point of the head to the tail was five and a half feet long.
The shell was covered with a tight, smooth, blackish skin, not
too firmly stretched to be moved about here and there. Along
the back there were five raised callosities, dividing the surface
into flat compartments. In the circumstances at that time this
was a welcome catch; the meat was dispensed in pounds at a
shilling sterling and was devoured, and although uncommonly
fat the taste of it was much inferior to that of the green
turtle.

flourishing forest-growth. This not being so generally
the case to the east of the mountains, every stranger
coming hither finds the western country pleasanter and
more to be desired. Over against Pittsburg land is already farmed and there are divers dwellings along the
high ridge of the steep hill looking towards the Monongahela. At the foot of this hill marble is found,
probably resting upon rock of a gneiss species. This
marble is blueish, becoming paler higher up the mountain. At the same time it is harder, denser, and of a
finer grain than the common limestone, similar to it in
color, on the east side of the mountains. Along with
it occurs a fine and beautiful liver-colored marble. It
is said that lime burnt of it does not absorb moisture
so easily or fall away so rapidly in the air; the reason
likely is that it is not thoroughly burnt, since as yet
there is nothing known in America of adequate lime-
furnaces. Above the marble lies a coarse slate, which
higher up the mountain becomes finer and passes into
a strong vein of the most beautiful coals, in turn
covered with a stratum of coarse clayey slate, white or
variegated in color. There follows then, almost to the
ridge of the mountain, a deep bed of laminated and
very micaceous sand-stone.

The coal-bed mentioned, midway of the hill or
mountain, is so much the more noteworthy because
elsewhere coals are to be dug for at a depth, and is
proof of what great changes have taken place in the
surface of this region. This appearance proves of itself that America must be older than it should seem to
be by the arbitrary assumptions of more than one illustrious man; for years must pass before so wide a
stratum of coal is formed, (according to the general

opinion, from plant-mould accumulated and changed), and this again covered with such deep layers of other mineral species; and how many more years would still be requisite for a stream to sink its channel, below this coal-stratum, 60-80 ft. deeper?—The singularity of this coal-bed is an item of great convenience to the inhabitants. The coals dug out are merely poured into a trench furrowed in the steep wall of the mountain, and thence rolled down to the edge of the river, where they are immediately taken in by the boats lying ready. The vein of these coals is 10-12-18 ft. wide, and extends throughout the length of the mountain. The coals are clean, light, and glistening, not so glassy as those of Wyoming, but more combustible and without any disagreeable smell. A part of the fuel for the garrison having been taken from this mountain, the vein has been worked a considerable distance; but for convenience fresh spots are continually being trenched. Moreover, the coals are the property of the land-owners, who, for the trifling payment of a penny the bushel, allow any one to fetch them away. The great supply will be uncommonly advantageous in the future settlement of this region, contributing as it will to the more general cultivation of the land, less wood having to be reserved. Also the use of the minerals here will be facilitated, and these coals will even form a considerable article for export. But coal is found not only here but in almost every hill on both sides the Ohio throughout the western country, and most of the mountain valleys contain coal-beds.

But with other minerals also are these remote regions richly and variously supplied. Iron and lead are found at many places near the Ohio and its tributaries. Lead occurs frequently at the surface; on the Siotto, 400 miles below Pittsburg, there is great plenty of it; from this and other places similar the Indians fetch their supply for war and the hunt; they fuse out the ore merely in their common fires. Here and there specimens of copper * have been found, and as the story is, of silver also.

Petroleum occurs in several ways; but there is a spring in particular, near Alleghany Creek 90 miles from here, which is heavily saturated with it, and the broad creek is for a long distance covered with the swimming oil. In the neighborhood of the Crossings, on the Youghiagany (commonly called the Yach) a mine is worked which is said to contain silver and lead. The owners are the Messrs. Downer and Lynch. A silversmith perseveres there, who sells the people silver utensils ostensibly fabricated from this domestic ore. But according to precise accounts this artful silversmith appears to be using the gullible country people for his own advantage.——Generally speaking, with the passage of time there must and will be discovered more and more on American soil not only the treasures of the earth but everything necessary for trade, crafts, and household economy. For, little as is known of America there is already ground for the assertion that nothing essential is lacking, and there is good hope of finding what has not yet been discovered.

One of the greatest gifts of nature, for the immense tracts of country lying this side the mountains, is the

---

* According to Carver this metal appears most frequently about Lake Superior.

salt-springs, already found at sundry places. It is remarkable that in the whole of eastern North America,
or between the Atlantic ocean and the mountains, no
traces of these have so far appeared. There are a few
dirty salt-spots, or plashes, of no great importance, (at
the foot of the more easterly mountains and among
the mountains), which taste mildly of salt and in warm
weather show a white skim. Wild animals and domestic cattle are the first to find these out, and they
like to keep near them. On the road from Pittsburg
to Virginia there is, near a brook, a salt-spring from
which a good quantity of salt has been boiled, but this
spring is often overflowed, and the water fouled and
made unusable for some time together. The attempt
was made to divert the spring and dig it out elsewhere,
and it was very nearly ruined in consequence. However, other improvements may be made, or by refining
the salt obtained the profits may be increased. Between here and Lake Erie, at a distance of some 60-70
miles, there are many salt-licks, which is the name
given such spots, because the buffalo and deer are accustomed to lick up the crystallized salt. It is said the
Indians have long obtained their salt from such places,*
although the use of it is not universal among them.
For the supply of the mountains and adjacent regions,
salt might still be fetched from the coast, whither it
is brought partly from Europe, partly from Tortuga
and other of the West India islands. But with the increasing population of the more remote interior parts
of this vast country, it would be no slight incon-

---

* By others it is asserted that the Indian nations never used
kitchen-salt until they learned the custom of the Europeans.

venience to bring so necessary an article 1000 miles
and more from the coast. This difficulty will now be
obviated through the use of the salt-springs so numerous in the interior of the country. The new colony at
Kentucky has already set up its own salt-boiling establishments, and thus supplies itself in greatest part
with the article, which will be of all the more importance so soon as they can obtain it in sufficient
quantity to make a more profitable use of their surplus
of meat.

The Western Country, Frontier Plantations, Kentucky &c.

The Ohio country, between the mountains and the Mississippi, or what is commonly called 'the West country,' is estimated at 15-20,000 English square miles. But by this is understood especially that tract of country from the Ohio south; for the whole extent of the western territory, which by the last treaty of peace is relinquished to the United States, between the river St. Croix, the Lake of the Woods, the Mississippi, and the Ohio, embraces some 400,000 English square miles of which however almost the fifth part is to be reckoned out, as included in the immense inland lakes and other waters.* All settlements which

---

* By the latest survey of the United States, of the year 1785, it is stated that the territory of the Republic amounts to about 1,000,000 English square miles, containing 640 million acres of land. From this deduct 51,000,000 acres for water surface and there remain 589,000,000. That portion of the United States to the west of Pensylvania, from the river St. Croix to the north-western part of the Lake of the Woods; thence by the Mississippi to the mouth of the Ohio on the west, thence along the southern side of the Ohio to Pensylvania, embraces 411,000 square miles, estimated to contain 263,040,000 acres. Deducting 43,040,000 for water surface there remain 220,000,000. Of this tract the officers and soldiers of the establishment have received 150,000 acres, and other troops serving in the last war 414,720 acres. 80,640 acres are appropriated for the maintenance of public schools. The waters lying north-west of the Ohio, but included in the territory of the United States, cover 43,040,000 acres, of which Lake Superior 21,952,780 acres, and

17

so far have been made by Europeans in the actual
western country are confined almost wholly to the
south and east sides of the Ohio. Beyond, that is to
say on the northern and western banks of the Ohio
and the Alleghany, and as far as the neighborhood of
the Canadian lakes, the Mississippi, and the Illinois,
there are (or were) no fixed establishments as yet.
All that country is still regarded as in the possession
of several Indian nations, and as such is stubbornly
claimed by them and murderously defended against
any actual or prospective encroachments. They were
willing to sell absolutely none of this land, so as to
preserve their hunting range from any further cur-
tailment than is already the case.*   The land lying to

Lake Michigan 10,368,000. The total of the waters found
within the limits of the 13 United States amounts to 7,960,000
acres, therefore the total water surface of the country is
51,000,000 acres. Lake Ontario alone contains 2,390,000 acres.
Hamb. Polit. Journal, October, 1786. An acre of land contains
43,600 English feet in the square. An English square mile 640
English acres.

* However, at the time of my visit there were already several land-surveyors at Pittsburg who were making preparations to go down the river in order to take up land partly on
the east side of the Ohio, and partly on the west or Indian
side. Their business is to seek out good land at the expense
of adventuring companies, survey it, mark the lines, and make
notes. These companies or private speculators buy the land
of the state of Virginia, expecting to sell it or lease it to individuals. The land-surveyor has his travelling expenses paid,
and receives besides a certain portion of the land surveyed.
Mr. Van Deering has commissions to survey 300,000 acres, of
which, as he says, 6000 fall to him. All who go out surveying
or looking for land on the west side of the Ohio must be careful to avoid meeting any Indians, who forbid absolutely all
land-surveying on this side, and would kill any one they found

the south and east of the Ohio has been in part ceded
by them through treaty or sale, and in part has been
merely usurped by Europeans. At the beginning, indeed, the limits of the several colonies were marked
off by the mother country; but with the growth of the
colonies the territory so fixed was to be conquered
from the Indians or bought of them from time to
time, they having never given up their rights and
claims to suzerainty. A part of the land assigned
by Penn's charter to the state of Pensylvania is included in this Indian territory and is still in their
possession. The boundary of Philadelphia extends
60 miles west and north-west of Pittsburg, and
embraces therefore a considerable tract on the north
side of the Ohio and the Alleghany. On the part of
Pensylvania there is little disposition to purchase this
land by munificent gifts, and the Indians are as little
inclined to fling it away; and thus it cannot be brought
into cultivation except through the shedding of blood
and the continual unrest of the settlers first established
there. And after a time this will be the case also with
the extensive country lying to the north and west of
the Ohio, given over to the United States by Great
Britain under the last treaty but without the privity
and consent of the Indian nations interested, who
therefore feel themselves in no way bound to regard
that treaty and withdraw from their forests and hunting grounds, unable or unwilling to comprehend how
any foreign power has the right to appropriate to

there.—These journeys are made in canoes or flats, and all
necessaries must be taken along, since there can be no de-
pendence on anything but what is found in the woods; therefore a good hunter is an indispensable member of the party.

others what they are in possession of by inheritance
from their remote ancestors. Hence they will for a
long time offer resistance as much as in them lies, and
even now they lose no opportunity of cutting off all
who venture on the north and west banks of the Ohio,
suspected as coming in the quality of land-seekers ✚
and surveyors.* However, the Congress has already
determined upon a division of this still unpossessed
land which, falling to the Congress under the treaty
and lying beyond the limits of the old provinces as
hitherto fixed, is called Congress-land. From this tract
will be taken the bounty-lands for the troops of the
states of Maryland, Delaware, Jersey, Connecticut,
Rhode-Island, Massachusetts, and New Hampshire;
the remaining states have enough waste land of their
own for the purpose. By a resolution of the Congress †
this soldiers' land is to form a new state of itself, including all that country from the Big Miami up to
Lake Erie, with Pensylvania to the east and the Ohio
to the south-east, a tract nearly as large as Pensylvania.
So has the Congress declared, and there is only lacking
the consent and the cession of the Indians.

Among all those settlements begun to the west of
the mountains, none hastens more swiftly to comple-

---

* According to the latest accounts from America (of the
year 1786) the Indians are letting it be known, by numerous
murders committed along the frontiers, that they are unwilling their lands should come into the possession of the Americans. They will not be bound by treaties between England
and the United States, and they will in no way cede their land.

† New and remarkable resolutions of the Congress touching
the establishment and setting-off of ten new states, from the
whole of the western country, are to be found in Appendix
No. 2.

tion or is more attentively regarded by the whole of America than the new colony at Kentucky. I make no scruple therefore to set down here the information regarding this colony which I was able to assemble at Pittsburg. Before the war and even during it, but altogether within the space of a few years, nearly 20,000 people had gradually removed from the frontier regions over the mountains to help increase the plantations there; and now that the war is ended numbers of people are going thither daily and by every road; we met them everywhere. This general emigration is to be explained in several ways; partly by the desire to escape the taxes imposed during the war and still increasing; again, a propensity for a free and unrestricted mode of life, fear of punishment and of the law, necessity or the spirit of adventure, but chiefly from the honest purpose of providing for growing families. The owner of a small estate nearer the coast sells it, and with the proceeds he can purchase 6-8-10 times as much land beyond the mountains, and is able to leave to each of his children as much as he himself formerly possessed, having first by their help brought the land into an arable state.

The Kentucky is a large river; it takes its rise in the Alleghany mountains under the name of Warrior's Branch, is joined by several other streams, and after a course of more than 400 miles unites with the Ohio, being 200 yards wide at the point of junction. Its current is throughout wide and deep and not rapid. Along its banks everywhere there is said to be the best land, the woods shading them yielding the finest timber. From this stream the whole extensive colony takes its name, but about its mouth, from the generally tempting circumstances, the settlement is thickest and most numerous. As is the case commonly, the first houses of these colonists are merely of logs laid one over another, which however keep off the bullets of the Indians, against whom, so far, the settlers must be continually on their guard.

Among the first to settle there, a certain Henderson ✚ won for himself a particular regard, but he brought them to the observance of a few general laws, and made the beginnings of a separate republican organization ; and in the course of time it will be a question whether or not they will recognize the authority of the state of Virginia in whose jurisdiction they lie.* The rapid growth of the population in these farther regions is already causing vigilance and anxiety in the old, provinces. Thus Pensylvania has made a law by which it is declared high treason for any one soever, in the western territory of the province, to go about establishing **independent communities**. But it is, and will continue to be difficult for the Congress or the individual states to keep dependent these beginning western states, which having no great advantage to expect from the United States will never be inclined to give

---

* An English journal of this year, 1785, gives the following news: Extract of a letter from Danville in Kentucky, May 31, 1785—"Our second Assembly has just opened. It is decided "to ask of the state of Virginia a formal Act of Separation. "Sundry laws of the Virginia Assembly, which are very bur- "densome to this region, compel us to adopt this measure "earlier than would have otherwise happened, although in the "end it may be the better for us. This new state is to be "called the Commonwealth of Kentucky; and at the present "time contains by estimation 30,000 souls; but before the "separation takes place the number will be vastly increased."

heed to their commands and help bear their burdens.
These putative subjects will, so soon as they feel themselves strong enough, without doubt follow the example of the mother-colonies, and desire to be and be
as independent. And have they not as much right?—
They are separated by extensive and impracticable
mountains, and their trading-interests will still more
set them apart.—Plans are made already for the establishment of several towns in Kentucky. The Ohio-
Falls, or rapids, are mentioned as a particularly advantageous site.* This is not really a water-fall, but
only a place where the river forces through rocks and
shallows with such vehemence that laden vessels cannot be taken through; although with high water the
difficulty is not so great. The boats are here commonly
lightened and a part of the cargo sent forward a certain distance by land to be taken on again below the
falls. And so here, it is believed, there will arise of
itself a ware-house and trading-town for commodities
coming down the river.

But many of these new colonists, even after they
have come half across America, find no abiding place
in Kentucky; some of these restless people, I am told,
push on farther to the Illinois, the Wabash, and the
Mississippi, and there mingle with what still remains
of the French colonists. These incessant emigrations,

---

* A detailed account in regard to the country, the rapids,
and the trade of the Ohio is to be found in Thomas Hutchins'
*Topographical description of the river Ohio, Kenhawa, Sioto,
Cherokee, Wabash, Illinois, Mississippi &c.* London 1778. 8.
He travelled through these parts before the war, under orders
from the British government, and his is the best and only
map + of that country.

of which there will be no end so long as land is to
be had for little or nothing, hinder the taking up of
manufactures in the colonies; for it is more befitting
the spirit of this population, and that of all America,
to support themselves on their own land necessitously
but with little work, than to live better continually employed for wages. This roving about, this propensity
for an independent life in the remotest parts, is not
without its advantages to those more regular and industrious classes of people who take the places of the
emigrants and carry on what has been left unfinished
by them.* These farthest colonists are rough and un-

---

* The first residents, or planters, in Pensylvania, who came
over from Europe, desired to introduce at once the most
finished manner of cultivating the land, according to the English fashion, and began the preparation of little tracts, making
them absolutely clean with unspeakable trouble and waste of
time. There was to be not a stump, stone, or thorn left on the
land. The small area which in this way they were able to
subdue was, notwithstanding the newness and fertility of the
soil, insufficient to supply them with the expected or the necessary maintenance. Thus many allowed themselves to be discouraged and returned to Europe where they found fewer
difficulties and more productive harvests for their work. But
others who had no place in Europe to retire to, and through
poverty were compelled to attempt anything, plowed and
sowed the land, between the stumps or among the trees but
recently killed. The rich and easily worked surface returned
a better harvest than they expected, and richly repaid the
slight labor spent upon it. Thenceforward this mode of cultivation was generally adopted and those who settle in the
farther regions still go about their farming in that way; and
some of them do no more, but give up their plantations, thus
roughly begun, to other families, and move on to repeat the
process elsewhere.—" In Pensylvania the impulse still con-
"tinues to migrate to the southern and western country."
Hamb. polit. Journ. May 1786.

lettered, but by mettle and intrepidity they make up
for what, in the stern conditions, must perhaps be
lacking in the items of good manners, peaceableness,
order, and the social virtues. Hardened by their manner of life and not accustomed to particular comforts,
they are best adapted to offer resistance on the occasions of inroads by hostile Indians; and often the remote countryman thanks them for the safety and quiet
in which he farms his acres.

The trade of these new colonies will be perhaps not
inconsiderable after a time. The raw products of their
soil, for the most part good, must supply them with
what they need from abroad. The former they will
send down stream, and the latter they will most conveniently have brought them from above. For the
navigation up the Mississippi and the Ohio is extraordinarily tedious and difficult. The Spaniards have
long since made attempts, but without result, to make
easier the navigation against the current of the Mississippi. Considering how immense is the interior
country, the Ohio and the Mississippi are not sufficient
to distribute wealth and plenty everywhere alike.
Populous and powerful states these western parts will
likely see arise, but the weightier advantages of the
foreign trade, producing wealth more rapidly, will redound only to the profit of the colonies along the coast.
Besides, at the present time there are reasons why
the trade of this interior country should be greatly
hindered, the mouth of the Mississippi (the single
great stream flowing through that immense land),
being wholly in the hands of the Spaniards.* The

---

* Contention with Spain, over the shipping and duties on the
Mississippi, has already begun, in the year 1784, and still
continues.

posterity of the new western states must and will seek
to make the mouth of the Mississippi free.

Particulars and circumstantial accounts regarding
the origin and natural condition of this new colony at
Kentucky I had recently from America, in a description
drawn up by John Filson, of which I have given an
epitome in the *Gelehrten Anzeigen,* Erlangen; but the
repetition, in the Appendix, No. III, will not be un-
acceptable.

Among the natural curiosities of the Kentucky
country, the wonder of all travellers has long been
excited by the numerous large teeth and bones found
there, of an animal at this time existent neither in that
region nor anywhere in America. The place where
these were first discovered lying in great heaps is a
low hill on the east side of the Ohio, 2-3 miles from
its banks and about 584 miles below Fort Pitt, reckoning by the course of the river. At the head-spring of a
little brook, where also there are several large salt-
plashes, the heavy tread of the buffalo congregating
there, what with the help of wind and weather, brought
to light this heap of bones, which lay buried only a very
little way beneath the surface. The quantity of the
bones is said to be very considerable; but judging by
what lies quite exposed or protrudes from the earth,
several persons have estimated that there must be there
skeletons of at least 12-15 animals. But how many
more might be found below? This was likely a numerous herd of animals which found here their common grave.—Touching the one-time owners of these
bones, the native Americans show quite as much ignorance as that so far displayed in the conjectures of
the most respectable naturalists. The enormous size

of the bones and the elephant-like tusks found among
them most naturally gave occasion to regard them as
the remains of elephants formerly native to this part
of the world or brought hither by chance and come to
grief; and there was all the more ground for this
opinion, in itself not at all contradictory, since in so
many other regions similar elephant-skeletons have
been found where the race of elephants was at the time
as little indigenous as in America. But on a more
exact comparison between these bones from the Ohio
and other bones and teeth derived from actual elephants, certain differences were observed which aroused
fresh doubts. It was found particularly that the thigh-
bones discovered on the Ohio were thicker and
stronger than those of the elephant as known today,
that the tusks were somewhat more curved, and especially that the crowns of the molar-teeth were furnished with wedge-shaped ridges, which is not the case
with the elephant. Influenced by these several circumstances, but more especially by the last mentioned,
the learned Dr. Hunter * believed himself warranted
in supposing that those American bones and tusks belonged to a carnivorous animal larger than the known
elephant. From the likeness of those relics to bones
found in Siberia, Germany, and other northern
countries of the old world Raspe † sought to show the
probability that they are the remains of a large animal
(elephant or not) of a singular species, and originally

* *Philosoph. Transact.* Vol. LVIII. 1768.

† *Philos. Transact.* Vol. LIX. 1769. Dissertatio epistolaris
de Ossibus & Dentibus Elephantum, aliarumque Belluarum, in
America boreali &c. obviis, quae indigenarum belluatum esse
ostenditur, I. C. Raspe.

meant for colder regions, the whole race of which for reasons unknown has become extinct. Daubenton and other savans subscribed to this opinion, and Mr. Pennant even believed this indeterminate animal might yet be found somewhere in the interior, unexplored parts of America, and therefore in his Synopsis called it the American elephant. The matter wants further clearing-up, ✚ if indeed remains of the hippopotamus are not found mixed with those of the elephant on the Ohio, thus giving rise to errors. At Pittsburg I saw in the possession of an artillery-officer a thigh bone, a tusk, and a molar-tooth, which he himself had brought thence. The thigh bone, notwithstanding it was quite dry and had lost something here and there of its substance, weighed not less than 81 pounds; at its middle, where it was tolerably flat, it measured only 20 inches, but at the lower joint two feet six and a half inches in circumference.—The tusk was three feet and a half long and nearly four inches in diameter at the lower end, but it was not a complete tusk; however, in this specimen I could discern no curve.—The molar-tooth, which I received as a gift, weighed six full pounds, and its crown was armed with three high, wedge-shaped apophyses.*—The two other specimens were given to the Library at Philadelphia, where I came upon them later.—As a secondary matter it deserves to be men-

---

* This molar-tooth, which is at the present time in the splendid collection of natural curiosities belonging to Privy Counsellor Schmidel at Anspach, is quite distinct from elephants' teeth compared with it by the Privy Counsellor, both as to weight and the entire structure—The molar-tooth of an elephant mentioned by Sparrmann weighed only four and a half pounds. See his *Travels,* p. 563.

tioned that the officer who had them, in order to get
these three pieces taken from the place of their discovery two miles to a boat on the Ohio, gave one of
his soldiers the modest pour-boire of 1000 paper dollars, worth 2400 Rhenish florins.—Besides this molar-
tooth I have seen at Philadelphia, (in the collection of
Mr. du Sumitiere), others which had been found in
other parts of America; these were all alike, and in
some of them the high continuations of the crown were
especially sharp, but in others more worn away. And
if by further discoveries of elephantine skeletons in
divers places in America it appears that this sort of
molar-tooth was general, the supposition will be
strengthened that there was at one time a distinct
American species of elephant.—It has only recently
become known that these places on the Ohio are not
the only ones in North America where remains of this
sort are to be found. Teeth &c have come to light on
the Tar river in North Carolina, near York-town in
Pensylvania, and in Ulster county in New York.
Moreover, Catesby mentions an elephant's tusk that
was dug up in South Carolina; Kalm, a whole skeleton
found in the country of the Illinois; and others have
been discovered in South America. The greatest store
of fossil-bones from the Ohio is owned by Dr. Morgan
at Philadelphia. By reason of the impracticable distance it was formerly a hard matter to come by them,
scarcely possible except by a long way about, sending
them down to New Orleans and around by sea to
Philadelphia. But Kentucky now becoming more
settled, there are better hopes of soon securing an
exact knowledge of these remarkable accumulations of
bones.—It would be superfluous to repeat the several

conjectures which have been ventured in explanation
of this heap of remains of an animal so wholly foreign
to the country. Recourse was had to inundations, remarkable changes in the climate, the earth's centre of
gravity, and the earth's axis.—The American hunters
are content to explain the death of these animals, taken
to be elephants really, by the severity of a winter
which they were not able to withstand; and in support
of their opinion they say that very often uncommonly
hard winters kill in quantities other animals ranging
in this part of the earth.*   But it is at once seen that
so local a cause cannot have worked the destruction of
these animals in the warmer climate of South America.
However, no one was happier in his conjectures on
this subject than the author ✚ of the *Essai sur l'origine
de la population de l'Amerique,* Tom. II. p. 298, who
(whether in jest or earnest is not known) regards all
these bones as nothing less than what remains of a
troop (equipped with six-pound molar-teeth?) of
fallen angels, according to his system the original inhabitants of the earth in its first and glorious state,
until for their transgressions they and their dwelling
place the earth were condemned to a common ruin,
and hereupon the remnant of the purified planet was
made fit for the reception of the present improved
race of the children of men.

I return again to the regions about Pittsburg.   In

---

* During the very hard winter of 1779-80, (among others,)
there were found dead here and there great numbers of deer
in the interior woods of America and in the mountains; often
many together, by frozen springs where in other seasons they
had been accustomed to drink or to lick salt. And during that
winter other animals and numbers of birds succumbed.

several excursions beyond the Alleghany we had occasion to observe the goodness and riotous fertility of
the soil in its original undisturbed character. The
indigenous plants had a lusty, fat appearance, and they
grow vastly stronger and to greater heights than is
their habit elsewhere. In a new-made and unmanured
· garden there stood stalks of the common sun-flower,
which were not less than 20 ft. high, measured 6 inches
in diameter, and were almost ligneous. The forests
were of chestnut, beech, sassafras, tulip-trees or pop-
lars, wild cherry, red maple, sugar-maple, black walnut, hickory and its varieties, several sorts of oak, the
sour gum, the liquid-amber or sweet-gum, and other
trees known along the coast but here growing still
finer and stronger. The forests are for the most part
quite clear of undergrowth, which is equally fortunate
for the hunter and the traveller. We were shown several trees, described as of an unknown species, which
appeared quite like the *Gleditsia triacanthos,* but had
no thorns.—Among the somewhat rarer trees are to be
reckoned the papaws,* which chiefly grow in moist,
rich, black soil, often called after them ' papaw-soil.'
They are slender trees, with a smooth, white bark, and
beautifully leaved. Their smooth, egg-shaped fruit
when over-ripe is not at all unpleasant, but by no
means to every one's taste. The fruit has an odor of
pineapples, but the bark and leaves a disagreeable
repulsive smell.

The sugar-maple is largely used by the people of
these parts, because the carriage makes the customary

---

* Annona glabra. Gron. *Virg.* p. 83. Annona fructu lutes-
cente lævi &c. Catesby II. 85?

sugar too dear for them. The tree grows more numerously here in the mountains than in the country
nearer the coast; and one sees now and again in the
woods gutters and troughs by means of which the sap
is collected. The Indians also are known to make use
of the sugar, and they boil it down on the spot. Others
prepare it for sale, at one and a half to two shillings
Pensylv. the pound. It is brown to be sure, and somewhat dirty and viscous, but by repeated refinings can
be made good and agreeable.* A domestic tea is prepared from the leaves of the Red-root (*Ceanothus
americana*), which is really not bad to drink, and may
well take its place along with the inferior sorts of
Bohea tea. Jonathan Plummer in Washington county
on the Monongahela during the war prepared himself
more than 1000 pounds of this tea, and sold it for seven
and a half to ten Pensylv. shillings the pound. His
method of preparation he kept secret; probably he
dried the leaves on or in iron-ware over a slow fire.
By better handling, more careful and cleanly, this tea
could likely be made greatly more to the taste than it
is. At the beginning of the war, what with general
prohibitions and the enthusiastic patriotism, the importing of Chinese tea was for some time rendered
difficult, and attempts were made everywhere to find
substitutes in native growths; this shrub was found
the most serviceable for the purpose and its use is still
continued in the back parts. Along the coast this
patriotic tea was less known and demanded, but it will

---

* More circumstantial accounts in this regard are to be
found in P. Kalm's description of how sugar is made in North
America from several sorts of trees. *Schwed. akad. Abhandl.*
XIII.

soon banish from many houses in the mountains the
foreign tea which is now become cheaper. The use
of tea is everywhere quite common.

Besides the elsewhere commonly known sorts of
wild American grape-vines, there is found on the lower
sandy banks of the Ohio a particular vine, of a squat,
bushy stem, which bears small, round, black, and sweet
berries, and has been observed nowhere else by me.
Ginseng and both varieties of the snake-root occur in
plenty and are industriously gathered. Of other
medicinal plants there are found the *Collinsonia,
Veronica virginica, Lobelia syphilitica, Aralia racemosa, nudicaulis, Spiræa trifoliata, Actæa racemosa,
Asclepias tuberosa, Aristolochia frutescens,* &c, and
numberless others which I have cited elsewhere in a
list of North American sanative remedies. What with
our short stay at a season already advanced, the list
of the remaining plants met with in this region would
be too uncertain and insignificant to be given place
here. We found only a few autumn plants in bloom
and those well-known; but spring and summer in the
mountains and swamps of this western country would
certainly afford a rich harvest, not only of rare plants
but of those unknown. Among other things these
forests would supply many new contributions to the
order of mushrooms, of which uncommonly large
specimens are sometimes found. I saw a white *Lyco-
perdon,* which weighed two and a quarter pounds, and
was in diameter a foot and eight inches. Extraordinarily large specimens of *Boletus parasiticus* also occur.

Fruit is still a rarity, here as well as throughout the
mountains. Near to the Fort was an orchard, planted
by the English garrison but since wholly neglected,

18

and this was the only one for perhaps a hundred miles
around.   In it were several varieties of the best-tast-
ing pears and apples.   The common reproach that
America is unable to produce as good fruit as Europe
will certainly not apply to this region.   In the woods
around there are many wild bees, and on a still, warm
evening one notices quite plainly a pleasant smell of
honey.   The hunters are accustomed to gather honey
incidentally.   The field-crops of the region are maize,
wheat, spelt, oats, buckwheat, and turnips.   With the
present trifling number of the inhabitants the worth
of their produce is not great, and the income from
lands is inconsiderable.   Mr. Ormsby, our host, owns
a tract of land along the Monongahela some miles in
length; but only 18 indolent families are settled on it,
who are required to pay a third of their harvest as
rent.   But being careless whether they raise much
more than they themselves need or whether the owner
bids them go or stay, and having so far no competitors
to fear, what they render is very insignificant.

The inhabitants of the surrounding mountain-woods
are bears, wolves, the fox, the lynx, wild cats, now and
then a red tiger (*Felis concolor, L.*) raccoons, opossums, and deer.   Elks are much rarer; and the buffalo
likewise have been frightened farther off, preferring
besides the flatter country.   Deer * are already growing scarcer in the neighborhood, but it is nothing uncommon for a man to bring down at times 10-12 in a
day.   Liberty of hunting being unrestricted, their numbers will soon become still more diminished.——It is

---

* By this I understand the 'Virginian Deer' of Pennant,
or according to Zimmermann the 'Virginian Hart.'

hardly to be believed, the number of grey and black
squirrels we saw, at this time in movement, migrating
from the frontiers towards the coast.* Failure of the
nuts and acorns, it was said, was the reason for this
migration, which brought about the death of many
thousands of these animals; for innumerable quantities
of them were shot. At Wheeling alone two lads within
three days brought down 219 of them. At our tavern
we had squirrels at every meal, baked, stewed, and in
pastries. From this migration it was prophesied at
the time that a hard winter would follow, and in reality
this was the case.—Beavers were here and there found,
also otters, minks, and ground-hogs; but I could not
be clear whether by ground-hog, here in the mountains, is understood the same as what is elsewhere in
America called ground-hog (*Arctomys Monax, Schreber*), or whether, as appears more likely, a sort of
badger is not meant. I make mention of this so that
others may be informed, on occasion, of the confusion
of names in America; for the *Arctomys Monax* is at
one time called ground-hog and again wood-chuck,
and according to Kalm † the name ground-hog is given
by others to a badger-like animal.—A smaller animal
of the mouse-species is said to keep in the woods, but
nobody has caught it or made it his business to settle
what it is.

A few Indian families, of the Delaware tribe, were
living at this time close by the Fort. Accompanied by
an officer of the garrison I visited their chief, Colonel

---

* Vid. Counsellor Schreber's *Saügthiere*, Abth. IV, 770. Of
the rarer fox-squirrels (p. 774) none was observed in these
herds.

† Kalm's *Travels*, II, 332.

Killbuck. It is well known that the Indians are very
proud of warlike titles, and take pleasure in hearing
themselves called Colonels and Captains. The Colonel,
whom we found in a dirty and ragged shirt, had the
day before returned from a long hunt, and was now
refreshing himself with drink. He spoke a broken
English, and brought out with pride a few letters
written to him by his son and his daughter, both of
whom, at the expense of the Congress, are at Princeton
for their education.—At the beginning of the war,
Colonel Killbuck, with a few families of his nation,
parted from the rest of his people, (who were generally on the side of the English), and betook himself
hither. Among all the Indians these were very nearly
the only ones who declared for the American party.—
Their whigwhams were contrived, merely for summer,
of poles and the bark of trees; they would build better,
they said, against the winter. There were about a
dozen huts. Their beds of bear-skins were spread on
the ground about the fire which in every case was burning in the middle. The flesh-pot is never taken from
the fire except to be emptied and again filled, for they
are always eating and are bound by no fixed times.
The walls of all the huts were hung with bones, corn-
stalks, and dried venison, which forms especially their
maintenance. One of their more important men was
Captain Whiteye; who was strutting about wrapped in
a checkered blanket, with rings in his nose and his
ears, and sumptuously adorned with colored streaks
down his face; for, along with one Montresor, a
quarter-blood Indian, he had this morning had an
audience with the commanding officer. General Irwin
had several times, and again today, given them to un-

derstand that they could leave the Fort if they desired, peace now being declared and their presence in several ways being burdensome; but they seemed not at all inclined to go, apprehending perhaps not the most friendly reception among their people.—A young, well-formed, copper-brown, squaw was beating maize in a wooden trough before one of the huts: her entire costume consisted of a tight petticoat of blue cloth hardly reaching to the knees, and without any ruffles; her straight black hair hung loose over the shoulders, her cheeks and forehead nicely dawbed in red. She seemed very well content with the society of her co-adjutor, a brisk young fellow who except for two rags appropriately disposed was quite as naked as the ingenuous beauty. Other women were occupied in pleating baskets, shelling corn, or in some such way, for as is well known, the men give themselves no concern about domestic affairs. The surplus of their crops, their baskets, and straw-pleated works they exchanged for whiskey. There were several by no means ugly faces among them, and their color is not of a uniform brownish-yellow.—Mistress Grenadier, an Indian woman lives in a house of her own, built after the European manner, in the orchard of the Fort. She is no longer young, but still shows the traces of a faded beauty which formerly elevated her to the companionship of an English, and later of an American General. Her daughter, with all the advantages of youth, is not so attractive as her mother. By trade with the Indians she has become rich, and still prepares for sale moccasons (shoes of buffalo-leather) and sundry beautiful articles made of colored straw.

The Indians are generally hated here quite as much

as they are pretty well throughout America. But this
hate does not always spring from the same reasons,
much less from those altogether just.——It is beginning
to be extensively and learnedly posited that none of the
Indian tribes, as many of them as are still scattered
throughout the whole of broad America, have the remotest right to the land wherein they and their fore-
fathers for unthinkable ages have lived. I have seen a
few outgivings on this subject in the *United States
Magazine* ✚ which sound strange enough. For example,
" The whole earth is given to man, and all the children
" of Adam have an equal right in it, and to equal parts
" of it." The right of earlier possession and of heredi-
tary possession is accounted non-sense, ✚ and after all
manner of digressions, the main proof continues, " that
" the revealed law has given the earth to man under
" the fixed condition that he use it in the sweat of his
" brow. Now the Indians do not use their extensive
" woods in the sweat of their brow, but only hunt
" there. Therefore it is plain as day that they have no
" right to the land and it is permissible to drive them
" out at will. For it would be as ludicrous to seek to
" buy the land of the buffalo and deer which inhabit
" the American wilds as of the roving Indians ; for if
" wandering about in the forest gave a title to it, the
" buffalo and deer would have as good a one as these
" Indian nations." On the same page the philanthropic
author admits that a German who finds along the
thickly settled Rhine no bit of free land for himself
and his family, following the natural law may sure
enough, in the less populous Pensylvania, justly demand an allotment of land for nothing ; but at the same
time he discreetly mentions that nobody would give

him the land. Because, says he, for the common peace
and the security of property, general laws are preferred
by states, according to which one man may possess an
acre of land, or none at all, and another may own
thousands without being set at defiance because the
property is unequally shared.

But are there not similarly accepted laws as between nation and nation, ancient and sacred laws, regardless of complexion or faith? Is not that reasonable for one which is right for another? Is not the
reproach, that he fails to cultivate large possessions,
to be brought against the citizen of the United States
as well as against the Indian, and no question raised
as to title? In his bitterness against the poor Indians the same author continues: " They are devils in
" the guise of men; without truth and without faith;
" to be won by no kindness; breakers of promises;
" barbarous in war, &c."—Mere abuse, which touches
others besides the original inhabitants of America.
He lets fall this judgment however: " These nations
" are so far degenerated from humanity, so insus-
" ceptible of every magnanimous feeling, so extrava-
" gant in all their boundless passions, so faithless, so
" incapable of civilization, that for the good order and
" well-being of the world it is dangerous to allow them
" to dwell in it longer."—The author is loud in his
professions that it would give him pleasure to know
that the whole race was exterminated—but with singular mildness he contents himself with proposing:
" that instead of making treaties of peace with them,
" and thus tacitly granting them the rights of nations
" and of property, they should without ceremony be
" compelled to give up the land of their fathers, to

" withdraw into the cold regions of the North, and
" never again show themselves below the sources of
" the streams falling into the Mississippi and the Ohio
" —there should they languish and decay." Who would
expect to hear so unrighteous a judgment, put forward so unashamed by a citizen of the states, only now
become free, regarding thousands of his fellow-men?

That the Indians are not so entirely incapable of all
betterment is proved by the efforts, not fruitless, of the
Moravian Brethren on the Muskingum, and by those
of the French and Spanish missionaries in Canada and
in Florida. But without the influence of religion it
often happens that from other motives Indian families
here and there come to live in the neighborhood of
Europeans and to concern themselves less with hunting, which had been their custom from their unstable
and unsocial manner of life.

Thus there are living now as citizens on Nantucket
the descendants of the Indians of those parts who, like
the white islanders, support themselves by whale-fish-
ing. Divers families are scattered along the coast of
Massachusetts; and but a short time since other
families were living on Long Island, quietly and harmless, by what they made from their corn-fields, by fishing and by the sale of baskets. That was the case in
several other provinces besides, where for the fish and
clams they for a long time kept to the coasts and
streams, until the numbers of the European colonists
constantly increasing drove them out and they were
obliged to withdraw to the interior. It is however true
that even where they were content to live quietly and
peaceably in European neighborhoods, they never
showed an inclination to adopt the customs, way of

life, or modes of livelihood of their neighbors.
Whether there was lacking in them a natural spirit
of imitation and ability to discriminate between better
and worse, or whether they were restrained by the
peculiar pride which they possess in no small degree,
I will not attempt to say. Whatever the reason, they
sought everywhere to maintain their independence in
all ways, and so fled from every closer bond of association with Europeans, so soon as they began to fear
the slightest inconvenience or restraint.—But with all
their unpliableness, their moral character is not so
black as it is painted in America; and it appears that
native Europeans who have had opportunity to know
them intimately are willing to do them more justice in
this regard than Americans born, who on all occasions
manifest for them an inherited and bitter hatred.
They possess and practice virtues for which, in their
meagre language, they themselves have no name. They
are hospitable and courteous and show respect for
every man who conducts himself conformably in their
regard; they are grateful and sensible, and if they seem
not to be so, it is merely because they set a worth different from ours on complaisances and gifts; they are
stedfast and trustworthy friends and are true to their
promises. It would not be difficult to support all that
has been said by examples, if I cared to assemble anecdotes. They can hardly be reproached with ever having broken treaties voluntarily and unprovoked, at
least in no way less conscienceless than what is customary with other and civilized nations. But once
aroused, their desire for vengeance and blood knows
no bounds, until they believe themselves indemnified
for wrong suffered.

Their wars are fierce and barbarous; and on this ground, among others, it is sought on the one hand to excuse the general bitterness against them, on the other to disseminate and maintain it, the true reason being only envy and greed of the lands still in their possession. Their unmanly and dastardly way of making war is fulminated against in America, but as against European foes, (as is well enough known from the history of the last war), every Indian device was allowed and made use of.—It is called inhuman if the Indians, without discrimination, murder the able-bodied man, his wife, innocent children and still more innocent cattle; but a similar vengeance is practiced against the families of Indians; their dwellings are burned and their lands devastated; so that by Christian example the horrors of their wars are justified. All the faithlessness, cunning, deception and treachery, suspicion and ardor of vengeance which are pictured in high colors as the marks of the Indian character, will certainly appear in milder light to every unprejudiced person if there is taken into the account all the wrong which they on their side have suffered, all the blood which has been shed among them, all that liberty and ease which they have lost through the European colonists, all the territory from which they have been driven, and the consuming maladies which have been introduced among them. They hold carefully the remembrance of all the oppressions and deception, of all the numberless instances of trickery practiced against them and blood shed by the Europeans among them, treasuring it up as a warning for their descendants who may thereby demand vengeance for past encroachments and be on their guard against future.—

But it is neither my intention nor my right to speak for the Indians. I leave this willingly to those who go about among them intimately and know that they, like all other nations, are supported by natural, by prescriptive, and by fancied rights; are proud in their conceptions of their privileges, and direct accordingly their dealings and their behavior.

There are, however, Europeans who are greatly attached to the rude way of life among the Indians. One of the inhabitants of Pittsburg at this time was in his youth taken captive by them, and lived with them for some years; and the pleasure he took in their customs and their careless and idle life got so strong a hold upon him that after he had been released, with other captives, he returned to them again secretly, and had to be brought away a second time by his relations. There are many examples of such captives who did not care to be released; and also of Europeans who of their own accord live among them, exchanging without regret all the advantages of civilized society and convenience of life for the unrestricted freedom which is the Indians' highest good.

Of the former works of the Indians, remains are still here and there to be found, which give evidence of great patience and often of no common inventive powers, when it is considered that they lacked tools and what they had were insufficient. General Irwin possessed a tobacco-pipe made of a soft, blackish kind of stone;* it had a curved stem, with mouth-piece,

---

* "Near the Marble river is a mountain whence the Indians "fetch a red stone which they use in the fabrication of their "tobacco-bowls. There is found in that region also a black,

perhaps six inches long, the whole made together.
Although this had no ornament as is sometimes the
case, the work was rather neat and the boring of the
curved stem must have cost no little time and skill.
The Indians who had presented this pipe to the General, set a high value on it, and declared it to be very,
very old. There are found also, but rarely, little
figures, porringers, and other utensils of the same
material, which if not tasteful are always laboriously
made. The Indians no longer concern themselves
with the fabrication of such things; getting all their
little needs from Europeans, this branch of industry
has become quite extinct among them.

Of the medical knowledge of the Indians the opinion
here and there in America is still very high.* The
greater number, but not the well-informed, are convinced that the Indians, mysteriously skilled in many
excellent remedies, carefully and jealously conceal
them from the white Europeans. As always so here,
people are deceived by the fancy that behind a veil of
mystery there lie hidden great and powerful things.
I see no reason to expect anything extraordinary or

"hard clay, or rather stone, from which the Naudowessies
"make their household utensils." Carver.

The bowl seen by me looked and felt like steatite. Mr.
Kirwan supposes that the white and yellow Terre à Chalumeau
of Canada is a sort of meerschaum.

* This ungrounded but ancient misconception Dr. Benjamin
Rush of Philadelphia some time ago undertook to combat.
See his *Oration delivered February 4, 1774, before the Ameri-
can Philosophical Society, containing an Enquiry into the
Natural history of Medicine among the Indians in North
America.*—A translation of this readable essay is to be found
in *Samml. auserles. Abhandl. für praktische Aertzte,* IV, 267.

important, and I am almost certain that with the passage of time nothing will be brought to light, if as is the case, outright specifics are looked for and presumably infallible remedies. I do not therefore deny in any way that we must thank the northern half of America for sundry medicaments of value, and I apprehend as well that every new remedy must be to the patriotic American physican a treasured contribution to his domestic medical store. Most of the diseases for the healing of which the skill of the Indians is especially praised are simple, those in which nature may work actively and effect the most salutary changes. The variety of diseases among the Indians is not great and is confined chiefly to fevers and superficial injuries. The observers and panegyrists of the so much belauded Indian methods of therapy are commonly ignorant people who find things and circumstances wonderful because they cannot offer explanations from general principles. The bodily constitution of an Indian, hardened from youth by vehement exercise and by many difficult feats, demands and bears stronger medical excitants; and endowed originally with more elasticity, the physical system of an Indian often rids itself of a malady more promptly than that of a European, weaker and softer, is able to do. Their weaklings succumb in early youth, and those who survive all the hardships of a careless bringing-up owe it to their better constitution. The medicines of which they make use are few and simple, potent naturally or through the heaviness of the dose. A mild repeated purgative the Indian knows nothing of, and with him the effect must continue at least a day or maybe two days without stop. The most of their praised specifics are purgatives, perspiratives, or urine-stimulants, which they use not sparingly at the first approach of disease, and in this way often check the progress of the malady. But success does not always attend the treatment. Certainly, cases enough occur where the prescription is agreeable to the malady, and great benefit is suddenly experienced. Such instances are then noised abroad until the story of one and the same case becomes so varied and magnified that it is regarded as a daily and hourly occurrence, proof of the medical skill of the Indians, and so the craving after their mysteries is continually renewed and maintained. On the other hand it is not remarked how many Indians fall unhappy sacrifices to their over-praised methods of cure. It is not observed that inflammatory fevers, small-pox, and other violent diseases ravage unspeakably among them, because their received methods can effect nothing in such cases, more than chance being necessary in the treatment. It is not observed how most of their chronic patients leave the world as a result of carelessness and unskilful handling. The Indian, when he falls ill, has recourse first to his roots and sacredly regarded herbs; he purges and sweats inordinately; fasts for days together; leaps into cold water, and submits to conjurings. Should he conquer his disease by arousing another—well and good, the medicines have done it. But should these first general means prove in vain, he knows not what to do further, uses promiscuously what strikes his fancy, and chance not being favorable to him, gives himself up to despair and his destiny.—And what should lead us to think that a people as rude as the Indians, so heedless and without foresight, could be more fortunate in the dis-

covery of specifics and more successful in applying
them than nations which by their united efforts and
assembled experiments have not yet learned how to
work wonders? Or why are we to believe that the
American soil is more beneficent than the rest of the
earth in the bringing forth of specific means? The
Indian lives truer to nature, if living wild and un-
constrained may be so called. His way of life subjects
him to a number of miseries; he suffers alternately
the extremes of hunger and fullness, cold and heat,
activity and relaxation, all which must work in his
body powerful and mischievous changes. Is he exposed to fewer diseases merely because he has less
knowledge and skill in the treatment of them?—Civilized nations live softer and more meticulously, and
bring upon themselves a greater number of maladies.
But also are they not able to remove or alleviate a
greater number of maladies, and to prolong the lives
of weaklings, who elsewhere perish?—But however
true these things are, and however grounded the
charge that the Indians jealously keep secret their
specific and wonder-working remedies, the burden of
accusation is in some measure lessened by their gen-
erous readiness to produce without reward their manifold roots, barks, and herbs for the behoof of those
needing aid, even if they do not indicate whence they
got them. They show at least no selfish and mer-
cenary views, which are the commonest motives among
the no less numerous mystery-usurers of more civilized
and enlightened nations. A speaking example of this
has been just now afforded in Pensylvania and adjacent parts by a certain Martin, who boasted of possess-
ing an all-powerful but secret cure for cancer. This

aroused the credulity and won the confidence of his
people so much the more because of the clever pretext that the discovery of the root (according to him
the medicine came from a root) had been communi-
cated to him in confidence by an old Indian at Pittsburg.   Although shrewd and impartial physicians at
Philadelphia found good reason to doubt the highly
praised worth of the remedy in genuine cases of cancer, the incredible number of imaginary or pretended
cases of the disease, news of which came in from all
parts, was astonishing.   Never before had so much
been heard of this malady.   But it was certain that
fear and prepossession caused the anxious patient to
fancy every obstinate or rooted impostume must be
cancerous, and it was to be expected of the purveyor
of the famous remedy that he, for his advantage,
should claim everything to be cancer and thus multi-
ply his cures.   However it was by no means clearly made
out that the medicine used by him was in reality taken
from nothing but a root.   But he sought to spread
abroad this belief, and almost every year made a
journey to Pittsburg pretending to dig his mysterious
root there from a particular hill on the Monongahela.
Since I had come from Philadelphia, the attempt was
made to search out this root for me, and I was shown
the region whence it was believed he got the root;
I found there in great quantity the *Sanguinaria cana-*
densis (blood-root) and the *Ranunculus sceleratus L.*
Both roots have corrosive properties, and from many
other circumstances too numerous to mention, it is
highly probable that Martin made use of one or the
other, if only to conceal other and more powerful constituents mixed in, for it was supposed that he added

arsenic to his medicine.*   Both plants are very common in other parts of America, and the blood-root is here and there used as a remedy for warts and in cleansing slight sores.—It is to be wished that the physicians in America, who have already in other matters, shown their patriotism in many noble efforts, may also have a patriotic eye to the completer knowledge and more general use of their native materia medica.   It betrays an unpardonable indifference to their fatherland to see them making use almost wholly of foreign medicines, with which in large measure they might easily dispense, if they were willing to give their attention to home-products, informing themselves more exactly of the properties and uses of the stock of domestic medicines already known.   They would then have the pleasure of showing their fellow-citizens how unreasonable it is to envy the poor Indians their reputed science, and they would be working usefully for the community and beneficently for the poor if they made it their business to further the employment of the manifold wealth afforded by nature in its precious gifts to them.

---

* After Martin's death, in 1784, Dr. Rush discovered & published in the second volume of the *Transact. of the Amer. Philos. Society,* that his cancer-powder consisted of white arsenic and a plant ingredient.

19

Return from Pittsburg

We had now spent seven days at Pittsburg, had industriously examined the country around and collected all seeds and plants that came to our notice.* I should not fail to mention the courtesies and assistance rendered us by the officers of the garrison; and I must especially acknowledge our obligations to the Commander of the Fort, General Irwin, ✚ and to Colonel Bayard. We returned this afternoon, September 13, to Turkey Creek Settlement. One of the old inhabitants there assured us that he had often made the following experiment. If in the middle of summer the water of Turkey Creek or, as he says, that of most of the other mountain streams, is whipped and beaten with a stick, and then if a fire-brand is passed over, a mist is enkindled and a faint evanescent flame runs over the entire width of the brook. But the experiment did not succeed when I was by, and I do not know through what chance the observation was occasioned. If it is true, it may be that the abundant pit-coals in the mountains, or the petroleum here and

---

* But it was labor lost. We committed two chests full of stones. plants, seeds &c to waggoners who promised to deliver them within a fortnight at Baltimore, whither they were bound. Not until after fourteen months did these boxes reach Baltimore, and then plundered of everything which seemed of importance to the conveyers, and the rest disordered and marred.

there found, had the greatest share in this phenomenon.*

Hard and continuous rains and a bad road delayed our journey; and the halt in these woods was all the more dismal and tedious, since returning we were obliged to follow the same road as we had come.— There was already heavy hoar-frost almost every night in the mountains—Wolves and bears had within a few days done much damage in these parts among the calves, sheep, and hogs, which are let run night and day regardless in the woods. As little thought is taken to protect these animals against danger by keeping them in stalls as the people themselves give to warding off thieves. Nowhere are doors barred for the safety of those sleeping within; for in these patriarchal regions where the general poverty does not yet compensate the trouble of stealing, few thieves so far find a support.

Dr. Peters, already mentioned above, we found on our return at home. He boasted that he had on his book for a year's praxis almost 200 Pd. Pensylv. Current, but unfortunately cannot collect any money from the people, that being a scarce article in the mountains, and he has no use for what they bring in kind. He makes a charge of two Spanish dollars for inocula-

---

* It was not known to me until later that Dr. Franklin had made the same remark in accounts given by him of swampy brooks in Jersey and elsewhere, and that this phenomenon shows itself in a good many slimey streams where *combustible effluvium, or marsh-air,* is contained in the water, that being the material cause. Several examples of this sort are given in Fried. Knoll's entertaining *Naturwunder;* See, his chapter *Entzündbares Gewässer oder lustige Feuersbrünste auf Quellen und Flüssen.* ✚

tions. How much of an apothecary he is, I know not, but he had neither whiskey nor bitters in store. He would hear nothing of pay for the breakfast we and our horses had had, and was so gracious as to heal in a masterly way our vehicle which had suffered from the ailments of the road.——With much difficulty we came this time over the rocky and boggy Laurel-hill. The extraordinary heat of the day oppressed us, and along the whole road, 14 dreary miles, there are only two places where water is to be had, and we had the ill luck not to find them. On the other side of the Laurel-hill, in the Glades so-called, we accidentally got out of the direct road, as night was already beginning to fall, and the road we were following led us into a narrow, level valley. Two lads who met us assured us, with a friendlier manner than that customary here, that we should be welcome in their father's house which was near by. When we reached the place, there appeared Mr. Herrman Husband, (for this was the name of the strange màn), barefoot and dressed in worn and dirty clothes. The reception was courteous, with no waste of words and with no impertinent questions—almost the American habit. I should have been rather perplexed how to volunteer our history had not Mistress Husband, while she was making ready the coffee for supper, shown somewhat more of a natural curiosity. Suddenly, as we sat about the fire, the talk fell on the mountains, their valleys, inhabitants, soil and the like, and I was astounded to hear our host, until then sitting still and reflective, all at once begin speaking with enthusiasm, judiciously and not wholly without learning. So far I had met no one, not even among those citizens of the United

States better housed and clad, who appeared to have
given so much attention to the mountains. However,
Mr. Husband was over-interested in the regularity
and straight line of the Alleghany which he compared
to a solid wall, reckoning off-hand that the foot-hills
of the mountains signified neither more nor less than
the little inequalities made by the protruding stones
of a wall. He estimated the width of the Alleghany
as from the foot of the Dry Ridge or Willis's Mountain to the western foot of the Chesnut Ridge, (thus
including the Laurel-hill), counting this one single
mountain-wall, and hence some 80 miles in breadth.
Then taking the one, two, and three-mile jutties as so
many eightieth parts of the whole, he compared them
to the projecting stone-points of a wall, say four feet
in thickness, and found that the apparently formless
off-shoots from the chief mountain wall are merely to
be regarded in relation as so many jutting stone-points,
of half an inch or more, in a wall of the thickness
mentioned, and therefore are quite insignificant. I
could at the moment make nothing of this vindicatory
estimate. He then spoke much of Woodward's and
Burnet's ✚ systems, of the central fire and other igne-
ous and ætherial hypotheses, and his talk became continually more astonishing. But among many just and
reasonable observations he made, it was plain that his
ideas as a whole turned about an axis and were directed
towards a main object which I could not by questioning discover. He mentioned that he had travelled
more than 400 miles along the Alleghany southwards,
and would within a brief space undertake a similar
journey, in which he most courteously invited me to
join him. I enquired what was the purpose of this

journey. " To complete a chart of the mountains,"
was his answer. I asked if I might see his sketches
for such a map. He promised I might examine them
the following morning. I could hardly wait for the
morning, and rejoiced at the chance which had brought
me to the acquaintance of this singular man. I
eagerly reminded him of his promise, and he drew
forth from the bed dusty papers, spreading them out
before him in a hesitating manner. The course of the
Alleghany through Pensylvania and Virginia was
pretty exactly set down; but not without surprise I
saw that he had continued this chain of mountains
northwards beyond the Hudson, then westwards below
Hudson's Bay nearly to the Pacific Sea, and thence to
the west of the Mississippi to and through Louisiana
and Mexico, and finally had sketched in still another
chain through Florida and Georgia making with the
first a complete quadrangle, through which the Ohio
and the Mississippi spread their numerous branches.

Upon my question what warranted him in making
the mountains of the northern half of America run a
quadrangular course, I received the very unexpected
answer:—" Not I but the Prophet Ezekiel so set
" down the walls of the New Jerusalem,"—and immediately he began, step by step and mile by mile, to
expound how the Prophet Ezekiel has delineated with
the utmost exactness the geography of America and
its future states. Now I knew my man, and his
allusions of the day before to walls, masonry, and
gates were no longer a mystery, the subject of his
extravagances being in this manner revealed. All
further objections and questions were in vain, for I
was continually referred to Ezekiel the Prophet. With

this as basis he had placed the new Jerusalem within
the four great mountain-walls, and indicated in fair
quadrature the twelve tribes which according to him
and the Prophet were to be the ruling nations of this
part of the world. But Ezekiel has measured space
for only twelve tribes, and the United States are
thirteen, I objected. Herrman Husband was in no
way perplexed at this question: for the United States,
said he, have nothing to do with the New Jerusalem,
which will form a kingdom to itself and will bring
into vassalage all provinces and peoples from the
Alleghany, or the eastern wall, to the Atlantic Ocean.
—Fortunate it is for the Congress and the entire
thirteen United States that they know nothing as yet
of Herrman's and Ezekiel's prophecies, and careless of
the subjugation threatening them, live on tranquilly
in the sweet, giddy pleasure of their new-won freedom,
and will so continue long to live. On his chart Herrman had christened the several regions of the future
kingdom with Ezekiel's names. The Mexican Bay,
stood there as the Waters of Contention, the Gulf of
St. Lawrence and the New England Coasts as the fish-
stocked waters of Engaddi unto Enghain, &c.—So
wholly was he absorbed in the glory of this future
kingdom that it was quite impossible for him to admit
a reasonable thought, so long as the chart lay on the
table, and had I not interrupted he would have read
me his descriptions and explanations. But Ezekiel
out of the way, Mr. Husband was again master of his
thoughts. The loneliness of his mountain sojourning-
place, lively powers of imagination, and a certain degree of erudition had doubtless given the man this
singular humor, who besides was naturally of a rest-

less and enterprising spirit. He lived formerly in
North Carolina, where he played a considerable part in
a company of men who shortly before the outbreak of
the war drew much attention to themselves and caused
great disturbance. They called themselves Regulators, ✚ and had undertaken nothing less than to demand
a reckoning of the Governor of the province, at that
time General Tryon, in the item of certain imposts and
the use made of them, intending also to abolish other
ordinances which they believed to be unlawful and
arbitrary. Whether it is true, I cannot say, but I have
heard several persons declare these Regulators became an unlucky sacrifice to their reasonable, if blus-
tering, opposition to the oppression which threatened
them, laying themselves open to persecution. Their
complaints and grievances did not prevail, their purposes were falsely represented, and they were treated
with the utmost severity. The war coming on, however, many of them are said to have remained worthy
and zealous friends to the royal government. At the
time, Husband could only escape through precipitous
flight the punishment in store for him. He betook
himself hither into the mountains, where under a
changed name and wearing strange clothing, he contrived to avoid further persecution, until the general
war breaking out assured him peace. Instead of
matters of state he concerns himself now with prophecies, of which several have appeared in Goddard's
Maryland Calendar under the name Hutrim Hutrim,
or the Philosopher of the Alleghany. In one of these
he had calculated the time of his death, but has already
lived some years beyond the term. He is a Quaker,
and was occupied with iron-works in the mountainous

part of North Carolina. He told me of solid iron,
which admits of cutting, found (but rarely) in North
Carolina.

We found the road pretty good through the remainder of the Glades until in the evening we came to
Marshall, the smith's, at the foot of the Alleghany.
Our horses needed shoeing. But we were obliged to
be patient spectators until he had leisurely devoured
his meal; we gained nothing by asking him in a
friendly way to help us on, since the night and a bad
road lay before us. He was an American-German
gentleman!

In these Glades, described above, in reality a broken,
elevated valley between the Alleghany and the Laurel-
hill, all sorts of grain are cultivated. Maize, however,
does not everywhere come to complete maturity, and
the people are accustomed to plant only so much of
the commonest sort as they count on eating green.
When the maize has just formed its 'ears', and the
grain is still soft and full of sap, the Americans hold
it to be a delicacy; the ears are boiled or baked in the
ashes, and eaten with salt and butter, and in the towns
cried for sale as 'hot corn.' But in this valley there
is a variety of early corn which developes smaller indeed, but does better. Much summer wheat is sowed.
Winter wheat must be got into the ground very early,
the end of August or about the first of September.
When we first came over the road we saw wheat just
sowing at a certain place, and after 14 days, on our
return, it was already several inches out of the ground.
A light hoar-frost is observed in the Glades during the
summer, once or twice in almost every month; this
summer more than formerly.—The inhabitants know

little of sickness. But they, (as others of their countrymen and from the same cause), are very subject to
rheumatick complaints; letting their horses and cattle
run in the woods at night, according to the general
custom, in the morning if they wish to use them they
must often go far to find them through dewy grass
and wet bush, and thinly clad besides. There are coals
and limestone in this valley, but no traces of petrifactions in the limestone.—The *Helianthus tuberosus* is
here and there grown in gardens and from it a tolerably good thin beer is brewed, and a syrup also is
boiled. Of fruit-trees there were few to be seen, and
as little industry observed in the item of gardening—
In the woods along the road we remarked no trees
conspicuously distinct from those of the lower parts
of the country towards the coast.

From the Glades the ascent is by no means steep to
the ridge of the Alleghany; only four miles from
Marshall's to the opposite foot of the mountain, along
which runs a branch of the Juniata, and following this
it is three miles more, a level road mostly, to the first
cabin. Crossing the Alleghany we found nothing but
sand-stones, (grind-stones, whet-stones, cos), whitish
intermixed with red, grey, reddish, and blackish; the
last named variety shows something of a fine mica, but
the others none of it or much less. The loose stones
lie as plates, half an inch to four inches thick, along
the road, or stick up out of the mould-earth. On one
of these plates I found the impression of a cockle
scallop; but these must be very rare for notwithstanding all my searching and turning over of stones I
could find no other along the road; they are perhaps
to be found more numerously only in particular spots.

—We reached the cabin mentioned towards sunset. As before, there was nothing to be had. It was 13 miles to the next house, and we concluded to await the rise of the moon which would appear about midnight. It began to rain and there was much thunder, and lying on hard deal-boards we had to go hungry through the night, man and horse, and hungry keep on over the Dry Ridge which now appeared to us doubly dry and barren. The remark above-made was again confirmed, the nearer we approached the east side of the mountains. That is to say, on this side the Alleghany one misses the more general prospect of black and rich soil which distinguishes the regions beyond. We breakfasted with a Bonnet, four miles from Bedford; he was of French origin, made bad coffee, had odorous butter, but read to us from a French grammaire, and brought out Welleri Opus Mago-Caballisticum which he believed to contain much hidden wisdom if it could be understood; I referred him to Herrman Husband for enlightenment. In the afternoon we came again with pleasure to the little town of Bedford.

As ore-bearing spots in the neighboring mountains there were mentioned among others the following:

Sinking Valley, much lead ore, which is said to contain by test one and three quarter ounces silver in the hundredweight.

Colonel Chiswell's Mine, on the Virginia boundary in Augusta County on Hosset's River; a lead mine which has been known some 20-30 years.

Dennis's Creek, alum schist, which the people use for dyeing and tanning.

On the Conemaugh copperas is found; and there is said to be a salt-spring nearby.

they feel none of the oppression of a cringing poverty
and have no anxiety as to a maintenance. They seem
content and gratify themselves and others by the
cleanliness which prevails in their insignificant dwellings as well as by their simple dress and behavior.

Here and there old Indian tombs are found in these
mountains. These are merely large heaps of stones,
which have arisen through the friendly casting-on of
a stone by each Indian passing by.

We spent the night at a Mr. Elliott's an agreeable
man, not without good sense. He had made many
journeys deep into the western country and told as an
eye-witness, how there are found there ancient graves
and ditch-works, often comprising an acre of land.
These are at times rectangular, at times oval, their
high, steep bulwarks still plainly enough visible. The
Indians of those regions know nothing whatever of
who made them, their uses, or age.

Not many years ago a saga of Welch Indians ✚ was
spread abroad by certain Canadian travellers. They
claimed to have found in the extreme western parts
of North America Indian families speaking Welch or
Old British, and having a knowledge of the Bible.*

---

* Similar reports appeared very recently in the London
Chronicle, by which they were taken from a Connecticut
journal: "that the American General Parsons had discovered
in the western country remains of buildings and fortifications
of brick and stone, which prove that these regions must have
been once settled by civilized nations, or visited by them
before the discovery of Columbus. In the same sheet it is
further mentioned that a Mr. Adair who has lived long among
the Indians and is familiar with their language, cites many
words and forms of speech, particularly the names of their
gods, which must be Hebraic. But it is still more remarkable

These accounts were repeatedly published in English magazines, and the possible roads and opportunities already indicated how these people could arrive thither out of Britain, before the truth of the story was yet established, which at the present time is regarded doubtfully and with reason.

From Elliott's, six miles this side Bedford, it is eight miles to the Crossings, the road between steep mountain sides which seem only to open to let the Juniata through; then over the Alequippe, a high, precipitous wall, and thence four miles along a narrow ridge or foot-hill overlaid with red whet-stone. On both sides of this projecting foot-hill flows the Juniata, and turns about the point (at Colonel Martin's) in such a way that on one side the direction of the stream is opposite to that on the other; and at one place three miles from the Crossings, where the distance across the ridge is only half a mile, the river may be seen flowing in both directions. We continued the way we had come, over Crossing-hill, Rays-hill, and Sideling-hill, and spent the night at MacDonald's tavern, where the coffee is drunk out of tin-ware, there are potatoes to eat, and straw to sleep upon, and a prodigiously dear reckoning.

Here we were introduced to still another domestic tea-plant, a variety of Solidago.* The leaves were

---

what the President of Yale College, in Connecticut, relates in an address recently printed. That is, an inscription on a rock at Narraganset in New England, having long been matter of observation; was during the last war copied and sent to an Academy in France by which the characters were pronounced Phœnician." *Sit fides penes auctorem.*

SOLIDAGO suaveolens; foliis lanceolato-linearibus, integerrimis, acutis, subquinquenerviis, punctatis, glabris, tener-

gathered and dried over a slow fire. It was said that around Fort Littleton many 100 pounds of this Bohea-tea, as they call it, had been made as long as the Chinese was scarcer. Our hostess praised its good taste, but this was not conspicuous in what she brewed.

In order to visit the Warm Springs, so famous in America, I parted here with Mr. Hairs, my travelling-companion, and rode quite alone from MacDonald's to Waller's on Licking Creek, and over Scrub Ridge to the Cove, which I have already mentioned above. There are here a few, but very weak and insignificant salt-licks at the eastern foot of Sideling-hill, and farther to the east not a trace of them. Licking Creek gets its name thus. These 'licks' appear only as faint, standing ponds, which in warm weather evapo-rate and leave somewhat of a salt-deposit. The soil where they are found is said to be mostly a blueish sort of clay. Something similar was mentioned to me by Herrman Husband. He described salt-rock, as a grey-black species of stone which according to him is found wherever there are salt-springs and is every-where the same.

The road to the Cove led over hilly and mean pine-land. The Great Cove has the Blue Mountain to the east, the Tuscarora to the north, the Scrub Ridge on the west, and lies between these mountains 16 miles long and 1-3 miles broad.

---

rime ciliatis.—Virga aurea americana, tarraconis facie & sapore, panicula speciosissima. *Pluk. alm.,* [Plukenet, Alma-gestum], p. 389. tab. 116. f. 6.—A species similar to this grows about New York, and has a pleasant odor of anise, noticeable also in the plant here, but weaker; no doubt because it was already late in the season and it had suffered from the cold.

It is mostly Irish families who live here, and a few Germans at the northern end. The land in the deeper hollows and along Cove Creek is good, and bears all the crops customary here. But this season the maize had suffered from the cold. Particularly spelt is much raised hereabouts, and is said to yield commonly 30 bushels for one, which is vastly more than their wheat does. Their spelt is used solely as feed for horses, for which purpose, unthreshed, it is certainly better than oats. Also, at the first cultivation of fresh rich land it is used in preference to wheat which on new land grows too much to straw. The people believe that spelt does not make as good or as white flour as wheat, but the reason is the lack of the requisite shelling-mills.

Now past the middle of September the leaves of most of the trees and shrubs were beginning to fall, and those still remaining on the trees have exchanged all their summer-green for divers other colors. I scarcely know more richly colored landscapes than the American in their autumn attire. Of the multifarious growths, some change hue earlier, others later, purple, scarlet, pale-red, yellow, and brown through all their shades. In among them berries and fruits of all manner of tints make parade, and the indescribable number of different species of aster and solidago, at this time in full bloom, helps to embellish the splendid coloring of this autumnal picture.

The entrance into the Cove is not so much by highways as narrow 'bridle-roads.' In the Valley itself they use, however, little wagons for farming purposes furnished only with block-wheels, and these every farmer can make for himself without great trouble by

20

sawing disks out of fairly round timber-trees, and
boring a hole in the middle for the axle.   To the south
the Cove is bordered by Canalaway Settlement whither
a pretended silver mine drew me out of my way.   Two
miles from Canalaway Creek, near Stillwell's, was the
place where the work was carrying on.   In the east
side of a hill they had sunk a shaft six fathom deep
which was already drowned out and they were at this
time engaged in drawing off the water through a deep
ditch, which cuts through a heavy bed of coarse, black
slate, containing spath-veins and flecks of marcasite.
The real promoter of this work, one Christopher Brandon, was absent; the owner of the land, Robertson, a
smith, who foots the cost, seemed a good deal vexed
at the continued failure of the ingots Brandon had
been a long time promising him.   Six men were working there.   They brought me some spath-crystals which
they called amber because, warmed or rubbed, they
said straws were attracted to them, but the experiment
did not succeed with me.   This spar crackles in the
fire, but does not burn to gypsum, and seems rather
to be a talky spar or cauk.   Here and there on the
surface of the hill there lay a sort of weathered, soluble
spar in the form of a hardened powder; this they
called, on Brandon's authority, **the leader**, and on it
grounded all their hope of finding silver.   The hill
runs from north-east to south-west, and consists of
the blue limestone breaking in thick scales.   Over both
slate and limestone there is a thick stratum of iron
ore which at one time was soft, for iron tree-roots are
dug out of it; that it to say, where this iron-ore in its
soft state had permeated such tree-roots, hardened
about them, and, after the roots had rotted, filled up

the space. A strong vein of iron crosses the slate from north-east to south-west, in which are found large, white marcasite-nodules and white quartz. With continued dry weather the slate shows a partly white, partly green mould (copperas and alum), and the water rising out of it has a strong vitriolic taste. The people who were digging there knew nothing of what sort of ore they expected; they wanted silver straightway, and appeared very well content with the shimmering look of the marcasite. I alarmed them with my conjecture that they would likely be digging long and deep for silver in vain, and that perhaps, if the slate does not lie too flat on the limestone, they might find coals.

Canalaway Settlement has existed only 25 years, and is already fairly populous. Most of the inhabitants of this district are Irish families who almost everywhere are indolent and unsystematic farmers. One can imagine that they must farm scurvily when they are blamed even in America, where in general agriculture is not carried on to the best advantage. They cultivate their land until it is quite exhausted, and then take in a new piece of land, letting the old lie. Never think of clearing up waste land and bringing it into cultivation, until driven by necessity. Are quite careless of sowing or intending more than they think their families will need; and hence with much good land are in danger at every failure of going hungry. Of cattle they have plenty, but feed them badly and so get little use of them. I am almost certain that the owner of 200 acres of land lives very little better than the owner of but 20 acres in Germany. However, they live and live content, and appear to console themselves

for the conveniences they lack by the less labor they
expend.

Through fertile valleys and over a few barren hills,
consisting wholly of limestone soil and growing almost
nothing but white-oaks, I came to Hancock-town on
the Potowmack; a small place begun shortly before the
war and numbering only a dozen houses. It belongs
to Maryland which province here runs very narrow,
for but a mile and a half from the town I crossed the
boundary-line, already hewn out of the woods, between
Pensylvania and Maryland, and the river which here
is as much as 2-300 yards wide forms the boundary
between Maryland and Virginia.

On the Virginia side it is six miles more from the
river to the Warm Springs, the road continuing
through limestone hills and their woods of white-oak.

Warm Spring Hill, a steep but not high mountain
running from north-east to south-west, consists of a
quartzose species of rock together with the already
often-mentioned laminated whet-stones (cos, grind-
stone, grit-stone). The lower hills on both sides the
valley contain species of limestone. The deeper, middle
part of the valley, in which is the watering-place,
shows something of iron; on digging a cellar recently
a coarse sort of blood-stone or manganese ore was
found, which as it lay was neither rich nor heavy.
And almost everywhere digging is done near the
springs of this valley, a black slate is found which is
partly micaceous and also contains sulphur-pyrites in
pockets and flecks; in other places jet-black and brittle
like coal; and again splitting in fine plates and good
for every use. In this region there is said to have
been found an octahedral manganese ore (*minera ferri*

octaëdra), of which I saw a few specimens later at
Philadelphia.

And now for the famous water itself. This is
known by no other name than that of the Warm
Springs; but it is far from warm, not more than 14-16
degrees above temperate, or between 70 and 72 degrees
of the Fahrenheit thermometer. Thus I found it in
the morning at 10 o'clock when the sun was shining,
and in the evening after sunset. That it does not
freeze in winter is remarked as a great curiosity, and
this may be the reason why the name was given. The
water tastes and feels cool. It has no especially marked
taste; closely observed, something like that given a
quart of water by a few drops of tartar emetick. It
contains no air or gas, is bright and clear, and shows
neither in the springs themselves nor in their outlets
any conspicuous deposit giving metallic constituents.
In short, but for its reputation it would be taken for
nothing more nor less than common smooth water.
It is said to have been tested by a Dr. Thomas who
found only about 4 grains sulphur to 4 quarts. The
water does not foam readily with soap. There are
8-10 different springs, which rise near together from
the foot of the above-mentioned hill. Of their efficacy
I can say little more than of their constituents. The
waters are recommended for old rheumatick complaints, and for accumulations of the gall, and are
thought to be harmful in pulmonary diseases. The
patients who resort hither drink as much as they like.
It cannot be said that this water has any further effect
on the body than what would follow from any other
water taken in quantity, increasing the excreta. It
appears that force of habit and the mode, and the pro-

pensity for dissipation and change, attract more guests to these springs than any established proofs of their curative qualities. At Augusta (also in the farther and mountainous part of Virginia, but 120 miles south of here) there are also some springs, similar to these in taste and content, but said to be greatly warmer— so warm that it is unpleasant to bathe in them, so warm that an egg (but only after 24 hours) becomes eatable if immersed in them. At Augusta the houses are not so numerous as here and therefore there are fewer visitors.

The little place grown up about these springs is called **Bath-town**, which is as yet in poor circumstances, made up of little, contracted, wooden cabins or houses scattered about without any order, most of them with no glass in the windows, being only summer residences. Not a building of stone, although stone is to be had there in plenty. The place lies in that part of Virginia called New Virginia, because as a frontier and mountain region it was later settled; the land belonged to the well-known Scottish Lord Fairfax, recently dead, who possessed great estates in land here and about Winchester. This singular man withdrew in his youth from his father-land, where gifts of fortune and posts of honor were in store for him, and retired to the solitudinous woods of America to live his own life in his own way. A disinclination for European pomp and the social constraints, and an inordinate fondness for solitude and love of the chase brought him to this region. His house near Winchester was of two rooms only; he had another here at Bath-town, whither he was accustomed to come for the cure, which was the largest in the place, had four

rooms, and served as ball-room and assembly-room for
the guests at the baths. There were no other public
buildings here. Over the only spring used as a bath
there is a thin boxed covering, and other bathing-
places are merely stuck about with branches of trees.
The number of guests assembled here during the past
August ran to 560; but very few of them came for
their health or the water; they seek society and dis-
traction, and make little journeys on horse-back of
2-300 miles, for frequently acquaintances living very
far apart have appointments fixed for Bath-town. At
this time there come many merchants and keepers of
taverns and boarding-houses, who stay during the
season to serve the guests, but these notwithstanding
find few conveniences here. The public amusements
are horse-racing, play, and dancing; at the balls one or
at most two blacks supply the company with woful
horn-pipes and jigs. The inhabitants of the place
themselves possess almost nothing but their cabins
which they let to the visitors, living in winter on what
they can earn during the 'genteel season.' They are
besides very indolent and careless, so much so that
nobody has taken the trouble to set out gardens and
attempt vegetables and other things they need, but
they all prefer to bring in everything from abroad.
The season was now over ✚ and the merchants gone;
and at this time, what seems incredible for a place in
Virginia, not a pipe of tobacco was to be had in the
whole town.

Among the thin-shale sandstones lying about the
springs, I found by accident two showing plain impressions of pectinites and entrochites; I could find no
more and these which I had happened upon were unheard of wonders to the inhabitants.

The hill to the east of Bath-town contains shaly sandstones, sandy clay, and coarse, reddish quartz; beyond are other hills of the same structure, tolerably high, to the west; and then the North Mountain which here near the Potowmack is not high, consisting chiefly of broken and barren hills, but still keeps its direction unchanged from north-east to south-west. In the valleys rough sorts of slate are found, the farms are scattered, the cabins wretched, and the inhabitants for the most part Irish. A few miles from Leek's Mill, I again met with the grey limestone, in the great limestone valley,* passed to Shepherdstown on the Potowmack, and across the river to the foot of the South Mountain, where the road turns to Fredrick-town, the whole way over limestone soil.

I was now again out of the mountains and might hope to be somewhat less burdened with tedious questions which, while in the mountains, one must submit to from every man. At bottom one cannot be offended at the curiosity of these remote people, who very seldom see strangers among them and do not know all that goes on in the rest of the world, but it can hardly be expected of the traveller that he should, with the patience of a saint, allow himself to be examined by every fool every day and all the time. Was it a stone I picked up or a plant I broke off, some one assailed me with questions. Are you a miner? A goldsmith? A doctor? Are you buying land? Where have you come from? How long have you been in the country? Where do you live? Are you married? How old are you? What is your name? Where have

* See above, p. 230.

you been? Where are you going? How tall are you?
Besides this irksome questioning, they have a still more
tedious custom of getting everything, inquiry or
answer, repeated. For this purpose they make use of
a single word, nowhere else customary: *Nan!*—which
Nan! is the first reply to anything said, no matter how
slowly or plainly; and by *Nan* it is desired that what
has been said may be heard again, as if insidious questions or unconsidered answers were to be guarded
against—at least that is the semblance, albeit it is
nothing but ill manners.

In this limestone valley and in the neighborhood of
Shepherdstown, which place itself is not small, there
are a few other rather considerable towns, among them
Hagars-town or Elizabethtown already of importance.
It lies in Maryland and has much inland trade, and
many houses mostly stone. **Winchester ✚** stands to
the south of Shepherdstown, on Virginia soil, but is
smaller and still of insignificant importance. The
especial products of this region are cattle, grain, and
hemp; and tobacco is gradually winning more place,
since, contrary to expectations, it grows well on the
rich soil of these mountains.

The Potowmack at Shepherdstown is pretty broad
and deep, however in the winter of 1781 it was seen to
freeze so fast that a part of Cornwallis's surrendered
army could cross in the morning with wagons and
horses where the evening before boats could still be
used. Four miles from the river one passes through
Sharps-borough, a small place only 17 years old; the
land-lord is the minister of the place. Here begins
the ascent of the South Mountain which is composed
of several moderately high ranges, the valleys fertile

and already a good deal tilled; the road passes by
many farms and through pleasant landscapes. The
species of rock of the South Mountain are quartzose
and gneissic; in the valleys there is limestone. Midway of the mountain stands **Middletown**, a little place
of perhaps 20 houses, 13 miles from Sharpsborough
and 10 from Fredricktown. The east side of the
South Mountain is a long and gradual slope, leading
to another broad, open, and well-settled limestone
valley, whence the several hills of the range have the
look of a low, undulating mountain-chain.

Fredrick-town. The inland towns of America are
in general little known; it is the occasion therefore of
a very pleasant surprise to come upon a spruce little
place where it had not been expected. The country
about Fredrick-town is pretty level, without being
monotonously flat. To the west is the South Mountain, sufficiently distant to present a pleasing prospect
to the eye; to the east there runs another, parallel
range of low hills; north and south the broad valley
lies open, in all directions well-cleared and rather thickly
settled. Good clay soil overlies the grey limestone,
and gives an excellent account of the seed entrusted
to it. The town was begun only 18 years ago, but
counts already some 2000 inhabitants and 300 houses,
has several good buildings, and is even adorned with a
few towers. The streets run regularly by the four
compass-points. Few of the houses are of wood;
most of them are of limestone or brick, the brick being
preferred here, as making drier and healthier dwellings. The area of the town was formerly the property
of the Delancy family. ✚ But during the Revolution
the eldest of the family, by inheritance the land-lord,

declared himself on the side of the King, and so lost his
rights; and the state of Maryland, on the payment of
a seven-year ground-rent by the residents, has ad-
judicated to them as their possession what they once
held under lease from the Delancys. The place cannot yet boast of any especially important trade. The
inhabitants are engaged in crafts and in agriculture.
There are some iron-works and a glass-furnace in the
South Mountain, but the product of these is neither
good nor sufficient, not so much from lack of materials
as of workmen. There is no navigable stream in the
region near by; the Monocasy, a small river four
miles north of here, is of too little consequence, and
the Potowmack, eight miles to the south, is obstructed
there by the neighboring falls. Baltimore and Georgetown, both distant only some 50 to 60 miles, supply
this place with what they need from abroad.

The greatest part of the inhabitants are Germans,
and the people are of all manner of religions; those of
the English established church, the Presbyterians, German Reformed, Lutherans, Catholics, and a few other
sects, have each their house of worship; also there is
a Latin School here, and a handsome town-hall.

Dr. Fisher at Frederick-town (also Apothecary and
at the time Sheriff), told the following remarkable
story and all those present confirmed it. A farmer,
Jacob Sim, living 8 miles from the town, was eleven
years ago in the month of July bitten by a rattle-snake.
Every year since, in the same month of July, he has
fallen ill and feverish, the skin over his whole body
becoming spotted blue and yellow. Carver observed
something like this, and mentions that it happens commonly that after the bite of a rattle-snake not only the

wounded part grows swollen, but the swelling extends gradually over the whole body, and makes it of as variegated a color as the snake; and further he speaks, as if certain, of **an annual return of the symptoms shown in the first instance.*** Everywhere I informed myself of the rattle-snake, and the copper-belly, (also called moccason-snake), the bite of which is quite as poisonous. The different accounts given by the country-people are of one accord that these noxious beasts are much less numerous than they once were. In the more settled parts almost all of them that showed themselves have been killed, and it is not so dangerous a feat as might be thought. The rattle-snake betrays itself by the characteristical noise of its tail. The attention is aroused and the snake is reconnoitred. It seldom seeks to run off, but rears up in a posture of defence. It may be safely observed at a distance, and if stones or sticks of wood are at hand it is easy to kill it or at least lame it so that it cannot glide or venture any more dangerous springs. Precisely speaking, the snake does not bite except with its mouth wide-open, and springing, strikes at the object with its eye-teeth, placed in the rear upper jaw. It does not follow after, and is not easily roused to attack, unless come upon suddenly in the high grass or the bush. Nobody runs from it farther than is needful to get beyond the danger of its first spring. It can spring scarcely farther than its length, but can repeat its spring several times, (this rarely happens), in quick succession. For the rest, its gait and movements are slow. Even children are not afraid to attack it with stones or

---

* Carver's *Travels,* English edit. p. 449, 450.

sticks. The hogs, which everywhere run loose about the farm and in the woods, are deadly enemies of rattle-snakes, and eat them greedily. The snake strikes at them in vain, either the poison has no effect on the hogs or the teeth do not penetrate the fat skin. Many of the snakes succumb to the fires, kindled either purposely by hunters or new settlers, or neglected by travellers. Snakes are said not to go out of the way of fire, but to rear up and hiss until enveloped. The copper-bellied snake is more dangerous and more dreaded because it gives no warning but attacks in silence. However, by no means every wound inflicted by the rattle-snake or the copper-belly is certainly fatal. It is nothing uncommon to hear of persons being bitten, but they seem seldom to die of the bites. Different circumstances are to be taken into account, through which the danger of the bite may be diminished or increased. It is generally regarded that the poison of snakes in the warmer parts of America, in Virginia, Carolina, &c., works more swiftly and more dangerously. And that further, in one and the same region, (and hence in the southern provinces) the sharpness and activity of the poison are heightened by the heat of summer, and thus a bite in the warm summer and autumn months is by so much the more dangerous. It is altogether probable that the exterior heat may have an important influence on the fluids of the snake, these being acted on differently according to the heat of the surrounding body. And it is quite as likely that something may be due to the corruptions in the juices of the human body occasioned by the hot season. From these reasons, then, snake-bites, especially in the autumn and in more southern parts, and generally during the summer months cause worse symptoms, but in the cooler seasons of the year, even on cooler days of summer, are less dangerous; which is confirmed by Carver and others. And moreover the greatness of the danger is in some sort determined by the situation of the wound; oftenest it is the foot or the leg which is bitten, and at times the thickness of the clothing, the boot, or the shoe, affords enough protection. Or it may be the poisonous drops expressed on the entrance of the tooth are lost in the fat tissue without being taken up into the blood. But should the tooth strike a more important blood-vessel or lymphatick channel, the pernicious poison must be spread more rapidly and surely over the rest of the body.

The general symptoms which follow the bite have been described at length by Carver and by others before him.* The shivering which immediately follows the wound may well be the effect of fright. Were the circumstances not so various, the efficacy of the poison, the activity of the wounded body, the conditions of the wound itself, and the season of the year, it could not be easily explained why so many are bitten without the least ill consequences, others recover after more or less significant symptoms, and others (but rarely) succumb on the spot. Dr. Garden saw a negro bitten in Carolina fall dead after 15 minutes. And without such a diversity of circumstances it would be impossible to make anything of the great number of remedies, of all descriptions and often

---

* Descriptions of the snake, of the symptoms and remedies are to be found in Kalm's account of the rattle-snake, *Schwed. Akad. Abh.* XIV, XV; in Linnaeus, *Amoenitates acad.* Vol. II, Diss. XXII. Radix Senega; and elsewhere.

apparently trifling, which by one and another are recommended as most excellent for the snake-bite. It will not be superfluous to set down here the sundry remedies for the snake-bite which in different parts of the country were pointed out to me and praised.

They are as follows: *Collinsonia canadensis* (Horse-weed). *Cunila mariana* (Penny-royal). *Cynoglossum virginicum. Hydrophyllum canadense. Convolvulus purpureus* (Purple Bindweed).* *Gentianae species* (Sweet Bazil). *Eryngium aquaticum. Sanicula canadensis* (Black-snake-root). *Ribes nigrum. Hypoxis erecta.† Uvularia perfoliata. Pyrola maculata* (Pipsissawa). *Phytolacca decandra* (Cancer-root). *Asarum canadense & virginicum* (Coltsfoot). *Spiraea trifoliata* (Ipecac). *Actaea racemosa* (Black-Snake-root). *Sanguinaria canadensis* (Blood-root). *Thalictri species. Ranunculus repens & alii. Scrophularia marilandica. Polygala Senega* (Virginia Snake-root). *Hieracium venosum. Prenanthes alba* (Dr. Witt's Snake-root). *Serratula spicata & squarrosa, Solidago canadensis. Erigeri Species* (Roberts' Plantain). *Aristolochia Serpentaria* (Rattle Snake-root). *Quercus nigra* (Black Oak). *Iuglans alba & nigra* (Black and white Wallnut). *Acer Negundo* (White Ash).‡ *Veratrum luteum* (Rattle Snake-root). *Osmunda virginiana. Adiantum pedatum. Hypnum castrense.* Of these divers plants the roots mostly are pounded or ground and ordered to be laid on the

---

* With the juice of this plant, according to Catesby, an Indian having smeared his hands took hold of a rattle-snake and fingered it without fear or injury.

† *Aletris farinosa* (Star-root).

‡ *Panax quinquefolium.* (Ginseng.)

wound; but of some, the leaves and bark also. Merely
the inner bark of the white oak is laid on the previously
scarified and salt-rubbed wound. Of the black and
white wallnut the inner bark is to be beaten and the
fibre twisted into a cord and this bound about the
wounded limb above the bite. The bark of the white
ash is burnt, the ashes made into a paste with vinegar
and applied to the wound, and at the same time a
decoction of the bark and the buds is to be drank.
But among all the above-listed plants the Aristolochia
Serpentaria and Polygala Senega have especially held
the general esteem; and to these must be added the
Roberts' Plantain, which has been praised by several,
particularly the worthy Dr. Otto at Bethlehem, from
positive and often confirmed experience, having many
times been of excellent use where signs of the poison
taken up into the blood were already plainly manifest.
This plant, little known as yet, grows well in hilly
regions and is found in plenty about Bethlehem; it is
raised there foresightedly in gardens, so as to be found
in the night if occasion arises. Its leaves have a bitter,
sharp, biting taste. They are applied, freshly crushed,
to the wound and often renewed, and also a decoction
made of them is copiously administered.

Another tried remedy was made known not many
years ago by Caesar, **✝** a Carolina negro, who was rewarded by the state of North Carolina with his freedom and a considerable sum of money. Having been
many times tried, the especial efficacy of this remedy
seemed to be admitted. It consists of the roots of the
Hoarhound (*Marrubium album?*) and Plantain (*Plan-
tago major? vel lanceolata?*). These roots are mixed
in equal parts, and three ounces of the mixture boiled

in two quarts of water until reduced by half; the
patient takes a third of this decoction three mornings
together on an empty stomach. It reduces the symptoms, and if continued effects a complete cure. If the
fresh roots and simples are at hand they are pounded
and expressed and a large spoonful of the juice given
daily. Two spoonfuls are said to be sufficient for a
cure. The herbs and roots, after expressing or boiling, are laid upon the wound, or as a substitute a leaf
of tobacco steeped in rum. Both of these plants are of
European origin and grow in America as aliens, only
in the settled parts and not in the wilds. How the
negro got a knowledge of them is not certain; perhaps through some European?—for both plants have
been of old praised and used in the treatment of wounds,
and besides, one of them, the **Hoarhound** (*Marrub.*),
has been greatly commended for the bite of noxious
animals and mad-dogs.

Among all the remedies used exteriorly the most
effective and reasonable are: the application of a liga-
ture immediately above the wound; the sprinkling on
of salt and pepper, gunpowder, or tobacco; timely and
repeated cupping, the searing of the wound, on the
spot or as soon as ever it can be done: these remedies
are now and again used with good results by the
country-people or by surgeons. And the fat of the
rattle-snake is at times rubbed over the wound, but
from this very little indeed should be expected.

A rattle-snake of uncommon size was killed in the
year 1778 in Redstone Settlement, a part of the above-
described Glades. It was 18 ft. long and the strip't
skin measured two and a half feet in breadth. There
prevails a tradition among the country-people in

21

America that a dog which has been bitten by a rattle-
snake always grows young snakes in his liver. Dr.
Bond of Philadelphia, on whose authority I am telling
this, made sport of a farmer who declared it to be so.
The matter came to a wager. A dog was to be three
times bitten by a snake and then, after some time, to
be killed. Dr. Bond and several other gentlemen were
invited out to see. There was plainly observed on
the dog an unnatural swelling in the region of the
liver. The body was opened and, to the astonishment
of the Doctor and of those present, in the superficies
of the liver a worm was found at least 1 and a half
feet long, and of the thickness of a little finger; several others a foot long and 6-7 still smaller. It was said
that they showed a resemblance to the snake, but unfortunately they were not preserved. A second time
the same man sent to Philadelphia a dog bitten by a
snake. Dr. Bond opened this one also, in the presence of several savans and physicians, and the same
kind of worms was found in the same part of the liver.
But nothing was done further to determine the nature
of these worms, the existence of which may have been
due to anything rather than to the snake-bite.

Among the snake-species often appearing in the
mountains as well as in the low country are: a Viper,
so-called here, (*Coluber,* scut abdom. 120-25 squam
subcaud. 50-53.) It is in length two feet and more.
The head and back are blackish-brown with whitish-
yellow spots some distance apart, passing into black
at the sides. The belly is yellowish-white with irregu-
lar blackish touches. Its habitat is in thick bush or in
gardens. Its bite is held to be poisonous. If it is
vexed, or in the act of striking, its cylindrically round

body becomes flattened. The Garter-snake (*Coluber Tænia,* Scut. abdom. 145-48. squam. subcaud. 60-65). It is some three to three and a half feet long. The black-brown back is set off by three beautiful, pale yellow, narrow stripes running from the head to the tail, plainly enough distinguishing this snake. The Green Snake which is also distinct by its color, and does not grow large. The Black Snake, (*Coluber Constrictor L.*), and several others which I had no opportunity to examine closely. I saw a two-headed snake on Long Island, preserved in spirits of wine; it was doubtless, (as well as that mentioned by Carver), an abortment.

In the mountains one hears much now and again of a Horn or Thorntail-Snake which has at the end of its tail a horny sting with which it can not only give man and beast fatally poisonous wounds, but can kill trees struck by its sting. But in regard to this I have no reliable evidence. Preserved in spirits of wine by a New Englander I saw on Long Island a two-headed snake. Carver also mentions one. They were both, likely, abortments.

In a hill of the South Mountain, seven miles from Frederick-town, silver was dug for a few years ago. However nothing was found but lead and iron; and several enthusiasts, who had let themselves be convinced, dug themselves penniless in the business. After they had gone a considerable depth, no workmen were to be had under 5-6 shillings a day and keep, and the work was given up at a loss of some consequence.

From Frederick-town I passed, over the York-town road, 11 miles north through limestone soil; then turned to the east over Rocky-hill, to reach the copper

mine lying back four miles from this road, owned by
Dr. Stevenson of Baltimore. The ranges of hills bordering this limestone valley run likewise from north-
east and north-north-east to south-west and south-
south-west, are very low, and next the valley contain
a black, coarse, white-veined slate, mostly limestone
schist. Large fragments of quartz are numerous hereabouts. Farther to the east there begins a greenish
species of slatey-clay stone, now harder and again
softer, observable until 16-18 miles this side Baltimore.
The covering of these hills is generally thin, reddish
sand and clay, showing small-stemmed trees, mostly
white-oak and sassafras. In the valley-bottoms there
are good meadow-lands and many fine farms. This
whole region was now empty of blooms.

There had been no work done for some time at the
copper mine. However, I obtained several small pieces
of ore. It was copper glass-sand ore with feldspar and
a talc crust. It is called here ' silver-grey copper ore.'
The stone in the rubbish was red feldspar with quartz
intermixed. A 10-12 fathom shaft has been sunk,
and a vein worked 16-18 fathoms in length. The ore
is found for the most part only clustered or in veins of
inconsiderable and very changeable breadth. It strikes
directly through hard rock; no timbering has been
done therefore, but the work has had to be very slow
and costly. The ore was said to yield 75 in 100. It
was shipped raw to England. Dr. Stevenson had long
been offering a half interest for sale, having been at
great expense latterly for up-keep.

From the copper mine to Tutteral's Tavern (three
miles) there lay by the road greenish sand-stones with
reddish flecks, and at one place a bed of a blackish-red,

dense, and heavy species of stone which had the look of limestone but was not so, being apparently a clayey talky slate.

From Tutteral's, a solitary tavern standing by the road, it is 39 miles to Baltimore. The road continued east, over low hills, which lie in ranges running mostly north and south with a few deviations. They are neither high nor broad, with undulating ridges, and all of them covered with the reddish sandy-clay soil. A few autumn flowers excepted, *asteres* and *solidagines*, there was nothing to be seen the whole day but sorry cabins, barren hills, and unsightly woods. The first 9 miles the greenish stones were still found. The next 6-8 miles there appeared beautiful, white, shining quartz, at first showing green veins or flecks but farther on quite pure. The soil then changed more to a red clay with small particles of mica. Near Allen's mill, 18 miles from Baltimore, there began a tract of pale clayey soil, very micaceous; at this place a rather high wall of quartz and mica mixed, or foliated gneissic stone. Two miles farther, white clay full of mica, and white quartz in fragments. Here the observation was again confirmed, which I had already made in other parts of America, that mica is found in greater quantity in the stones and soils nearer the sea-coast, diminishing towards the interior country.

The last seven miles this side Baltimore there appeared along the road fragments of a soft, coarse, iron-bearing stone, more or less mixed with mica, varying greatly in composition, hardness and color. Some of these had the look of serpentine; others on the contrary struck fire on steel. They were all more or less green. This greenish stone, which begins in

the hills before Frederick-town, seems to continue as
far as the neighborhood of Baltimore, sinking deeper
and deeper. Where wells are dug in that region the
green stone appears at various depths beneath the
overlying sand and other species of stone. At such
times also much greenish earth is dug up, which tasted
to me something like copperas. The same kinds of
greenish earth and stone are found along the Cone-
gacheag road, many miles out from Baltimore.

Notwithstanding the numerous hills it is plain
enough on coming from the mountains that one is
travelling over a surface sloping to the sea.

Baltimore. Rapidly as Philadelphia grew to its
present importance, Baltimore seems to have hastened
after. It is hardly thirty years since the town was
established, and already it may be counted among the
larger and richer American cities. It numbers almost
2000 houses, for the most part built of brick neatly
and conveniently; and this number is very nearly
equal to that of all the houses in the remainder of the
province of Maryland. The inhabitants are estimated
at 12,000 and more (and again at 15,200). The advantageous situation of the harbor at the mouth of
the Patapsco river and at the upper end of Chesapeak
Bay, gave the first occasion for the founding of the
city. It is safe and commodious; can ride ships of 17-
18 ft., and has the great advantage, placed as it is almost in the middle of the province of Maryland, of
lying near to a part of Virginia and Pensylvania, between the Delaware the Susquehannah and the Potowmack, and at the same time nearer and more convenient
for trade with the regions in and about the mountains
than any other of the cities on the coast. Therefore

Baltimore has already drawn to itself the whole trade
of southern Pensylvania, that part lying this side the
Susquehannah, and also the greatest part of the trade
of back-Virginia; because the inhabitants of these districts (as well as those of the eastern peninsular and
of the whole of Maryland) find here the most convenient market and many willing buyers for their very
considerable produce; for, Philadelphia excepted, there
are nowhere in that country so many merchants
gathered together, and ready to take up what is offered.
Old experience has been here recently confirmed, that
the more the commerce of a state is assembled in one
place, so much the more is gained for the common
good in manifold ways. The few merchants of the
province were formerly scattered here and there about
the country, and were in no position to carry on business with energy; as in some measure is still the case
with the state of Virginia, which had not, nor has,
any large trading towns, and continually looks to
foreign lands for the most of its needs. Thus Baltimore, soon after its establishment, got to itself the
name of one of the most important trading-towns in
the whole of Chesapeak Bay. But nothing was so
favorable to the commerce of the place as the last war.
The situation of the harbor assured it against the
sudden attacks of hostile craft; larger ships could not
approach without circumspection and danger, and
smaller dared not venture alone as far as the end of so
spacious a bay. So Baltimore became the general
depot of imports and exports for the middle part of the
American states. During the first years of the war the
Congress for some time fixed its seat here. From
these and other causes, the population, the consump-

tion, and the number of magazines still more increased; more houses were built and house-rents rose
uncommonly high, as they are at the present time. The
extraordinary price paid for ground in the city is an
argument showing how profitable trade has hitherto
been and what is expected in the future. In several
places next the harbor each square foot of ground
yields a guinea a year in rent. I was shown a spot,
where a ware-house is just now building, 30 ft. front
and 30 foot depth, and the rent paid was 90 guineas a
year. There was building in all quarters of the town,
and at the same time care is taken for beautifying in
the items of pavements and lights. Work and activity
were to be seen everywhere.

The Point (properly Fell's point) is the south-eastern end of the town; a narrow tongue of land extending into the Bay; this part of the town being
distinguished by the water and masts surrounding it.
Here especially is all the shipping business done.
Whenever, according to the first plan, this point is
wholly united by buildings with the rest of the city,
the length of the city will be nearly two miles; but at
this time a marshy channel still divides the two parts
and is neither ornamental nor contributory to good
health. In the harbor there were lying at the time
some 50 vessels, although many on the approach of
autumn had sailed with their cargoes. This is as
yet a free harbor; ships pay only a very trifling duty.
By the Chesapeak Bay Baltimore has an easy communication with the Eastern-shore (the peninsula
lying between the bay and the ocean); with the numerous rivers and coasts of Virginia; and (by the Elk
river) with the Delaware, the distance being only 10

miles between 'the head of Elk,' the most convenient landing place on that river, and Christiana Creek which falls into the Delaware.

Baltimore exports chiefly: flour, maize, salted meat and other articles of food, all kinds of timber, and tobacco. For this last article there is an Inspection-house at the Point to which all hogsheads for export must be brought for examination and registry. In the future the mountains will supply iron and copper for export. The trade in flour to the Spanish islands was during the war by far the most profitable. A barrel of flour, costing perhaps four Spanish dollars, brought at the Havannah 25-30-36 dollars; and notwithstanding many of these flour-ships fell into the hands of the English there was a considerable profit if only one out of six escaped the enemy and returned safe. The war, which elsewhere had an opposite effect, was there-fore favorable to the trade of Baltimore, proving, among other things, how advantageous to the state company-agreements may be. The dangers which caused the individual merchant to fear utter ruin from those numerous enemies swarming about the sea, were diminished when many contributed to the fitting-out of a vessel. The results of these combinations were fortunate; Baltimore won a name, (and its merchants wealth), and regard and merit in the eyes of the country. For the considerable loans subscribed with great readiness by the merchants here and at Phila-delphia, formed almost the sole support of the ener-vated Congress during the last years of the war, and were the only means of maintaining the war at a time when all manner of difficulties delayed the collection of taxes, (insufficient for the needs of the state), and made the prosecution of the war doubtful.

Just at this time, however, the trade of Baltimore and of the rest of America, is in an uncertain condition. The profitable trade in flour came to an end with the peace; and the prohibitions against the entrance of American vessels into their West Indian possessions, issued by England, France, and Spain, (a chance which America seemed hardly to expect from the inimical Britain, and certainly not from the amicable Gaul), must of necessity cause a certain disarrangement in the commercial system here, plans being thereby made idle which looked to the most profitable outcome. However, the speculative and now independent spirit of trade will shortly find new channels and new outlets.

The object of the merchants of Baltimore, as of American merchants generally, is exports and imports. They neither intend nor desire to be manufacturers, and do not care to see such among them or very much to encourage them. For the more wares are fabricated in the country itself, so much the less would the merchant have to bring in. Increase of the population generally, and of the planters particularly, is their sole wish, or, what comes to the same thing, increase in the consumption of foreign articles and in the production of domestic. But in any event the manufacturing of the finer wares, requiring time and labor, would be as yet a fruitless undertaking, since the price of labor is so high, the working hands are so few, and those few so lazy. Certain branches of the heavier manufactures, however, such as glass, iron &c, might always be set up to better advantage in the southern states where negroes, whose work is to be had for so little, could be made use of under the direction of a few white men.

The advantages which Baltimore has hitherto derived from its trade, as the most productive source of
its prosperity, will arouse the envy and the imitation
of others. The city therefore cannot forever boast of
the exclusive trade of the Bay, and can scarcely continue to develop with the rapidity so far observed,
but from its situation it must remain always one of
the most important commercial places. Alexandria
and Georgetown on the Potowmack, and Norfolk at
the entrance of the Bay, (which during the war lay
in ashes, but is now beginning to revive), and other
Virginia towns besides are greedy for commerce, and
these must all do an injury more or less to the business here, although they can never raise themselves to
a similar greatness. The merchants of Baltimore are
not careless of these things, and in order that their
trade may not be again distributed or seen to fall into
other hands, they have expressed the wish that a
' Board of Trade,' or commercial collegium, be established, the members of which should have the capacity
and the experience to hit upon regulations for the
maintenance and strengthening of their commerce.

Soon after its settlement, the number of the inhabitants of Baltimore was increased by many French
families who came hither from Acadia or New Scotland. This province having long since been given
over to England by the crown of France, all the French
families there remained in undisturbed possession and
in the full enjoyment of all rights and liberties along
with the other colonists newly brought in from Great
Britain. But they afterwards, despite of their oath of
allegiance, letting their secret and rooted enmity to the
English government and nation be seen on all occa-

sions, and even stirring up the Indians continually to barbarities against their British neighbors and fellow-colonists, it finally became necessary to take measures for sending them out of New Scotland entirely, in order principally to bring them from under the influence of Canada, (at that time still under the sceptre of France), by the inhabitants of which they were instigated to all manner of treachery. They were accordingly apportioned to other provinces of North America; the most of them came hither, where they live together in a particular quarter of the town, the most unsightly, they being in general neither well-to-do nor enterprising, although they have the same advantages, rights, and opportunities as the other citizens.

A Roman Catholic church stands on one of the heights outside the city; where two other churches, but half in ruins, are to be seen also. The family of the Lords Baltimore, who formerly owned the whole of Maryland, being of the Romish faith, there have been long settled in this province a greater number of people of that religion, although they had no especial rights to the exclusion of others. At the time of the persecutions which the Roman Catholics had to suffer during the last century, many considerable families fled to Maryland; and therefore if genealogical registers were of any use in America the greatest part of the Roman Catholic families would have reason to be proud of theirs, when very many others might be perplexed how to give the history of their fathers and grandfathers. It is supposed that the number of the Catholics, in comparison with those of other beliefs, is throughout the whole province as 3 to 1. The Jesuits at one time owned many fine estates in this province, and although

the Order itself has been abolished the priests of this
society are still in possession of their excellent and
lucrative lands.

All of the United States, on the establishment of
their new form of government, have made tolerance a
fundamental law, solemnly declaring that every inhabitant has complete liberty to serve his Creator in
any manner to him seeming good, in so far as his religious principles are no disturbance to the public peace
nor detrimental to his fellow-citizens. Properly, therefore, in none of the states, particularly in none of the
more southern states, may any religion whatever be
called dominant, even if one or the other through the
majority of its adherents might so regard itself. Freedom is guaranteed to all alike. But before this revolution the Episcopal or English established church enjoyed the greatest advantage, its clergy (consecrated
by English Bishops) being supplied by the British
government with a constant and often very considerable support. This maintenance was furnished in part
by the publick treasury; but also raised here and there
by special imposts, to which those of other beliefs were
obliged to contribute as well as members of the established church. This was the case in Maryland, where
the Catholics in like proportion as the Protestants must
pay taxes for the support of the Protestant clergy; a
circumstance which occasioned no little secret bitterness. Then the Revolution put a stop to these allowances on the part of the magistracy, and the ministers
of the established church had, under the new government, no income except from their perquisites and
the voluntary contributions of their congregations. In
divers places, but not universally, it had long been a

regulation that considerable pieces of the best land be set apart for the behoof of the church and its ministers, the revenues so accruing being applied to their support.

'Glebes' of this sort were in part occupied and tended by the ministers themselves or they might let them. In the tobacco colonies they often yielded gratifying returns. But where this is not the regulation, the ministers of the established church depend chiefly on the caprice and generosity of their parishioners; a circumstance which is the cause of no little vexation to them, they seeing themselves now placed upon a footing with the clergy of the other religions, of whom formerly they had so greatly the advantage.

So it has happened that the clergy of the established church in several of the provinces, but especially in Maryland and just now when the Assembly is about meeting, are zealously engaged in bringing matters around again so that they shall not only receive their allowances from the civil power immediately, but, drawing a sufficient support from the public revenues, that they may be independent of the caprice of their congregations and have no further care in the matter of the love and good dispositions of their parishioners. These expressed wishes and proposals have been the occasion of much debate in public and private assemblies. Similar proposals, it is said, were recently laid before the Virginia Assembly, but by it were rejected with indignation.

The following were perhaps the opinions most generally expressed in this business. When a state has granted those of all beliefs whatsoever full, equal, and impartial rights, they cannot then ask for more, and have no ground of complaint. But was one or another society of Christians, through special protection or favor on the part of the state, to be preferred before the rest, there would thus be sown abroad the seeds of envy, emulation, disorder, bitterness, and finally, perhaps, of murder and war. No religion conduces really to evil; but what is here and there laid to the charge of this or that religion is to be ascribed either to the oppression which in one country it was exposéd to, or the presumptuous pride with which in another it sought to control. No religion being privileged, and the followers of teachings the most diverse being held, (through common rights merely civil), to good order and the observance of the laws, the result will be that the spirit of persecution, oppression, and hate will be unknown. America has already experienced the woful consequences of neglecting such maxims. The Presbyterians of New England, having withdrawn from Europe for the sake of freedom in religious matters, were shortly thereafter observed to be so far deceived by jealousy and the desire to dominate as to show quite as much intolerance of the peaceable Quakers as that against which they had striven in England and by reason of which they had come away from their fatherland. In Maryland and Virginia, so long as the British form of government gave the Episcopal Church preferance, support, and a revenue, there were very similar if not such violent manifestations. Numerous as the divers sects in America are, the new states have notwithstanding the weightiest reasons for granting them due freedom. For a great many years there have been no instances, among the most opposite of them, of dissensions and strife; none having to control the others, nor desiring to control, they were all at peace.

Was there disturbance, it was because one or another had a special influence in the management and organization of the state. It has been remarked that almost all the sects coming off from the established church worked for independence with more unanimity and determination than those which had a closer connection with the mother-church, being often led off in that way, and by their clergy who were paid by the old government. Everywhere indeed obedience to the civil powers was heard preached from the pulpits, but different men had different ideas of the civil powers, according as they looked to keeping or losing their rich benefices. It is believed further that the clergy is corrupted by inductions and fixed allowances; in free states, that is to say, the clergy would soon begin to neglect their clerical business, mixing in worldly or political affairs, or would be led into idleness and a disorderly life. But it is not contended that the laborers are not worthy of their hire, and that for imparting spiritual nourishment the servants of Christ and of the manifold churches should not expect a bodily support, only it is desired that the government in America stand apart, leaving to the people and the churches the determination of the worth of men, and who they shall be, who are to receive a part of their possessions as a willing remuneration for spiritual instructions given. The Government will assure these men that they all may look for protection and gratitude on its part, but for no privileges the one before the other.

From this regulation, people persuade themselves, there would (in America) arise many other advantages. The clergy will be more active in the performance of their duties, and the most worthy, the greater number likely, will be the better rewarded. There will not be seen every day so grievous a contrast between the preaching and the practice of ministers accepted and paid without any control of their terms of service; nor will there be heard from a proud, domineering priest exhortations to humility and abnegations unknown to him, and no red-cheeked, over-fed bacchanal will be recommending the virtues of moderation and continence, equally beyond his ken.

The ministers of the established church formerly paid by the state, who were sent over from England to America, were seldom what they ought to be. They were commonly held to be good enough for America. At one time they were almost the only scholars in the country, and they were expected to know everything; but when people found out that they either knew nothing, or of what they knew brought nothing into practice, this gave their numerous and increasing opponents many and lasting triumphs, and opportunity always to be marking down new blemishes in their doctrine. And so it happened that they were frequently deserted of their hearers, these joining in with other factions of belief. It is known reliably that in Virginia and Maryland all the religious societies coming off from the established church have been considerably increased by those discontent with their teachers. In Virginia, only 40 years ago, the proportion between the Dissenters and the established church was as 1 to 20; but in the year 1776 the number on either side was almost the same.

The constitution of America regards all religious societies, of what name soever, as arbitrary societies,
22

to which an equal rank, equal rights and liberties are
legally appurtenant.   Therefore should the Episcopal
party succeed in bringing their church again into a
close union with the state (of Maryland), receiving
through the state a special place and maintenance,
from that moment all other religious societies would
be held to be merely **tolerated Dissenters**, and this
would be a grievous thing as well as an injustice.
Should one Assembly, the members of which belonged
in a majority to one church, concede this party-advan-
tage, the case might be that another Assembly through
a preponderance of other denominations would change
everything again.   This would be a fruitful and fearful source of continual strife and contention.   Besides,
there are in this and other states many preachers as
well as congregations diversely denominated, who hold
themselves bound in conscience neither to receive nor
to give reward for the preaching and dispensing of the
gospel.   Was then the government to agree to furnish
pay from the public treasury to the preachers of the
Episcopal church, a part of this burden would fall
upon these and other sects; and it would be highly
unjust to make citizens pay for something about which
they have no concern.

These were very nearly the grounds of opposition to
the religious party-strife, recently stirred up by some
members of the Episcopal church.   For the rest, so
long as in America itself they will have no bishops,*

---

* According to published reports this is now the case.
"In December 1786 the Right Reverend Dr White of Pen-
"sylvania and the Right Reverend Dr Provost of New York
"were consecrated at London, as bishops for the United
"States, by the Lord Archbishop of Canterbury. Dr Griffith

the clergy of the Episcopal or English church must get their ordination in England.

Of the quantity of merchandise, which since the peace has over-stocked the American markets, there was one article apparently which showed no rapid falling off in vogue, that is to say, **Irish Servants.** Within a brief space many hundreds, men, women, and children, have been brought hither, where they looked to make their sudden fortunes, and to have their cost for passage and keep paid by the Americans. Most of these people were by false and illusory pretenses inveigled into emigrating,* and they find themselves deceived no little when on their arrival in America the skipper compels them to bind themselves out for several years to any person soever, who, on their making good the cost to him, will set them at liberty. This sort of Irish adventurers were at the time being offered for sale in the newspapers everywhere, and were being dragged about from place to place with this in view. It appeared however that nobody would willingly take up with the Irish, it being known from long experience that from indolence they leave one part of the world, so as if possible to live yet more idly in another. German servants † always found a readier purchase, being

---

"of Virginia will be the third American bishop, so as to make "complete the clerical organization of the Episcopal church "of these states."

* So with the German traffick. Vid Schlözer's *Briefwechs.* IV, no. 40. However the Irish, from the greater intercourse between the countries, should be better informed of what they have to expect, and less gullible.

† "Account of a German society established at Baltimore in "1783 by a Berliner, in the behoof of needy Germans who "without due care have gone thither." In the *Berlin. Monat-*

generally regarded as industrious people; they have this character throughout America, and are everywhere welcome.

At Baltimore I had the pleasure of knowing Dr. Wiesenthal, ✛ a worthy fellow-countryman, an old German physician. He has been here since almost the first beginning of the town, and for his private character as well as his attainments is generally esteemed. It is a pity that his years and infirmities restrict his activities too narrowly, already obliging him to take in a 'partner.' This is a very usual custom in America; physicians form agreements like merchants, and it is no matter if perhaps their methods are quite contrary; on the other hand, one gains at times what the other loses and they share the profit in the end. Almost all the doctors dispensing their medicines themselves and keeping their offices at home, it is in this way a considerable help to beginners, unable to set up for themselves, if they form a partnership with an older man, whose practice they at first assist in caring for and finally inherit.

I have already made mention, under Wyoming, of the saltpetre prepared in America; from Dr. Wiesenthal I received still further information, regarding the natural saltpetre found in America; and it will not be inappropriate to bring together here all I learned on that subject.

In the preface of the first volume of the American Philosophical Transactions it is stated among other things that the southern parts of North America are

---

" *scrift.* no. XI, 1786.—I knew nothing of this society at the time of my stay in Baltimore, October 1783.

so rich in saltpetre, or so favorable to its production,
that in sundry places it covers the surface in the form
of a rime, and that here and there in the mountains are
found 'mines of saltpetre.' During my stay in
America I had similar oral accounts, with the repeated
assurance that often completely developed saltpetre is
found in such places.

These reports coming neither from eye-witnesses
nor always from sufficiently well-informed persons,
credence could not be blindly placed in them; and the
less so, because very recently the general opinion of
the chymists was unfavorable either to the existence
or to the natural production of a pure saltpetre, although sundry travellers have affirmed that small saltpetre-crystals, produced and shaped naturally after
rains, have been found on the surface of the earth in
Pegu, Bengal, and certain regions on the coast of
Africa, and that in India, Spain, and elsewhere true
saltpetre has been got from the earth without the aid
of ash-lye. These accounts are now confirmed by the
following similar discoveries made in America.

In Wyoming I was taken to a rock from which at
one time saltpetre had been gathered by scraping. A
loose, fine-grained, species of sand-stone, associated
with a considerable quantity of mica, lay piled in
couches of varying thickness. The color of the stone
was in part greyish, in part reddish, the stone itself
being of different degrees of hardness; but on the
whole the side exposed to the air was the softest.
These rocks formed steep, rent walls, 25-30-40 feet
in height, and were the basis of a high mountain,
grown up in trees and bush, running along the Susquehannah river. Many narrow, perpendicular clefts

cut the rock-wall, often filled up with quartz-veins but oftener with stone of the same species as the cliff. Along the horizontal fissures, or laminate beds, there hung a white, tufted deposit which the people called saltpetre, but which tasted to me more like natron. This efflorescent deposit is restricted chiefly to those places where the rock overhangs, and appears only after warm and dry weather, being washed off by moist winds and rains beating against. These rock-walls were everywhere full of larger or smaller holes, made by persons collecting the material for the preparation of saltpetre. Several such cliffs showing this kind of exudation are to be found along the Susquehannah, up and down the river, and in consequence, at.the beginning of the war various saltpetre-boileries were set up in the Wyoming region, but were given over on account of the Indians or for other reasons. Now this deposit and the scraped-off sand are said to have been used in the preparation of saltpetre; my guide knew nothing of how the work was actually done; presumably ash-lye was used in the process.

Dr. Wiesenthal gave me more detailed and exact information in regard to natural saltpetre-crystals and saltpetre obtained without ash-lye. I give his account in his own words:

"At the beginning of the American war the uni-
"versal lack of gunpowder making it necessary to
"look carefully to what materials were to be found in
"the country, there were many projects published,
"some of them impossible, others ill-considered, a few
"promising something; until finally a man, who came
"from the Alleghany mountains, brought me a small
"quantity of saltpetre, mixed with some earth and

" little stones, assuring me that he had got it himself
" from the 'mine.' This material contained sundry
" entire specimens of saltpetre, large as a bean, and
" showing all the requisite properties. The general
" opinion being that saltpetre is a salt only to be had
" artificially, a mine of saltpetre was an important
" novelty ; and since a few years before an account had
" been received of such a mine, where from the high
" price of labor the work could not be carried on, I
" judged it worth the trouble to bring the matter to the
" attention of the Government so as to get an investi-
" gation set on foot. I was commissioned for the
" purpose, and undertook a journey into the mount-
" ains, where I first examined the old mine which had
" been at one time worked. Here the stone got out
" had been broken up in deep troughs with great
" pestles, lye-soaked, and the lye boiled, and saltpetre
" crystallized out, but not sufficiently to bear the costs.
" This place is on the other side of the southern branch
" of the Potowmack. I proceeded farther into the
" mountains ; not far from Patterson's Creek was the
" place whence the *nitrum nativum* had been brought
" me, from a hollow, or cave, in a rock (perhaps 20-
" 30 ft. high) in some places 6, 8-10 ft. deep, and from
" 10 to 15 ft. wide, full of a light earth and many fallen
" stones ; this hollow was grown over with trees and
" protected from rain beating in ; inside I found many
" small clefts in and between the rocks, large enough
" to hold my hand flat-open, and filled with small, loose
" bits of saltpetre such as had been brought me. Of
" this loose earth I took a bushel, leached it, and boiled
" the lye down to the half which on the following
" morning I found as if a thick brine, to the eye about

" as much as half the earth used. Then in order to get
" good crystals, notwithstanding this brine showed a
" crystal-formation, I made forthwith an ash-lye and
" poured it on, boiled it, and on its congelation ob-
" tained the finest and purest saltpetre-crystals. I
" showed the inhabitants there the manner of making
" saltpetre, and had the pleasure of seeing that many
" tons were afterwards made, much of it indeed with-
" out the help of ash-lye. To convince myself plainly
" of this, I had brought from the mountains about 1
" and a half bushel of earth, which merely by leach-
" ing and congelation gave 49 and three fourths pounds
" of the very best and purest saltpetre, the same I had
" the honor to show you."

In the following month of December I had the
further pleasure of receiving information quite conso-
nant with this, from Mr. Rübsaamen in Virginia. A
great store of the richest saltpetre-earth is found in
sundry large caves in the mountains of Virginia, where
there is protection afforded from wind and rain. The
floor of some of these caves and clefts is made up to a
depth of many feet, wholly of saltpetre-earth; no
attempt has been made to find how deep, because the
upper beds gave a sufficient profit. Mr. Rübsaamen
has not found any naturally crystallized saltpetre, but
the walls of these caves are often to be seen quite
covered with a white efflorescent deposit resembling a
thick salt-brine which has not had space to crystallize.
The rock in which these saltpetre-clefts were, is, (as
well as he can remember), a sort of coarse marl or
slatey limestone. The usage there, as commonly, was
to employ an ash-lye in the preparation of the saltpetre. But from experiments of his own Mr. Rübsaa-

men is convinced that this earth merely leached also
crystallizes into pure saltpetre, but with the loss of a
third to a half of what may be obtained by the help
and addition of ash-lye. This is the case because if
the leached earth is boiled of itself over the fire, a
great part of the saltpetre-acid, fixed only in particles
of earth, escapes unused for lack of an adequate alkaline basis. In the average there could be obtained in
this way 8-10 pounds of saltpetre from a bushel of
earth. No birds have been found in these caves and
clefts, although it has been the opinion of sundry persons that the alkaline element of the saltpetre must
have been occasioned by the droppings of birds long
accumulated and rotted. To be sure, there were seen
the dens and excreta of bears and foxes, but in amount
insignificant.

During the war tobacco-stalks ✚ were also used for
saltpetre. Several sorts of tobacco, on being burnt,
have the property of crackling and scattering sparks.
This sort, commonly covered with a white salt-dust, is
called ‘ Salt-Marsh Tobacco,’ grows chiefly in low
spots in Virginia and Maryland and, on account of the
property mentioned, is extremely disliked by the
tobacconists. From two pounds of the rough stems of
this sort, not previously used, more than an ounce of
good saltpetre-crystals are obtained by leaching. The
saltpetre seems to lie ready ; other kinds, it has been
found by experiment, yield saltpetre only on the addition of ash-lye, and then but very little. It appears
also that certain kinds of soil are better adapted for
supplying the tobacco with active saltpetre, which is
the case with some other plants, as turnersol, fennel,
borage &c. Besides, the tobacco-warehouses and the

houses in which it is dried, contain much saltpetre-
earth as well. But in the warehouses it is not the
upper layers of rotted and trodden leaves which yield
the most, but the earth lying somewhat deeper, and
this often without any ash-lye. Regarding the origin
of the natural saltpetre in the fore-mentioned mountain
parts, or how nature goes about to produce it, I will
not here form an opinion. The supposition that the
lixivial salt of plants can only be brought out by re-
ducing them to ashes has done much to sustain the
doubt as to the existence of a natural saltpetre. But
since it is more and more established by recent observations that nature without the aid of art can produce
a lixivial salt from plants,* and that this lies in part
already present in them † as well as in animal substances, there should be no longer any reason for astonishment at the production of this pure saltpetre in
the mountains of America; and the less so because it
can now and again be had from the aphronatron of old
buildings, old mortar, and old vaults. The observations of all chymists so far agree, that saltpetre is
hardly to be anywhere found except in earths or places
where there have been present rotted, (indeed entirely rotted), plants or organic materials. Whoever
therefore has any knowledge of the wild mountains
and forests of America where for unnumbered years
mouldering trees and plants have lain heaped up un-
touched and undisturbed, and further, whoever considers how in those wildernesses animals, serpents,
and insects live and die yearly in untold numbers, and

---

* Crell's *Neuest. Entdeck.* &c XL, 279.
† Ibid. XL, 149.

how all this material through unknown ages, in a
warm climate and a moist soil, has been quietly exposed to the most complete decay, to such a one certainly the development or production of an indescribable quantity of stable lixivial salt should be no matter
of astonishment, provided the salt can be produced in
this way. But should it be admitted, (and should the
later discoveries continue to offer confirmation), that
atmospheric air itself stands in the closest relation to
the acid of saltpetre, these rich saltpetre-mines are at
once made explicable.

The zeal of the Americans in the preparation of
saltpetre for the needs of the war was at its height
during the first years of the war, before the French
fleet had made navigation and imports somewhat
easier. That before that time much saltpetre was
really made in the manner above-described, is quite
to be believed, but there were sufficient reasons why
afterwards the fabrication should have in great part
come to a stand. The workmen for this business were
dear, as for all mine-work, and during the war scarcer.
For although not everybody joined the army, and
many sat in comfortable and careless ease at home,
they were nevertheless unwilling to go into the mountains to dig and boil saltpetre. And so the Congress
could never obtain it in sufficient quantity for making
the powder needed by its troops; but so as not to let
the spirit of the people sink, casks were often filled
with black sand and despatched about the country and
to the artillery. The saltpetre prepared in the country
reached a high price; and later, under the protection
of the French flag, saltpetre as well as powder could
be brought to America cheaper than it could be made

there. Before the war there were no powder-mills in
America. The American powder is said to be weak,
and not of the adequate effect. But this cannot well
be ascribed, as has been done in English journals, to
the faulty nature of their domestic saltpetre. According to these statements American saltpetre, which had
been used among other purposes for brining meat, had
shown injurious, corroding, and unhealthful properties.
Here and there indeed there may have been a failure
in the preparation, and the saltpetre not enough separated from other salts; but that which I saw at Dr.
Wiesenthal's was in appearance and to the taste altogether fine and pure.

In productions of the mineral kingdom the region
about Baltimore is likewise not poor. There are found
there rich beds of swamp iron-ore, good sand-stones
fit for squaring, all sorts of clay-earths, fine white and
grey marble, soap-stones, shorl-crystals, several varieties of breccia, and other species of stone, which I pass
over here having elsewhere * given a circumstantial
account of them. The flora of this region, judging by
what was still to be seen towards the middle of October, appeared to be very little different from that
about Philadelphia.

Several circumstances obliged us to spend a few
days longer in this neighborhood, and gave opportunity
for a little journey to Annapolis, the capital of Maryland, to Alexandria, Georgetown, and Bladensburgh.
The first six miles from Baltimore was altogether
through forest, mostly young wood. A forge near

---

* Vid. *Beyträge zur mineralog. Kenntniss von Nordamerika.*
§22, 23.

the Patapsco had for many miles around eaten up all
the wood, which was just now beginning to grow
again. Forges and other wood-consuming works will
at length be impossible of maintenance here, the wood
being taken off without any order or principle of
selection, and the second growth in this poor and
sandy country starting up slowly. The land would
have a still balder look, did not the forests consist
largely in sprout-shooting leaf-wood. Eight miles
from Baltimore we passed the Patapsco at a ferry, and
beyond the river kept on through monotonous woods,
very little cultivated land to be seen along the road.
The maize appeared everywhere in bad condition,
small, and thin like the soil; and besides, late frosts
and the general dry weather had very much held it
back. The roads are, or are intended to be, kept up
at the public cost, but are nowhere well cared for.
The tendance is left to heaven. Bridges and ferries
we passed today were almost all of them impracticable.
So long as anything **will do** in a measure, people in
America give themselves no further trouble. The
country through which we came was hilly, showing the
same species of rock as that around Baltimore. We
arrived late at Bladensburgh whither it is counted 35
miles from Baltimore.

In two or three public houses at which we stopped
on the way we found much company. It was about
the time for the election of the new members of the
Maryland Assembly, and the curiosity and interest of
all the inhabitants were aroused. Already in private
companies the debate was over the business the new
Assembly would have to be concerned with. One of
the most important matters at their next sitting will

be the payment of debts owed British merchants. The
current opinions in this regard are as different as different interests, and disposition or aversion to England, can make them. There were those who plausibly
sought to show that the payment of debts contracted
under the old government cannot justly be demanded
now under the new, and that all debts except those
made for the Revolution are to be regarded as extinguished. For by the Revolution the old form of
government, and everything dependent on it, has been
eo ipso annulled, done away with, and made of no
effect; the political constitution is transformed, and
the people have therefore ceased to be what they
formerly were; the obligations of debtors to their
creditors, existent under the old government, must
therefore cease to be valid and lawfully binding. But
under the new constitution of the state there arise
new social rights, under which each debtor is confirmed in the exemption become effective through the
abolishment of the old constitution. The senseless
and conscienceless nature of these propositions needs
neither explanation nor contradiction, but much pains
have been taken to establish their validity and to
spread them abroad for acceptance through newspapers and special pamphlets. It is always unpleasant
to pay old debts, and it is plainly enough to be observed that all the reasons are being diligently sought
out why the obligation should be set aside. The only
members of the next Assembly, of whom it is to be expected that they will vote for the payment of the
British debts, are the members for the city of Baltimore; it will certainly be incumbent upon them to
press the settlement of the old debts, because otherwise

the merchants there will be little likely to find new
credit in Great Britain; old debts being paid, as the
custom is, so as to make new ones. But the next difficulty is the question: how are they to be paid? Many
of the old debtors are now dead; others are ruined;
and it is held that such debts must be borne by the
community, because by the peace-conventions the obligation was assumed of paying all British debts without
exception. This proposition is zealously supported by
most of the merchants, who desire to see the total
debt, (to be regarded now as an obligation of the
whole state), paid by a generally imposed tax, hoping
that in this way the sums they owe may creep in with
the rest. Naturally the people in the country, upon
whom the burden of the tax would fall, are not of the
same opinion, although they themselves have borrowed
again of the merchants what these have borrowed in
England. From everything which has been said for
and against, it is plain in advance that there will be
very little disposition to assume these debts as a common burden. The result will prove this.*

Bladensburgh,—a small place on the eastern branch
of the Potowmack (here navigable only for boats and
shalops) has a tobacco-warehouse and inspection-
office. These tobacco-warehouses are, equally for the
planter and the merchant, convenient and safe public
institutions. They are distributed at suitable distances
on all the rivers and little bays in Maryland and
Virginia. Thither must the planters bring and deposit
all their tobacco before they can offer it for sale.
Responsible superintendents carefully examine the

---

* Has proved it. Little or nothing has been paid.

tobacco which is brought in, and determine its quality.*
The damaged or bad is condemned and burnt; but
that which is good and fit for sale is taken in and
stored, and the owner is given a certificate or note
showing the weight and the quality of the tobacco
delivered. The planter sells this tobacco-note to anybody he pleases, without showing samples of his tobacco,
and the purchaser, even if many miles distant, pays
the stipulated price without having seen the tobacco,
the inspectors being answerable for the quantity and
quality by them stated. The merchants take these
notes in cash payment for the goods which the planters
get from them; they are counted as hard money
throughout the province, and for that reason are often
tampered with, of which there have been recently 3-4
instances: however, the management is such that the
cheat cannot stand or go long undiscovered. By this
excellent and convenient regulation it was the case
even under the British rule that in Maryland and
Virginia no paper-money was necessary, without
which, as early as that, the other provinces could carry
on no internal trade. The Acts of Assembly contain
many long-drawn laws touching this branch of trade,
the ordering of the warehouses, oversight, inspection,
and export of tobacco.

* The Maryland and Virginia tobacco-planters distinguish
between several varieties of tobacco, according to the growth:
as Long-green, Thick-joint, Brazil, Shoestring &c. But in the
warehouses for the most part only two sorts are made out,
that is, Aronokoe and Sweetscented. The latter is known by
its stalk and better smell, and is on that account preferred;
it is raised in greater quantity in Virginia than here, in the
lower parts along the James and York rivers; the Aronokoe
is commoner in the upper regions of the Chesapeak Bay and
on the inland plantations.

The tobacco, before it is brought to the warehouse, is packed by the planters in hogsheads; and these, for the more convenient storage on shipboard, must all be of a prescribed breadth and height; the weight of the tobacco contained must be not less than 950 pounds, but more than this as much as they please; and really as much as 1500 to 1800 pounds are often forced into the hogsheads. The heavier they are so much the better for the merchants, four of these hogsheads, of whatever weight, being reckoned a ship's ton and paying a fixed freight, since the freight on vessels is counted by the space the goods take up and not by their weight.

The price of tobacco stood at the time at 29-30-32 shillings Pensylv. Current the hundredweight; during the war it was 35 shillings, or a guinea, and more; but at the last, when export was extremely difficult, hardly 18-20 shillings. The freight for a ship's ton, or 4 hogsheads, is now 7 Pd. sterling to England, or 35 shillings the hogshead. It was estimated that shortly before the war Maryland exported about 70,000 and Virginia about 90,000 hogsheads of tobacco; and was each rated in the average at only 10 Pd. sterling, it is a very considerable amount which these colonies gained yearly by this plant alone.

The planting of tobacco is a special branch of agriculture, requiring much trouble and attention, and in many ways exposed to failure. There are but few planters hereabouts who make more than 15 hogsheads in a year; most of them not over 5-10. An acre of land, if it is right good, produces not much over a hogshead. In Maryland there is far less tobacco raised than formerly; particularly because of the dis-

23

quiets of the war and the more profitable traffic in flour, many planters have been led to give up the culture of tobacco and to sow grain instead.

Hard by Bladensburgh there is a spring which has a strong content and taste of iron, and upon which the inhabitants have imposed the splendid name of Spa. Similar iron-waters are nothing rare in America; but neither in these nor in others observed by me, have I been able to remark any fixed air.*   Nor have I learned of any curative springs supplied with any sort of salt, if I except those yielding kitchen-salt, found in and beyond the mountains.

The situation of Bladensburgh is unhealthy, among swamps which surround it on all sides, and every fall obstinate fevers spread among the inhabitants of the region, which on the other hand is rich in manifold beautiful plants.   Negroes are beginning to be more numerously kept here, and the people show already a strong tincture of southern ease and behavior.   Also several plants are grown here which farther to the north are scarcely seen.   Cotton-wool (*Gossypium herbaceum*) and sweet potatoes (*Convolvulus Battatas*) are raised by each family sufficiently for its needs. The blacks raise ' Been-nuts ' (*Arachis hypogaea*) ;†

---

* However, a spring in the county of Botetourt, said to contain iron and much atmospheric acidity, is mentioned in the second volume of the *Amer. Philos. Transact.*

† This plant, with a few others of the same class, has the rare property of burying its seed-pods in the earth.   The bloom appears far down on the stem, and inclines towards the earth, in which the pistil buries itself, and matures round husks with 2-3 seeds, which are dug out for use.

Its origin being in a warm climate, it is not easily transplanted farther north; even in England attempts have been

this is a pretty hardy growth, which at all events stands
a few cold nights without hurt. The thin shells of
the nuts, or more properly the husks, are broken, and
the kernels planted towards the end of April in good,
light soil, perhaps a span apart. They must then be
diligently weeded, and when they begin to make a
growth of stems all the filaments or joints are covered
with earth. After the blooming-time, the pistils and
young seed-cases bury themselves in the ground and
mature under the earth which is continually heaped
upon them. The kernels have an oily taste, and
roasted are like cacao. With this view the culture of
them for general use has been long recommended in
the Philosophical Transactions, and the advantages of
making this domestic oil plainly enough pointed out,
but without the desired result. The wild chesnuts

---

made without result. In more southern countries it flourishes
astonishingly, and it is all the more valuable because it does
not require the best land, but prefers a thin, light, and sandy
soil. Besides what the negroes raise for their own use, planters
here and there in the southern colonies cultivate great quantities of them to fatten their hogs and fowls, which gain
rapidly on such feed.

It is believed to be originally an African plant which was
brought to the American colonies, particularly the sugar colonies, by the negro slaves; the blacks are very fond of them,
and plant them industriously in the West Indies, in the little
patches of land left for their use.

The oil made of these nuts is especially recommended for
keeping long at a great heat without becoming rancid. To get
a completely pure and good oil, no heat should be used in the
pressing. From a bushel of the seed, costing in Carolina not
much over 1 or 2 shillings sterling, nearly 4 quarts of oil are
obtained. In some parts they are called also 'ground-nuts'
and 'ground-peas.'

growing so generally in all the forests might yield a
fruit quite as useful for the whole of America. It is
known that in certain parts of Europe the chesnut is
of almost as important a use as the jaka, or breadfruit-
tree. The native chesnut-tree is found everywhere in
America but is not regarded except as furnishing good
timber for fence-rails. Its fruit is indeed small, dry,
and inferior in taste to the European great-chesnuts,
but in Italy these are had only from inoculated trees,
the fruit of the wild chesnut there, as in America, being neither large nor agreeable in taste. By inocula-
tion, then, there could be had quite as fine great-chesnuts here. But without that, on account of its great
usefulness this fruit has received some attention
from the Americans who eat it boiled and roasted, con-
vert it into meal and bread, and fresh-shelled and
ground use it as a kind of soap with plenty of water.

Unfavorable weather and the hope of finding in the
swamps along the several branches of the Potowmack
certain other particular seeds or plants made our stay
here also a few days longer. But we found very little
we had not seen. However we were fortunate enough
here to obtain a stock of acorns and nuts which elsewhere had failed. These with some other seeds we
shipped on board a brigantine bound from Georgetown to London, but which never came to port.

The family with which we put up at Bladensburgh
was quite American in its system, according to which
everything is managed regardless. When it was dark
they began to bring in lights; when it was time for
breakfast or dinner the blacks were chased about for
wood, and bread was baked. In no item is there any
concern except for the next and momentary wants.

Whoever travels in America will observe this daily.
For the rest, we lived in cheerful harmony, with two
tailors, a saddler, a shoemaker, a Colonel, and other
casual guests. A lady with a high head-dress did the
honors at table, and three blacks of the most untoward
look and odor were in attendance. Our European
ladies would be horrified to see about them negroes and
negresses in a costume which starts no blush here;
and besides, the disagreeable atmosphere would inevitably cause them vapeurs.

Eight miles from Bladensburgh lies **George-town**,
a small town by the Potowmack. As far as this the
river is navigable, and this gave occasion for the establishment of the place from which at one time much
was hoped. There is a tobacco-warehouse here; and
at one time the place had a good deal of trade, but this
was wholly in the hands of English merchants, who
had warehouses here and took out tobacco. On the
outbreak of the war they deserted the place, and
poverty has since been its lot; for nobody among the
inhabitants had capital or credit enough to set up trading. This autumn there came in a few English and
French ships to take out tobacco. The banks of the
river, on which the town stands, are high. Three
miles from here, up the river, are the lower, little falls,
and 10 miles above them, the great falls of the Potowmack. The fall of the river is some 130-150 ft. across;
at one place only is there a plunge of 15 ft. perpendicular height. The noise of the fall is with still weather
heard for a good distance. Just at this time means are
devising to make this fall navigable, either by weirs
or by blasting, or at least to establish convenient port-
ages; which would be vastly advantageous for the

country along the river towards the mountains and for
this place itself.   But to all appearance the carrying-
out of these fine but costly plans will not be so soon
accomplished.   Between the little and great falls many
fish are taken, or at least might be; for here the fish
coming up from the ocean find a *non plus ultra,* and
crowd together in great masses.   Between this place
and the opposite Virginia shore the breadth of the Potowmack is half a mile.   A grey species of stone, very
micaceous, strikes through the region from north-east
to south-west; the same is found likewise about
Bladensburgh and Alexandria; it is the continuation
of a similar but blacker stone seen about Baltimore,
and belongs to the first granite line extending along
the eastern coast of North America.   On both sides the
high banks, and for some distance from the river, sand
and rounded pebbles are the commonest soil, which
therefore is not the most fertile.   Iron-ore occurs
everywhere at the surface, in many forms.   To its development here a sort of rough breccia ('budding
stone') has contributed the most, cementing together
coarse sand and pebbles.   This is the case almost everywhere in the sandy hill-country of the coast, where
more or less iron-bearing earth is found distributed
under and in the upper strata.   From many circumstances, may it be almost believed that the plant-king-
dom has had a share in this phenomenon?   The depth
of the bed of the Potowmack as well as of the other
rivers in America, and the unmistakable traces of their
former higher-lying, shallower, but wider channels,
give continually weighty evidence for the great age of
the continent of America.

We crossed the river, going to Alexandria, whither

along the opposite bank it is reckoned eight miles; the
road is level and proceeds through long woods, among
which only a few tobacco-fields are to be seen. All the
fences were hung with the freshly pulled tobacco-
leaves, so as to let them wilt a little before taking them
to the drying-houses proper.

It is known throughout America that the common
sort of people in Virginia speak markedly through the
nose; and it is not imagination that we could already
observe this on the way to Alexandria. But a great
part of the New Englanders are also given to this
habit, which is at bottom nothing but custom and
imitation.

Alexandria, formerly called Belhaven, was settled
later than Georgetown but grew incomparably faster.
Like Georgetown it stands on the high and almost
perpendicular banks of the Potowmack, which for the
great convenience of shipping not only ebbs and flows
at this place but also somewhat about Georgetown.
From Alexandria to the mouth of the Potowmack,
where it falls into the Bay, the course of the river is
about 150 miles; and it is as far again from its mouth
to the bottom of the Bay; thus from here ships have
some 60 German miles to sail before they reach the
ocean. The situation of the town is, as said, not only
very high towards the river, but rather elevated above
the surrounding country, open and agreeable and better
placed for defence, should the necessity arise, than
many other Virginia towns. The streets are straight
and there are some 200 not unpleasing houses; the
number of the inhabitants may be about 2000 This
was next to Norfolk, even before the war, one of the
wealthiest and most respectable towns in Virginia; its

trade was flourishing and apparently is reviving again. Ships of all sizes are vigorously building there, and the carpenters are so greatly employed that they are not to be hired for less than two Spanish dollars a day. Many new buildings, wharves, and warehouses have gone up within a brief space, and new settlers are every day coming in, drawn by the activity of trade in which item Alexandria will perhaps in future, as hitherto, have the advantage of all other places on the Potowmack. However, the complaisance of the merchants has been recently somewhat disturbed by the stoppage on the part of Great Britain of all trade between its West India islands and the United States. A striking proof of the overweening and unreasonable expectations and demands of the Americans is, among other things, shown by the loud protest they have raised over this restriction of commerce. Having violently withdrawn from the British Empire they could still expect, now as before, to enjoy all advantages of trade equally with British subjects, could flatter themselves that Great Britain, (although plainly to the greatest injury of its Canadian and Nova Scotian colonies), must allow them an open competition in trade. Provisions are cheap but for that reason not always to be had, the price being so insignificant that people hardly take the trouble to bring what they have to market; for the same reason fish are a rarity although the river teems with them. The country-houses of the surrounding region are almost all built on heights; at present this is more a consequence of vanity and usage than anything else, (notwithstanding the first occasion was a necessary concern for health in the avoidance of low and swampy spots), for such a situation has this inconvenience, that often they must go miles for fresh water. On the contrary the Pensylvanians and others build their dwellings as near to springs as possible, and for a fresh drink forego the pleasure of freer air and a finer outlook.

Returning from Alexandria, by Georgetown to Bladensburgh, we found the road vastly more lively, since a crowd of horsemen and their attendants were hastening from all sides to Alexandria for the races which were shortly to be held. At Georgetown we saw *en passant* a case at law being decided on the tavern-porch. Judges, spectators, plaintiffs, defendants, and witnesses sat on the bench before the door, disputing and drinking. The matter appeared to be of no particular consequence, and was being adjusted more in a friendly way than by legal process; the costs, to the satisfaction of everybody, were placed with the host for punch.

We were by chance made acquainted with the peculiar manner in which the laws of Maryland and other provinces protect the citizen under charge of debt. To be sure, the creditor on his complaint has from the civil authorities an order for the arrest of the debtor, but at the same time the debtor, as far as he can, is allowed to make sport of the order and the creditor. The arrest of a bad debtor must be made by the Sheriff; but the Sheriff, even if he has the warrant in his pocket, may not open the door of the house or of the room in which the debtor is; may not raise the latch, although the door is not otherwise barred or closed. He must seek to enter the house by an open door and execute his order, or to take the debtor into custody in the street, if he lets himself be found there. But since it is a simple matter to guard one's house-door against the Sheriff so that he shall never find it open, there are numerous examples where debtors and bankrupts, subject to arrest, have in this way kept up a voluntary imprisonment in their houses for several years. In this condition they can carry on at home any sort of trade or craft without fear of disturbance; but by this indulgence of the law (and this is really the object of the law) it happens that many recover themselves, gaining time and finding expedients, who else in debtors' prisons would go to ruin, through loss of time and interrupted business, even if they had not been broken already. On the Sunday these voluntary prisoners may go at large where they please; on the Lord's day no Sheriff may touch them even in the open street.

Another example of the indulgence of these laws is the following: A man at Bladensburgh made proposals of marriage to a woman, then changed his mind of a sudden, and married another. Not long afterwards he repented at having jilted the first, took her to himself along with his first-married, and has lived with both for several years; both have children by him, and, what is more important still, they behave themselves in a very sisterly manner. None of the neighbors is offended with him, and no civil officer makes inquiries.

With sorrow I observed at Bladensburgh two striking instances of the sad custom, indulged in without thought or conscience almost throughout America, I mean the evil habit of giving the tenderest children and sucklings spirituous and distilled drinks. This happens partly with a view to relieving them of windiness and colicks, regarded as the sole causes of their importunate crying, partly (and this is absolutely without

excuse) to make them quiet and put them to sleep.
Spirituous drinks being so universally in use, nobody
thinks it harm to give them to children as well, and
no attention is paid the bitter injury done their health,
and how frequently there is occasion given in this way
for internal disorders and consuming diseases. I had
many opportunities to convince myself of this, and saw
many of our German women killing their children by
this practice, who following the advice and the custom
of the American women would on all occasions be giving their children quantities of rum, spirits, anise or
kummelwasser, and only to stop their crying. Besides
the injury immediately done, the worst feature of the
practice is the taste acquired in this way for brandy
and grog. Our host's five-year-old child seeks to get
hold of rum or grog wherever he can, and steals fur-
tively to the flask; we saw him almost every day stag-
gering and drunken; he was besides weak and thin as
a skeleton, just as another very young child of a
neighbor, addicted to the same vice. The parents
observed this but were at no pains to prevent it; and
the servants and other people appeared even to be
amused at the drunken children and to egg them on.
In general, children are badly brought up among the
Americans, living sporadically as they do, and the
servants here being only negroes, ignorant, careless,
and immoral, many evils are the consequence.

We returned by Annapolis, whither it is 30 miles
from Bladensburgh. The road lay at first over thin,
sandy hills, and then we came into a flatter country
where the sand is mixed with a large proportion of
good, black earth, producing excellent corn, wheat,
and tobacco. This is a most vexatious road for travel-

lers, from the endless number of cross-bars and gates
encountered, every landowner not only fencing in his
fields, meadows, and woods, but closing the public highways with bars, to keep in the cattle pasturing on the
road. Thus it was that in the short space of a mile we
often had to open 3-4 such gates, and with a horse un-
accustomed to the practice this must always mean a
delay.

We passed through Queen-Anne, on the Patuxent
(a narrow stream) where there is a tobacco-warehouse
and two or three insignificant houses, and 9 miles beyond came to New London on the South river, which
is more than a mile wide; the remainder of the road to
Annapolis was quite flat, sandy, and without stones.

Annapolis has not always had the honor of being
the capital of Maryland; the capital was formerly St.
Mary, on the river of that name, and scarcely more
than in name does the town exist; the site was found
inconvenient and the seat of government was removed
hither. Annapolis stands between the South-west and
Severn rivers, more properly on the latter river, on a
sandy height whence there is an open prospect towards
the Bay. The number of the houses is about 400, of
which some are fine and well-looking. The State-
house indeed is not the splendid building of which the
fame has been sounded, although certainly one of the
handsomest in America; but no less insubstantial than
most of the other publick and private buildings of
America. That it pleases the eye is due to its elevated
situation, its small cupola, its four wooden columns
before the entrance, and because no other considerable
building stands near it. It has only seven windows in
front, and is built of brick two storeys high. The

large hall on the ground-floor is tasteful, although
not spacious. At the other end, facing the entrance,
as is customary in State and Court-houses, there are
raised seats in the form of an amphitheatre designed
for the meetings of the high courts. For the rest, the
building has space enough for the rooms of the Provincial Assembly, the Senate, Executive Council, General Court for the Eastern-Shore, Intendant for the
Revenue &c. Next the State-house is a little building
of one storey meant for the publick treasury. It is
said to be a very strong and fast building; doors and
windows I saw well-barred and fixed—but with all
this the house is empty. The real Treasuries of this
province, throughout the war, were the tobacco-warehouses; the taxes for the most part being assessed and
paid in tobacco and other produce, because the people
had no hard money and unfortunately have none still.
At one end of the town stands the house in which the
Governor lives, but another building, of an extensive
plan and designed for the Governor's residence, was
before the war begun by Governor Blagden, but not
finished, the Assembly judging the plan too costly;
the bare walls remain, known as the Governor's Folly
in memory of him. The streets of the town run almost
all of them radially towards a common central point
which is the State-house. They are not yet paved, and
with the sandy soil this occasions great inconvenience
in summer. Annapolis boasts of a play-house but of
no church, as indeed in everything regarding luxury
the town is inferior to no other and surpasses the most.
Shortly before the war money was collected for building a very handsome church, but the amount was later
applied to bloody purposes, and worship since has been

held partly in the State-house, partly in the play-house.
The situation of the town has been determined as 39°
25′ latitude and 78° longitude west of London.   There
is little or no trade, which is to be explained both by
the site and the character of the harbor.   The roads
leading into the interior are crossed by divers streams,
and the inconvenience arising from so many passages
by ferry has brought it about that the people prefer to
bring their produce to Baltimore and fetch thence what
they need, which they can do by unbroken land-car-
riage.   The harbor, into which fall no fresh streams of
any significance, is full of worms, which live only in
salt water, and these in a few months eat through the
ships' bottoms and render them useless.   At this time
there was not one ship of consequence here, but merely
small craft ; and the merchants of the place themselves
get the most of their stocks from Baltimore.   However, the harbor is spacious, and its mouth, (not over
4-500 yards wide), easy of defence.

The form of government of the state of Maryland
is not essentially different from that of the other states,
having like them a House of Assembly, a Senate, a
Governor and his Council.   The Assembly of the commons possesses really the law-making power of the
state ; the members are annually newly elected in the
counties, and during the meeting of the House receive
15 shillings current a day, or two Spanish dollars.   The
Senate cannot of itself make new laws, but can propose
them to the Commons, and also express its disapproval
of those brought forward by it ; for without the con-
currence of the Senate the resolutions of the Assembly
are without legal force.   The members of the Senate
are elected only every five years, but they meet as often

and at the same time as the Assembly. In the interim
the Governor, with his Council, is charged with the
execution of those laws approved by both of the state's
Assemblies, and in so far he possesses the highest, but
not an arbitrary, power, and must give a strict account
of any thing done by him without authority. In the
choice of the Governor there is an especial prudence
shown. He must have lived five years in the state, his
property must be five times greater than that required
of a Senator, and he can fill the office only three years
in seven. After all these and other careful measures
adopted with a view to having a wise, experienced, and
rich Governor, he finds himself none the less very
answerable and under manifold restrictions.

At present the taxes in Maryland amount in the
average to some 31 and a half to 32 shillings in the
100 pounds, or 1½ pro cent of the value of real
estates. However little this can be regarded as a
heavy burden, it is nevertheless held to be such, in
consideration of the fact that under the former constitution almost nothing was paid in taxes. Meanwhile it is fondly hoped that in future the public imposts will grow less again, but this will hardly be the
case.

It is well known that from the beginning of the
province of Maryland, the territorial lordship of the
province lay in the Baltimore family; after the death
of the last Lord Baltimore Mr. Harford, his natural
son, succeeded to all his possessions and estates but
not to the title. The general revolution offering an
opportunity, the state of Maryland held it convenient
to regard no overlordship as henceforth valid, and
consequently to declare that the rightful claims of the

heir of Lord Baltimore are null and void. A free and independent state is not indeed essentially obliged to justify itself in such a matter as against a private person. *Stat enim pro ratione voluntas.* However, Mr. Harford immediately after the armistice coming over from Europe to contest for his inherited rights, several grounds have been given for the action taken; among others, that during the Revolution Mr. Harford was living in Great Britain, a subject of a power inimical to the state, and hence was to be regarded as an enemy of the province. Mr. Harford was born and brought up in Europe, had never before been in Maryland, was at the outbreak of the war still under age, and is at present only 23 years old, and was guilty of no offence against the state of Maryland except that of being the lawful heir of his father who drew thence a yearly income of 20-25,000 Pd. sterling in ground-rents and returns from his domains.

The next Assembly will decide finally in this matter; but the outcome is easily to be foreseen when one remembers that a whole people is unanimously resolved its property shall no longer be held in fee-tail. The state itself, by and through the change in its constitution, has assumed the paramount right, has purchased the demesne estates of the family of Baltimore and applied the proceeds to the maintenance of the war; ground-rents are no longer paid, because another method of taxation has been adopted and has become necessary. Mr. Harford at most has no further hope beyond receiving arrearages up to the year of his majority; but even this is subject to as many doubts and difficulties as all other payments which Europeans are demanding of Americans.

Annapolis has the honor of setting up the first mint for small silver coin in the United States. A goldsmith here mints on his own account, but with the sanction of the civil authorities. After the decadency of the paper money, what with the general shortage of small coin, it became customary and necessary all over America to cut Spanish dollars into two, four, or more parts and let the pieces pass as currency. This divisional method soon led to a profitable business in the hands of skillful cutters, who contrived to make 5 quarters, or 9 and 10 eights, from a single round dollar, so that everybody soon refused to accept this coin unless by weight or opinion; the perplexity how to get rid of this cornered currency is an advantage to the goldsmith mentioned, who takes them at a profit in exchange for his own round coin. On the obverse of his shillings and half-shillings stands his name *I. Chalmers, Annapolis;* in the middle two hands clasped; on the reverse: *One Shilling,* 1783; and two doves billing.

Recently, after the Congress had fled from Philadelphia, and Trenton did not seem to it comfortable enough, the proposal was made to invite it to Annapolis. But the town having not sufficient trade or provisioning capacity, nor being large enough to entertain all the representatives of the United States with their adherents, it occasioned no little joy when a few days ago a courier brought the news that the Congress had decided to hold its interim-session here, and would assemble on the 25th of next October. But it will remain here only until quarters for it have been set up at Georgetown on the Potowmack and at Trenton on the Delaware; for at the same time this

24

illustrious assembly resolved for the future to remove
its residence every autumn and spring from one to the
other of these places. These solemn migrations have
given occasion to the bitterest gibes in the public
papers.

Maryland is behind none of the other states in excellence of climate, in variety and fertility of soil, or in
diversity of products. Its situation, almost at the
middle of the continent of North America, causes its
inhabitants seldom to languish from immoderate heat
or to suffer from disagreeable cold, and most of the
products of the rest of America thrive here under good
management. With Virginia it shares the advantages
of a spacious bay, which in regard to its size, safety,
and the number of its navigable streams can hardly
be excelled. It is convenient at all seasons of the year
and is seldom disturbed by the hurricanes of the south
or closed by the impassable ice of the north. Maryland
produces good maize and excellent wheat, hemp, and
flax. The more profitable culture of tobacco has indeed kept these articles somewhat under; but the inconvenience of wanting the most necessary things and
the uncertainty of getting them from other parts having been variously felt, more attention is now directed
to agriculture. Swine and horned cattle do well with
the most careless handling, and increase prodigiously.
The lands are more divided, and more uniformly, than
in Virginia, are therefore somewhat better cultivated
and are generally worth more, especially on the western side of the Bay where the soil is less sandy and
barren than on the Eastern Shore.

The whole province is divided into the following 16
counties; Ann-Arundel, of which Annapolis is the chief

place, Baltimore, St. Mary, Charles, Kent, Frederick, Prince George, Somerset, Dorchester, Worcester, Talbot, Cecil, Calvert, Queen Anne—and two other new ones, the names of which escape me. Those counties which have as yet no particular or aptly placed towns fix their Court-houses at some convenient place in the middle of the county, often in the midst of the forest, where at the appointed times numerous assemblies come together to transact business, as well as out of curiosity and the desire of company.

The country between Annapolis and Baltimore is for the most part flat and sandy; having gone 9 miles of the road, one notices a grey quarry-stone protruding from the soil and farther on much breccia composed of iron-bearing sand. The extensive woods consisted, throughout, of the twi-blade Jersey pine, and there were only a few scattered farms to be seen. A few miles this side Baltimore the Ferry-branch of the Patapsco must be crossed, near two miles wide, and the passage not agreeable as we made it, at night in a rain-storm and with drunken negroes. But it was far more unpleasant to learn that, of our collections made in the mountains and ordered hither, nothing as yet had arrived. We could no nothing but consign them, with the rest of our store, to the care of a friend here, for later expedition, and we left Baltimore troubled at having been at fruitless pains.

On the road to Philadelphia the first 10 miles are through a sandy clay soil, showing numerous fragments of iron-bearing stone. We put up for the night at a tavern standing alone by the road. A man from the Eastern Shore entertained us with many anecdotes regarding the 'dam'nd English dogs,' that is, the soldiers. Of all he laid to their charge nothing vexed

him so much as their stealing his fat hogs after having
in vain offered him money for them. But in an honorable and upright manner he acknowledged that he and
other American militia-men on their campaigns had
done as ill, taking cattle when they wanted them and
without having offered money, which besides they had
none of. In the morning, three miles from our
quarters, we passed an iron-foundry lying in ruins.
At one time swamp-ore was worked here, which the
neighboring marshes furnish in plenty; the war coming on put a stop to the business. One mile this side
Gunpowder-Creek the blackish granite began to appear, which, as at Baltimore, receives its color from the
mixture of a blackish scale-hornblende. The stream
itself, as we afterwards saw, has broken through a
deep bed of this stone, and it appears from the rock-
walls of the creek that the stone was originally laid
in strata. Farther on, at the ferry over the Susquehannah, there was still to be seen a related species of
stone, but of a lighter, greyer color. Only along the
deep beds dug out by the streams is there opportunity
to observe the underlying rock, which elsewhere is
covered with the common sandy soil composing the
level surface. Thus, for many miles along these roads
and in these parts there is a tedious uniformity of pine-
forest and sand. The Susquehannah at this ferry,
(called the lowest), is a mile wide, and has many
hidden shelves due to the lines of rock striking across.

Seven miles beyond this ferry we came to **Charles-
town**, on the North-East-Branch, still in Maryland.
It was a church-dedication day. Already we had met
on the road a great many country-people, all of them
well dressed, on horseback, and all sober although returning from the festival. The sun was not yet set

and the market not yet over when we reached the place, which contains not more than 40-50 houses. There was a superfluity of the best wares, the finest cloths and linens, and not less than five booths for silver-ware and jewellery to be seen. But the merchants who had come from Baltimore and Philadelphia, complained that they could hardly pay their tavern-scores, to say nothing of their expenses. Of gazers at the fine things, or of people hankering to buy, there was no lack, but the money was wanting. The court-days, which should have been held several weeks before (this is the capital of Charles county) must be still further postponed on account of the unfortunately general scarcity of money. For where no money is for settling debt-cases won, or paying costs and fines, or for 'instructing' attorneys, no court can be held. At the house where we put up, the fair damsels of the region waited a long time for music and the dance but in vain; not a fidler was to be impressed, and they would have been easily satisfied; the company was obliged to get home undiverted and unfatigued.

The place has no trade, notwithstanding large vessels can lie here; but tobacco is no more raised, and there is not much else that can be exported.

A few miles farther lies Head of Elk, on the Elk river. Near this little place General Howe and his army landed in the fall of 1777; the house in which he ate is pointed out as a curiosity, and the English are contemned here merely for the reason that after so many threats they failed to carry out what they promised, which, it appears, would have been preferred here. Shortly after we came into the jurisdiction of the

State of Delaware,

which formerly was also a part of the property of the Penn family (just as actually the Governor of Pensylvania is Governor of this state), but for the rest, the state or province exists of itself, independent of Pensylvania. It is called properly 'the lower states of Delaware,' ✝ and is made up of three counties only, New-Castle, Kent, and Sussex, which together occupy the lower and southern side of the Delaware and in part the peninsula formed by this river and the Chesapeak Bay (the 'Eastern Shore,' according to the Maryland and Virginia expression). In length this state begins 12 miles north-west of New Castle, and extends to the mouth of the river, in breadth it is nowhere more than 30 miles. Next to Rhode Island it is the smallest of all the United States; but is not so well peopled, the eastern or New England states indeed generally exceeding those more to the south in number of inhabitants, towns, and villages. The form of government of this state corresponds with that of Pensylvania, consisting of an Assembly, Executive Council, Governor and Privy Council. Also the laws, since the abrogation of the union, are about the same as those of Pensylvania. The complete separation of these states took place during the Revolution. This state furnished to the army only one slim regiment during the war; but at the same time maintained another, called a flying-corps; and such it was from all accounts. The troops of the state

were at the time not completely discharged from
service; and this, at the last election for members of
the Assembly, gave rise to violent dissensions. The
soldiers claimed that they had a right to cast their
votes in the election of these Members. The right is
granted by the law, if one has lived a year in the
province and can show property in the amount of 40
Pd. The first provision must be allowed, because the
soldiers, even if not natives, performed service for
that period or longer within the limits of the state; as
satisfying the second condition of the electorate the
soldiers held that the state, being in their debt for
several years pay, the sum amounted to far more than
the stipulated 40 Pd. But, said the citizens, so long as
you are soldiers we cannot grant you the suffrage, because soldiers are merely servants of the state, not
really members of it, contribute nothing to the needs of
the community, and fall under special laws and juris-
dictions—and particularly because what the state owes
its soldiers cannot be counted as actual property; which
last objection the soldiers from troublous experience
are unable to deny. Meantime, this quarrel excited
much anxiety and unrest, but remained undecided
until shortly after this the whole American army, by
promulgation of the Congress, was finally discharged
from service, and thus the soldiers became citizens
again; but in the interim the precaution had been taken,
at the last election, of ordering away all soldiers who
were at New-Castle. The upper part of this province,
lying towards Pensylvania, has good meadow-land
along the Delaware and the streams flowing into it,
and the higher land shows good wheat soil. The lower
part is sandy and infertile; at the mouth of the Dela-

ware the people support themselves by fishing, and by divers sorts of trade * with the in- and out-going ships and the assistance they render these. But it is strange to say especially of this little state, as several have done, that its sky is clear and its weather regular, as if in these items it was superior to the adjacent regions.

Christianabridge, the first place in this state we came to, 12 miles from Head of Elk, is of itself a small place but on account of the convenient communication to be had here between the Delaware and the Chesapeak Bay, may become more important. From here to Philadelphia the customary and shorter post-road goes by Newport, but this is a hilly and rocky road; a better and more pleasant is by New-Castle, and along the beautiful banks of the Delaware. This we chose and after five miles reached

New-Castle, the capital of this province and the seat of the Governor, but a little insignificant town on the high banks of the Delaware. Besides several churches it has few other seemly buildings, the whole number of which may be scarcely 200. There is no trade here and the inhabitants seem not to be active. The nearness of Philadelphia, which is only 30 miles higher up the river, is likely the great hindrance to the taking-up of large affairs. The boundaries of the county of New-Castle are so fixed that this place lies at the centre of an arc of a 12-mile radius. Five miles on, along the river where one continually observes good land, fine meadows in the bottoms, large wheat-

---

* Formerly, (and doubtless in future when duties are collected again), by smuggling and receiving smuggled goods.

fields above, much cattle, and neat country-houses, lies

Wilmington; a vastly better place, large and busy. We arrived there a little before sunset, having not far from the town been set over Christina Creek, which falls into the Delaware here. Wilmington is not only very pleasantly situated but also very advantageously for trade. Standing on a moderate hill based on rock, it has on the one side the Christina and on the other the Brandywyn Creek, these making a point of land, at the most elevated part of which is the town, the land thence falling away and flat to the Delaware, 2-3 miles distant; a splendid prospect towards the river and the farther shores in Jersey is thus afforded.

Brigantines as well as three-masted ships can come up Christina Creek to the town and lay-to very close in. The trade of the place, which begins to be considerable, is in grain, flour, and timber. The town contains some 400 houses, mostly good, neat, brick-houses standing close together in several straight streets; it has two well-supplied and roomy market-places, four or five houses of worship, and many new houses are on the point of building. The Swedish colony here, which gave occasion to the settlement of the town and conferred on Christina Creek its name, has preserved pretty well its language and usages; at least these are less deformed than among the Swedes of Philadelphia, many of whom scarcely understand any longer the speech of their fore-fathers.

Near to Wilmington the Brandywyn is crossed, over a good stone bridge. The name of this stream has been made immortal by the fight between Howe and Washington which took place at a little distance from here in the year 1777. The banks here are deep and rocky, and the narrow gorge through which the stream flows makes a view peculiarly pleasing and rough. The stone appearing at the surface is a grey, fine-grained mixture of quartz and black hornblende. Several mills are so conveniently placed on this creek that large shalops can lie close to them, and unload and load wheat and flour with great ease; the creek is not navigable beyond. Many good houses and fine country-estates are to be seen in this region, where twenty years ago it was all wilderness and nobody cared to buy. The flour-trade has now so increased the value of this profitable situation, that an acre of land on the creek fit for a mill-site costs 100 Pd. and more Pensyl. Current.

Over high ground, here and there rocky, at a little distance from the Delaware which is now and again in sight, one comes to Marcus-hook, a small village with a church. This country is distinguished by many well-kept live hedges which elsewhere in America are little in use as yet. The whole way from Virginia we noticed very few birds, some partridges (*Tetrao virginianus, L.*) and quails (*Alanda magna, L.*), falsely so-called, excepted. But for two days there have met us flocks of many thousands of blackbirds (*Oriolus phoeniceus*) which have begun their journey to the south, and where they settled they covered the trees with black. The wild doves had already gone south in the middle of the month.*

---

* The birds of passage, to which the American farmer most often pays regard, are: Columba migratoria, Turdus migratorius, T. polyglottus, Oriolus phoeniceus, Alauda magna, Al. alpestris, Picus principalis, Pic. auratus, Gracula Quiscula,

Twelve miles from Wilmington on this road and 14 from Philadelphia lies **Chester**, belonging to Pensylvania; a place of middling size to which the ships lying there, going to Philadelphia or coming thence, furnish some support. Here we saw a few fine mulberry trees, not often found elsewhere. The assertion has been made that these trees, like the walnut, better the soil in which they grow. With a view to the culture of silk, the elder Bartram made a few small but promising experiments; also, as du Pratz relates, successful experiments have been made by a lady at New Orleans, so that there is reason to hope that this domestic tree will one day be of great use to America.

Farther on, nine miles from Philadelphia, is Darby, a small village where in deep roads the grey rock was still to be seen, overlaid with a coarse, slatey, white stone. The 31st of October in the evening we came a second time to Philadelphia.

Philadelphia. During our absence a company of players had arrived. For many years America has enjoyed these diversions at sundry places. Travelling companies came from Europe to Philadelphia, New York, Charleston, and the West Indies; and Philadelphia, as also New York, had a special play-house, although the Quakers have always protested. The present company, under the direction of a Mr. Reyan, **+** was formed several years ago from the remnants of

---

Motacilla Sialis, Mot. Calendula, Loxia Cardinalis, Emberiza hiemalis & nivalis, Trochilus Colubris, &c. and a few others which are the more striking in the eye of the countryman either for the great flocks in which they come and go or on account of their distinct colors. But generally only a few land-birds remain the winter through in this region.

one that had gone to pieces, and made its first appearance at Baltimore. During this summer it had sought to take advantage of the presence of the British army at New York, but with trifling success. It then came here, where another evil star awaited it. An old law of the state of Pensylvania forbids public plays. When that law was passed Quaker principles had a stronger hold than now; for enlightenment is gaining ground here also, and the long sojourn of many foreigners, military men and others, has greatly changed manners, taste, and ideas, widening and increasing a disposition for all pleasures. A great part of the modernized inhabitants desired that plays should go on, which the others vehemently opposed as an unlawful and immoral innovation; so the general question was: will the play be countenanced by the government or not? The Assembly had recently met,—most of its members those who have been born and brought up in the country, have never seen a play, and therefore have few and wrong ideas as to the morality of the matter, or on the other hand Quakers and other sectarians who from their religious principles frown on all the pleasures of the rest of the world —to this assembly, then, representations and petitions were submitted pro and contra, and judgment was awaited.

A petition signed by very many of the inhabitants declares the dreaded licensing of the play to be a contemptuous abuse of the law; extremely sinful after a war just ended; * saying: that an authoritative approbation of this idle, licentious, pernicious pleasure would

---

* At Baltimore even during the war the play was legitimate.

be wickedly and ruinously inadvertent, showing the
greatest ingratitude to Providence; that the young
would be thus debauched, led away into dissipation and
every vicious tendency, and the taste for the orderly
and virtuous joys of domestic and social life be corrupted; that conjugal unfaith would be so occasioned,
disorder and extravagance be increased among the
citizenry, the spread and confirmation of true religion
hindered, &c. In a word the play is described as the
source and school of every vice, as the direct road to
Hell, and the certain means of destruction to the state.
Mr. Reyan on the contrary endeavored to convince the
House of Assembly of the good effected by plays and
of their influence on the polite and moral culture of
the young and of the people generally; he did not forget to titillate the ambition of the members of the
Assembly: " The most celebrated and greatest nations
" of the world, said he to them, have at all times had
" plays and loved them: and shall this young budding
" state, having in the most praiseworthy manner es-
" caped the chains of threatening servitude and the
" dangers of a bloody war, having made sure its claims
" to a rank and dignity equal to those of the other
" kingdoms of this earth, shall it in this regard think
" and act differently to them?—No! Policy says, No!
" —Sound reason says, No! and certainly the wisdom
" and magnanimity of the House will corroborate—"
No! the House of Assembly did not corroborate, and the
majority of the votes was against the play. And the
proposal fell to the ground, (from which Mr. Reyan
promised himself the best results, according to the
posture of affairs then), to lay a tax on plays, as had
shortly before been done in the case of billiards. The

House was not to be moved, and forbade the continuation of plays, which, despite the law, were given for
some time afterwards. In this state, as in many others
where for every matter a new and express law must
be made, it is only necessary to comply with the literal
sense, and the law may be freely mocked at. Concerts
were not prohibited, nor reading, nor dancing. ✚ So
concerts were advertised, a select piece to be read between the acts, and a ballet given at the close. I went
to hear one of these concerts and saw instead the
tragedy of 'Douglas.' The music was as customary,
and the actors and actresses came on with a bit of paper
in their hands which they did not look at and finally
threw away, but for the rest played their rôles as
formerly. This in a country which boasts of its laws.
There is no disavowal of the law ; there is no insistence
on its observance, but a quiet looking-on while means
are found to avoid it. Thus both sides are content ; the
one was pleased at making a law, the other at making
naught of it. However, this might not long be kept
up, for the Assembly having come together again, it
will likely pass a new law and interrupt this reading-
society.

The Assembly of Pensylvania,* which, as I have
mentioned, was at this time in session, held its sittings
in a large room in the State-House. The doors are
open to everybody ; I had thus the pleasure of being
several times in attendance ; but I cannot say that in
the strict sense I saw them sitting. At the upper end
of the room the **Speaker**, or President of the Assembly,

---

* It is called: General Assembly of Representatives of the
Freemen of Pensylvania.

sits at a table, in a rather high chair. He brings forward the subjects to be considered, and to him and towards him the speakers direct themselves when they open their minds regarding questions pending. He calls the Assembly to order, when he observes inattention, or talk that is disturbing, and puts the question when the matter has been sufficiently discussed pro and contra, and is now to be decided by a majority of the votes. The members sit in chairs at both sides of the table and of the room, but seldom quietly, and in all manner of postures; some are going, some standing, and the more part seem pretty indifferent as to what is being said, if it is not of particular importance or for any reason uninteresting to them. When the votes are to be taken, those in the affirmative rise, and those in the negative remain sitting. The members of German descent (if as is sometimes the case, from a lack of thorough readiness in the English language they either do not properly grasp the matter under discussion or for any other reason cannot reach a conclusion) are excused for sitting doubtful until they see whether the greater number sits or stands, and then they do the same so as always to keep with the largest side. Each county elects and returns yearly six representatives to the Assembly, the full number is thus 69;* but they are seldom all present.

---

* Pensylvania numbered formerly but 10 counties: City of Philadelphia, County of Philadelphia, Buckingham or Bucks, (capital Newtown,) Chester, Lancaster, York, Cumberland, (Carlisle,) Berks, (capital Reading,) Northampton, (Easton), Bedford, Northumberland, (Sunbury); to these there have been recently added six new counties, beyond the mountains: Westmoreland, Washington, Fayette, Franklin, Montgomery, Dauphin, and Luzerne.

The constitution of Pensylvania differs from that of the other states in this, that besides this Assembly, which is the real law-making power, it has not like the others a Senate or Upper House, (in imitation of the English House of Lords), but a Supreme Executive Council, of which the Governor is President, consisting of 12 members, elected also in the counties by turns. Pensylvania besides has been quite alone in setting up a Council of Censors, to which each county elects two members. It is the duty of these Censors to safeguard the Constitution, to observe what Assembly and Council undertake and what they carry out, to guard against encroachments of power, to criticize all abuses and changes, and to examine into the management of the revenues of the state. But information as to all this is to be had from the published constitutions of the several states.

Regarding the frequent changes of residence of the Congress, and especially in the matter of its annual migrations from Jersey to Maryland and from Maryland to Jersey, recently decided upon, the newspapers of Philadelphia have hitherto had no little diversion.

Under the protection of an almost unrestricted freedom of the press, which rightly used can be one of the solidest supports of the Constitution, there are every day lavished for the amusement of the public the bitterest mockeries over the high-puissant Congress, and nobody is held to account. The populace, which takes impudence to be liberty, would defend the author as well as the publisher against every attack, as was recently the case in a suit at law which Bob Morris, the celebrated financier, brought against the printer of the ' Freeman's Journal ' for an abusive article. I

give only an example or two to show how rudely the
Illustrious Assembly is handled. To the Defender of
the Fatherland, General Washington, the Congress decided to erect a statue on horseback, the work to be
done by the first artist of France, and the statue to be
set up at the meeting-place of the Congress. This
resolution was followed shortly afterwards by that
fixing two 'foederal-towns,' on the Delaware and the
Potowmack, in which alternately the Congress was to
assemble. Whereupon, in the 'Freeman's Journal,'
some one brought forward the hypothesis that the Congress migrating from one town to the other, the
mounted statue must necessarily go along; and very
likely this horse, as the Trojan, would be hollow-bellied
so as to lodge on the journey the gentlemen of the
Congress, and for the private archives of the same
there would be room in **a part of the anatomy** equally
so. Again, it was proposed to build a floating town for
the Congress, known to be poor and greatly in debt,
sending it and all its luggage down the Delaware from
Trenton, along the coast into the Chesapeak Bay, and
up the Potowmack to Georgetown, comfortably and at
a saving of heavy expense. It was announced further **+**
that at the earliest possible day there would be seen
swinging in America an immeasurably great pendulum;
for the Americans, having observed the unequal and
uncertain workings of the European machines of state,
having discovered the irregularities to which that political system is subject, had devised a **working mechanism** for keeping their affairs going in an orderly
course. The centre of oscillation of the pendulum hit
upon for this purpose would be somewhere in the
planet Mars, the weight to be composed of **certain**

25

particularly heterogeneous materials of great specific gravity known as the American Congress. This pendulum will swing through a space of 180 miles, between Annapolis and Trenton; but even the most erudite mathematician will be unable to calculate its true line of movement, since it will describe neither a straight line, nor a cycloid, parabola nor hyperbola, but will go **its own crooked way.**

These and many other similar anecdotes should plainly enough show that this sovereign Assembly gets no especial reverence nor, outwardly, any great honor in America. But in a political aspect as well, it appears from other circumstances that the Congress has neither the necessary weight nor the requisite solidity. It is therefore, in the very restricted compass of its activities, exposed to all manner of grievous vexations. It was to be expected of a people so enthusiastic for liberty that they should grant their Congress only a shadow of dignity, (a very perplexing circumstance when there is a disposition to be proud), and watch its proceedings with a jealous exactitude. The real business and the prerogatives of the Congress, in so far as it represents the common power of the United States, are: To declare war and conclude peace, to raise armies and give them orders, to contract alliances with foreign powers, to oversee the constitutions of all the states and preserve their relations to the whole; to **call** for and administer the revenues necessary to these ends, and to make public debts. In so far its activities may be compared with those of other sovereign powers, the Congress being bound to exercise care for the well-being and the safety of the community. But as regards the application of the means requisite, there are a

thousand difficulties in the way. Thus the United
States authorized the Congress to borrow money and to
pledge the honor of the nation; but to pay these debts,
there is no authority granted.* Each individual state
has it own independent government which is concerned
for its especial welfare and inner security; its own
laws, police, execution of justice, and all other institutions looking to the furtherance of the common good,
with no immediate influence on the general union of
the states, free and regulated according to its own
pleasure. It is competent to these governments of the
several states to resist all ordinances and proposals of
the Congress which are unpleasing to them; and if they
had not the right, they would do so none the less.

The power conferred by the people on the government of each separate state, and conferred by these
governments on the Congress is subject to incessant
change, in so far, that is, as the members of these assemblies are from time to time replaced by others. Thus
continually the private man is taking up the business

---

* This is still sorrily the case: The debts of the Congress
at the beginning of the year 1786 amounted to 54 million dollars, of which, distributed into 14 parts, 6 parts are due to
France, 3 to Holland, 2 to British subjects, and the remainder
to Americans.

The Congress, on the 2nd day of August 1786, determined
the budget for this year, the total 3,770,000 dollars in amount,
of which 317985 dollars for interest on the debts made in
France and Holland, 169352 dollars the costs of the Civil department, 168274 dollars for the Military department, 44294
for sundry other disbursements, and 1 million 392059 dollars
are needed for funds payable during the next year. *The Congress will with difficulty be able to effect the procuring of this
sum. Hamb. polit. Journ.* October. 1786.

of a statesman, and after a time returns to make place for another. By this arrangement it is desired to guard against the misuse of the highest power, which a constant body of statesmen might allow themselves to drift into. Every member of a Provincial Assembly as well of the Congress will be careful of approving an ordinance which as a private person he might hesitate to obey. He will be loath to impose heavy taxes, which must be a burden to himself as well; and will be slow to make an ill use of the public moneys, because similar action on the part of his successors would be disagreeable to him.

But also, generally useful institutions will be more slowly advanced if it appears that special interests are to suffer, and there will be a hampering of the best and wisest plans of the Congress. For it may give no decisive sentence, may not arbitrarily order. It can represent only under correction, make proposals and recommendations for the carrying out of which it must have recourse chiefly to influence, cabals, and crooked ways as was said before. And the Congress is very well aware of its increasing infirmity and its diminishing dignity; and does not fail to bring before the people, through hired authors, the necessity of increasing its prerogatives and widening its sphere of arbitrary action, even recommending a Congress to be made up of permanent members. All the newspapers contain articles in which are combated the ineptitude and groundlessness of the jealous suspicion which is almost everywhere entertained regarding the unquenchable thirst after grandeur of this illustrious Assembly.

Their place does not give the members of the Con-

gress any particular advantage or rank beyond their
fellow-citizens; nor can such posts be said to be very
lucrative, the allowances granted by the state, exclusive
of travelling costs, amounting scarcely to 1 Pd. sterling a day. However, an election to the Congress is
always honorable in itself, and after retirement remains a glorious memory, proof of the regard and confidence which one's fellow-citizens have for his capacities and zeal of service. The Deputies to the Congress are chosen from the Provincial Assemblies, the
number from each state being proportioned to its size,
the extent of its business and influence, but this may
not be less than two, nor more than seven. Whatever
the number of the Deputies from a state, they have together but one vote in the Congress, where the smallest
deciding vote is seven against six; they must decide
among themselves, by a majority of votes, regarding
the affairs of their state in relation to the Congress and
as regards the party in the Congress they think it salutary to support, provided they have not received defi-
nite orders as to their conduct, but this is generally the
case.

Nothing has so much damaged faith in the Congress,
or so diminished regard for it, even among its friends
and constituents, and nothing has caused more general
and bitter indignation against it, than the debts heaped
by it upon the states, and especially the woful after-
pains left by the paper-money issued under its warrant, which (with the hard regulations adopted in
support of its continually lessening credit) has sorrily
been the occasion of the loss of a great part or all of
the property of so many once prosperous families and
individuals. In vain the Congress offers in excuse that

other methods were not open to it by which to complete
the great work of freedom, and that certainly and alas !
the welfare of a few private persons must inevitably be
sacrificed (against the will of the Congress indeed) to
that of the whole community. However, the repre-
hensions of the upright are express, who regarded
other means as possible and proposed them, and the
complaints of suffering innocence continue.

There was a time when printed bits of paper were to
the people as valuable as hard coin ; for paper-money
had already been introduced in all the provinces,
(under the royal government and by the King's
authority), to the furtherance of trade, and was kept
readily in currency because the public was not deluged
with it,* as was lightly and superabundantly the case,
after the first years of the war, under the Congress.
However, these notes, dirty, decomposed, patched, and
unreadable as they came to be, scarcely to be handled
without contamination, are still deserving of a sort of
respect. The hope merely of the end to be gained gave
them a value, and during the first years of the war
this hope was certainly very much alive. At that time
the paper-money issued by the Congress and the states
was wholly esteemed and was reckoned without question as equal to silver and gold. But this kind of mint-
age being found to be so easy, new and other new
millions being struck off on all occasions in payment
of the costs of the war, credit began to weaken, and
could only be kept up for a short space by blind zeal on
the one hand and fear on the other. Sundry reasons

---

* Each province might issue only a certain amount, not exceeding its capacities ; and proportioned to the needs of its
trade and disbursements.

contributed later to its steady fall.   Opposition to the
war and mistrustful fear of its outcome, on the part of
the discontent; the preference of a trading nation for
the nobler, solider, and glittering metals, a preference
never extinct and hardly to be repressed by patriotism;
the obligation of the merchant to pay for his imported
European wares with sounding coin; the necessity of
supplying American soldiers in British prisons with
cash money, which their relatives wished to do even if
the Congress assiduously neglected it; and finally the
absolute impossibility, or at least the extreme improb-
ability of coming by a sure fonds on which in some
measure to base the credit of the rapidly increasing
paper millions; all these circumstances contributed pro-
portionately to the depreciation of the paper-money.
Then a few merchants, under some one of these pre-
texts, began to ask for their wares the customary
cash-price, or the double of it in paper-money.   Whoever had to buy, must submit to the condition, but in
his own business made use of a similar for his reimbursement.   But this device once adopted, the depreciation of the paper-money went forward irresistibly.   The
Congress sought in vain, with the whole fulness of its
credit, and by repeated and emphatic decrees, to stay
the pernicious evil, but all the measures adopted remained without effect, or the effect was of short dura-
tion.   Once the tormented Congress set an example of
the greatest tyranny, through a law for the maintenance of its paper, known as the ' Tender-law ' and forever to be abominated.   The value of the paper had
already considerably fallen, when it was proclaimed
that in the payment of old debts the Congress or
Paper-money should be legally accepted at its full

nominal value, paper dollars at the time being about as 50 to 1 of silver. Thus whoever before the war, or even later, owed 50 hard dollars, or had merely borrowed them, could now come off by the payment of 50 paper dollars, the fiftieth part, that is, of the true worth; the legally cozened creditor was obliged to regard the debt as extinguished, or refusing, to expose himself to informations and severe handling. It may easily be fancied to what great injustice and oppression such a decree must have given rise, which nevertheless did not accomplish the end proposed, the paper-money of the Congress sinking at last to **nothing**, repudiated by itself in some degree. The loss which the holders of the paper-money sustained by its yearly and daily falling value cannot be estimated, but there are great and woful complaints in this matter generally. It is indeed unpleasant for the Congress itself that its most zealous adherents and friends, misled by patriotic credence in its golden promises, have of all people lost the most. And it was discretion on the part of the members of most of the Assemblies, that they had their allowances paid not in paper but in natural products, as, for example, with wheat in Pensylvania, with tobacco in Maryland and Virginia; good proof that in these very Assemblies they were either convinced of the worthlessness of the paper, or felt the conveniency of making the most of the situation. But after all that may or can be said about the paper-money, it remains none the less true that without it, (a tax wrung from their subjects and certainly distributed very unequally), the Congress would have found it impossible to raise the money needed for the war.

At present the paper-money of the Congress is

wholly worthless, and will be preserved merely as a
curiosity of sad memory. Whoever cares to make a
collection of this diverse and multiplied money will
however get great entertainment from the proverbs and
emblematic pictures, and will observe, among other
things, how Father Priscian ✝ has been given a rude
cuff on the ear. For example, on an 80 dollar note of
the year 1779, there stands a tree, between the heav-
ens—and the waters, with the legend: Et in sæcula
sæculorum *florescebit.* The printing of the paper-money
was always done with great circumspection ; the paper
was specially prepared and delineated ; sworn persons
were present who carefully counted off the sheets, and
others signed each note with their names ; and the
blocks and letters used were destroyed after every edition. Nevertheless there was a deal of counterfeiting.

After the decay of the Congress-money, here in Pensylvania and in a few other provinces the State-money
and ' Loan-certificates ' kept a certain value. The first
is a sort of paper-money, which in Pensylvania was
issued in dollars by authority of an Act of Assembly ;
and the second, states' bonds for money borrowed of
the public, for deliveries made, and other services rendered : both are at this time received at the public
treasuries in the payment of taxes, but reckoned at
half value, the other half to be paid in hard money ;
but the certificates are not valid in the payment of civil
and military officers, of soldiers, or of sailors. But in
the common trade and negotiations neither passes ; and
further, there are certain taxes which must be paid in
gold or silver, as the lamp, night-watch, street, and
poor-tax, as also (according to the phrase of a decree
in German) die **Fines, wenn einer nicht Exerciren**

gehet, that is, the penalties of the militia-soldiers who do not appear for their weekly or monthly manoevres.

During my stay this time at Philadelphia I had the chance opportunity of being present at the marriage-ceremony of a young Quaker couple. The ceremony is very simple, but solemn. Bride and bride-groom sit in the meeting-house, before the whole assembly, which meditative and still, according to their custom, waits for what the holy spirit will let them know on the occasion through one or another member of the society. No one was inspired at this time, and after a long while of speechlessness the marriage-contract was read aloud slowly by one of the oldest persons present— for they have no installed and paid ministers—without preface or comment. Thereupon the betrothed silently joined hands, and then signed the contract read them, as was done also by the eldest of the congregation, the relatives, and others present, witnessing the transaction —and the ceremony was over.

In the matter of divorces the Quakers are as expeditious; but these take place among them less often. But married persons of other religions also separate in America with no great formality, either quietly or, after the event, by giving notice in the public prints of the conclusion reached. In the newspapers as well there are to be found not seldom advertisements of deserting and absconding wives, or warnings to the public from husbands not to give credit to their divorced or prodigal wives. But to be completely valid and legal, a divorce must be the subject of a special resolution in the Provincial Assembly, and it is not always that the trouble is thought worth the taking.

I should have been glad also to be a spectator at the

baptizing of a young and handsome Anabaptist, which
was announced for a cold Sunday morning of this
chilly November; but I came too late to the Schuylkill where the ceremony was performed. It was indeed very cold; but these good people do not believe
that the coldness of the water at a time of baptizing
can be injurious to the health, even of the tenderest
woman, as this candidate was.

At Philadelphia I could not be too circumstantial
with my acquaintances in telling of my journey to the
mountains. To many of these citizens everything I
had remarked, seen, or brought back with me was great
and surprising news. This is not to be wondered at,
what with the almost total lack of a precise geographical and topographical description of the country. Many
of the small towns and villages are scarcely known even
by name, and one might almost say that beyond the
range of their inhabitants and nearest neighbors they
are many times not known at all; and as regards full
accounts touching their situation, size, management,
history, trade, population, œconomy, and plenty or
goodness of their particular products, there are no
public reports whatever to be had. It is therefore
greatly to be wished that patriotic American scholars +
might soon determine to give an exact and complete
description of their fatherland. It would be received
thankfully by both foreigners and natives. According
to the plan which, on leaving New York, I had made
of visiting the most remarkable regions of the inner
and frontier parts of the middle provinces, I had now
travelled more than 1200 English miles in about three
months; this space of time, to which I was **necessarily**
restricted, did not permit me to linger as I should have

wished, making leisurely observations and researches. Very little assistance or information is to be had of the inhabitants, who on the whole are not much acquainted with the characteristical natural treasures of their country, and it is besides vexatious enough, when they begin to tell of this or that just when one is on the point of pushing on farther, having previously made inquiries in vain regarding the curiosities of the region or gone about looking for them oneself. These people, who naturally concern themselves only about what brings them in a profit, cannot conceive how a stranger might like to know of what to them are customary things; they think that one has merely come to see their fine country and their fortunate way of life. Moreover the season being late and the time not the most favorable for a mountain-journey, the sum of my observations did not correspond to my wishes or my expectations. My travelling-companion and I had been diligent collectors, had collected everything which came to our notice; but our journey ended, the pleasure of quietly examining what we had brought together was denied us, at least we had not the time to look into everything. The many difficulties we encountered, unknown to us before the event or fancied as of small moment, especially in the item of getting our baggage through the interior of the country, safely and at the right time from place to place, caused us the mortification of losing much outright and of seeing a great part of the remainder ruined or badly handled. Had we been able to foresee these difficulties (certainly great if through them the particular cherished design of a journey is made idle) we should, doubtless, have hit upon better methods in the avoidance of them. In the future, what with a better established order and quiet, and an internal commerce continually widening, other travellers will have less ground for similar complaints ; and the native savans least of all, (they being vastly more able to get about conveniently and easily), when they once begin to investigate the rarities and beauties of their fatheland.

At Philadelphia Mr. Hairs, ✝ my travelling companion hitherto, left me in order to seize the opportunity of returning to England by the last British fleet sailing from New York. But having determined to get some knowledge as well of the more southern provinces of the United States, and if possible of a part of the West Indies, I did not permit myself to be frightened by the approach of winter from setting out on a journey through Virginia to Carolina.

Appendix

No. I

Abstract of the Address of Professor Kunze of Philadelphia on the Purposes and the Progress of the Chartered German Society of Philadelphia in Pensylvania.   [Vol. I. pp. 613-629.]

No. II

Resolves of the Congress touching the Establishment of Ten New States in the Territory lying to the West of the Mountains.

[Vol. I, pp. 630-637.   From Bailey's Pocket Almanac, Philadelphia, 1785.]

No. III

Notice of *The Discovery, Settlement & present State of Kentucke and an Essay towards the Topography and natural History of that important Country*.   By John Filson.   Wilmington.   Printed by James Adams. 1784.   8.   118 pages.   [Vol. I, pp. 638-644.]

Notes

Preface—The continuation of the title of the Abbé Robin's New Travels is: " Also Narratives of the capture of General Burgoyne, and Lord Cornwallis, with their armies, and a variety of interesting particulars, which occurred in the course of the War in America. Translated from the original of the Abbé Robin, one of the chaplains to the French Army in America.

From such events let boastful Nations know,
Jove lays the pride of haughtiest monarchs low.

*　　　*　　　*　　　*　　　*　　　*　　　*　　　*

Busiris by Young.

Philadelphia.

Printed and sold by Robert Bell in Third-street.

1783—Price, Two Thirds of a Dollar."

[The translation by Philip Freneau.]

The picturesque Smyth (who is to be found in the biographical dictionaries under the name Stuart, having set up claim to descent from the Duke of Monmouth) offers material for a dissertation. A contemporary detractor charged him with having been a coachman in Virginia. Smyth's narrative is excellent reading; a close investigation alone would determine whether he was not often wide of the truth. Defoe could have shaped his Travels into a novel of impeccable verisimilitude. His title-page runs:

" A Tour in the United States of America, containing an Account of the Present Situation of that Coun-

try, the Population, Agriculture, Commerce, Customs
& Manners of the Inhabitants; Anecdotes of several
Members of the Congress & General Officers in the
American Army; and Many other very singular and
interesting Occurrences. With a Description of the
Indian Nations, the general Face of the Country,
Mountains, Forests, Rivers, & the most beautiful,
grand, and picturesque Views throughout that vast
Continent.

Likewise, Improvements in Husbandry that may be
adopted with great Advantage in Europe. Two volumes. London, 1784."

The edition of Chastellux examined by Dr. Schoepf
was the pirated one printed at Cassel. The first translation was in 1787, London and Dublin, supposed to
have been the work of George Grieve, who lived for a
time at Alexandria in Virginia:

"Travels in North America in the years 1780, 1781,
and 1782. By the Marquis de Chastellux, one of the
forty Members of the French Academy, and Major
General in the French Army, serving under the Count
de Rochambeau. Translated from the French by an
English Gentleman, who resided in America at that
Period. With Notes by the Translator.

πολλων δ'ανθρωπων άστεα και νοον εγνω. Odyssey, B. I.
Multorumque hominum vidit urbes, & mores cognovit.

Two volumes."

[The notes are of great value.]

If Schoepf had seen the complete work he would not
have been so scandalized. Chastellux is flippant at
times, and made no pretence to a knowledge of the
exact sciences, but few foreigners at that period had a

better notion of the true status of the United States.
The unfortunate Brissot also, who was in America in
1788. could not pardon Chastellux his lightness of
touch.

The Italian *conte* was Luigi Castiglioni, whose
Travels, immediately following those of Schoepf and
covering a wider territory (from Canada to Georgia)
are similar in treatment: the observations primarily of
a botanist with notes on conditions in general. A comparison of Schoepf with Kalm and Castiglioni brings
out Schoepf's merits strongly, his sense of proportion
and his gift for informing the commonplace and the
technical with an individuality. Castiglioni belonged
to the great family of that name, and was as thorough
a botanist, no doubt, as America saw for many years
after the Revolution. The title of his book was,

" Viaggio negli Stati Uniti dell' America Settentrio-
nale, fatto negli anni 1785, 1786, e 1787, da Luigi Castiglioni, Patrizio Milanese, Cavaliere dell' Ordine di
S. Stefano P. M., membro della Società Filosofica di
Filadelfia e della Patriotica di Milano.

Con Alcune Osservazioni sui Vegetabili più utile di
quel Paese. Milano, 1790."

[Two volumes, the greater part of the second being
careful descriptions of plants, arranged alphabetically.]

Captain Von Wangenheim of the Hessian Chasseurs,
published in 1787, at Göttingen, *Beschreibung einiger
nordamerikanischen Holzarten, mit Anwendung auf
deutsche Forste, mit 36 originalzeichnungen.* gr. fol.

The reference to Crèvecoeur's *Lettres d'un Cultivateur Americain* is to the Paris edition of 1787, three

volumes, ' traduites de l'Anglois '. Letter 47, dated
Baltimore, May 1, 1771, forms one of the " beautiful
and true " chapters, regarding the American, what and
who he is.

For editions of Kalm, see Winsor, *Narrative and
Critical History*, IV, 494 ; V, 244.

P. 15—Nicholas Dirx, called Tulpius, of Amsterdam, 1593-1674. There was a tulip carved in stone
over his father's house, hence the name. His chief
work, *Observationum Medicarum libri tres*, Amsterdam, 1641 ; Leyden, 1752, with augmentations.

P. 16—" It was remarked upon as a curious circumstance, that while, before the revolution, lobsters or
large crawfish had never been seen in this vicinity ; yet
no sooner had that struggle commenced, than numbers
of them left the continent of North America and came
to New Scotland. This gave rise to a standing joke
among the people of this place, that the lobsters were
good royalists." *Letters & Journals of Mrs. General
Riedesel.* Translated by William L. Stone. Albany,
1867, p. 190.

P. 22—Anburey tells this story of a Virginia officer
travelling in New England. Vol. II (ed. 1791), p.
62-63. Burnaby ascribes the method to Dr. Franklin,
and it is his version that Schoepf has followed. See,
Burnaby's *Travels through the Middle Settlements*,
(1759-1760). London, 1775, p. 83.

P. 28—*Beyträge zur Völker- und Länderkunde;
gemeinschaftlich herausgegeben von J. R. Forster und
M. C. Sprengel.* 3 Theile. Leipzig, 1781-1783.

It should not be forgotten that Johann Reinhold
Forster was for many years active in making America
known in Germany. See, Meusel's *Lexikon der vom
Jahr 1750 bis 1800 verstorbenen Teutschen Schriftsteller.*

P. 36—For some account of John Jacob Faesch, and
the colonial iron industry of New Jersey, see Edmund
J. Halsey, *History of Morris County, New Jersey.*
New York, 1882, ch. VII-IX; cf. also *American Ma-
chinist,* XXV, 409; XXVII, 240, 354, 451.

P. 42—" The flying machine sets out from Powles-
hook, opposite to New York, for Philadelphia, every
Monday, Wednesday, and Friday morning in summer ;
from November first, to May first, it performs the journey only twice a-week, and sets out on Mondays and
Thursdays. The waggons from Philadelphia set off
the same mornings. As the Machines set off from
Powles-hook early in the morning, passengers should
cross the ferry the evening before. The price for each
passenger is twenty shillings currency."
Patrick McRobert, *Tour through Part of the Northern Provinces of America &c.* Edinburgh, 1776, p. 56.

P. 46—Richard Peters, 1748-1828, first President of
the Pennsylvania Agricultural Society &c.

P. 56—*Dictionnaire Philosophique,* art. *Eglise* (vol.
39, pp. 500 ff., ed. Kehl).

P. 61—See, *An Account of the New-invented Pennsylvania Fire-Places &c.* Philadelphia. Printed and
sold by B. Franklin. 1744. Sparks, VI, 34-64;
Smyth, I, 127-129.

P. 65—Timothy Matlack, 1730-1829.

P. 70—John Fothergill, 1712-1780, of whom Franklin said, " I can hardly conceive that a better man ever existed."

P. 81—See, *Transactions of the American Philosophical Society,* II, 225 ff., article by Dr. Rush, on Tetanus—

" Dr. Schoepft, the physician general of the Anspach troops that served at the siege of York in the year 1781, informed me of a singular fact upon this subject. Upon conversing with the French surgeons after the capitulation he was informed by them that the troops who arrived just before the siege from the West Indies with Count de Grasse were the only troops belonging to their nation that suffered from the Tetanus. There was not a single instance of that disease among the troops who had spent a winter in Rhode Island."

P. 83—Adam Kuhn, of Germantown, 1741-1817; said to have been a favorite pupil of Linnaeus at Upsala; the first Professor of Botany in America.

P. 84—" A collection of anatomical models in wax, obtained by Dr. Abraham Chovet in Paris, was in use by Philadelphia medical students before the Revolution." Goode, *Beginnings of American Science,* Smithsonian Report, 1897, II, 413.

P. 87—" Then I dressed myself as neat as I could; and went to Andrew Bradford, the printer's. I found in the shop the old man his father, whom I had seen at New York, and who, travelling on horse-back, had got to Philadelphia before me."

Franklin: *Autobiography,* temp. 1723.

P. 87—Melchior Steiner, Race St. near Third; Charles Cist, Market St. near Fifth. See their advertisements, *Freeman's Journal*, Nov. 12 and Nov. 19, 1783.

P. 89—Thomas Spence Duché. See, Scharf, *Hist. of Philadelphia*, II, 1040.

P. 93—Arbustum Americanum: the American Grove, or, an Alphabetical Catalogue of Forest Trees and Shrubs, natives of the American United States. 12mo. 169 pp. A very rare book. Cf. Harshberger, *Botanists of Philadelphia and their Work*. Philadelphia, 1899, p. 80.

P. 95—George Glentworth, of Philadelphia, 1735-1792; after 1777 Senior Surgeon of the Continental Army, and Director General of Hospitals for the middle division.

P. 96—Letters from an American Farmer; describing certain Provincial Situations, manners, and customs, not generally known, and conveying some idea of the late and present Interior circumstances of the British Colonies in North America.

Written for the Information of a Friend in England.

By J. Hector St. John [de Crèvecoeur] A Farmer in Pennsylvania.

London, 1782.

The *Freeman's Journal* (Philadelphia) for Dec. 24, 1783, contains an advertisement dated 'New York, Dec. 1783' and signed

" St. John
Consul for the States of New York,
New Jersey, and Connecticut."

P. 98—Kalm's *Reisen*, Göttingen edition, 1757, II, p. 405. John Reinhold Forster's English translation, 2nd ed. London, 1772, I, 206-207.

P. 100—See, Gottlieb Mittelberger's *Journey to Pennsylvania in the year 1750* (Trans. by Carl Eben). Philadelphia, 1898, p. 117—"All English ladies are very beautiful; they wear their hair usually cut short or frizzed."

P. 101—The custom may have been general. Burnaby (ed. 1775, London, pp. 83-84) gives Massachusetts Bay as the locus. See also, Anburey, *Travels through the Interior Parts of America.* London, 1791, II, pp. 87-88. Letter XLIX, dated 'Cambridge in New England, Jan. 19, 1777'.

P. 104—Habermann, called Avenarius, Professor of Theology at Jena 1520-1590, whose prayer-book went through many editions.

P. 108—For a specimen of the later speech, see, *Proceedings, Pennsylvania-German Society,* I, 33-34—*De Olta un Neia Tzeita.* "Ich con on nix bessers denka os a pawr wardt sawga weaga de olta un neia tzeita. Suppose mer mista now widder tzurick gae iwer fooftzich yohr, un laiva we sellamohls? Denk a mohl drau, ainer het business in Pittsburg, un mist dort si in dri odder feer dawg. . . . . Eb mer awer om end feel besser laiva con ich net exactly sawga."

P. 110—This address was delivered Sept. 20, 1782, being the first commemoration address before the German Society of Pennsylvania. See, Oswald Seidensticker, *Hundert-jährige Feier der Incorporation der Deutschen Gesellschaft von Pennsylvania.* Philadelphia, 1882, Introd., p. 9.

For some account of the conditions noted in this address, see also Seidensticker, *Geschichte der*

Deutschen-gesellschaft von Pennsylvania. Philadelphia, 1876, pp. 21-40.

P. 110—For the early history of the German Society of New York, see, *Das Buch der Deutschen in Amerika.* Philadelphia, 1909, p. 682-83.

P. 138—See, Anburey, *Travels through the Interior Parts &c.* (ed. 1791), II, pp. 450-452—"In short, in laying out the plan of this tavern, they seem solely to have studied the ease, comfort, and convenience of travellers." General Phillips, says Anburey, was so much delighted with this tavern that he went out of his way forty miles to revisit it.

P. 138—Samuel Gustaf Hermelin, 1744-1820. See his *Berättelse om Nordamerikas Förenta Stater.* 1784. Ed. C. E. B. Taube. Stockholm, 1894, p. V, Letter of Count Creutz, minister at Paris, to King Gustaf III (Nov. 7, 1782)—"Le baron de Hermelin est parti pour l'Amérique. Il a desiré de profiter de la première occasion pour y aller, à fin de recueillir à temps les connaissances nécessaires et former des liaisons qui lui fourniront des moyens d'ouvrir des debouchés avantageux pour le commerce de la Suède avec cette partie du nouveau monde. Il m'a dit que le Président de la Chancellerie lui avait fait sentir que votre Majesté pourrait bien l'accréditer comme Ministre auprès du Congrès, aussitot que la paix serait faite entre les Etats-Unis de l'Amérique et l'Angleterre. Je lui ai conseillé d'agir avec le plus grand secret et la plus grande circonspection et nous sommes convenus ensemble d'annoncer son voyage comme ayant pour objet des découvertes de l'histoire naturelle à l'instar de

celui de Monsieur Kalm, et les lettres de recommanda-
tion que je lui ai obtenues en font mention."

The Baron Hermelin's reports are now deposited
among the State archives at Stockholm. This edition
is merely a selection from those papers.

P. 140—These pages descriptive of Bethlehem were
reprinted as Appendix I of a *History of the Rise, Progress, and Present Condition of the Moravian Seminary
for Young Ladies.* 1858. (See, *Hist. of Bethlehem.*
By Bishop Levering. Bethlehem, 1903, pp. 524-526.)

P. 141—See, Benjamin Smith Barton, ' Observations
on Some Parts of Natural History, to which is prefixed
an account of several remarkable vestiges of an ancient
date which have been discovered in different parts of
America.' London, 1787. For instance, bricked wells
discovered in Jersey by Swedes.

P. 145—John F. D. Smyth gives an interesting chapter on the Moravian settlements in North Carolina, as
they were just before the Revolution. *Tour in the
United States of America.* London, 1784, I, ch. 29.

P. 161—" Kalm relates (Travels, 1781 ed., p. 199,
vol. 2) that the " Stags " [wapiti] came down from
the mountains in 1705, and were killed in great numbers in the vicinity of Philadelphia. Regarding the
name " Stag," McKay, in his Zoölogy of New York
uses this as the common name for the wapiti. Ord, in
Guthrie's Geography (Amer. ed., 1815, p. 306), uses
the same name for it. Godman uses both this name
and " red deer " in his synonymy (Nat. Hist., vol. 2,
p. 294). " Red deer " was used by the backwoodsmen
to distinguish it from the Virginia or " wild deer."

Rhoads, *Mammals of Pennsylvania and New Jersey,* pp. 31, 39 [Caption, " Eastern Wapiti or Elk," pp. 29-47].

P. 172—A recent and full discussion of these facts of the early history of the Wyoming country is to be found in Harvey's *History of Wilkes-Barré.* Wilkes-Barré. 1909. Vol. II, ch. XI, ch. XII, and ch. XVIII.

P. 208—See, H. C. Grittinger. Iron Industries of Lebanon County, *Lebanon County Historical Society Papers,* III, 3-4.

P. 210—Cf. Smyth, *Tour in the United States,* II, 387-88 [Long Island]. " There is a very singular insect in this island, which I do not remember to have observed in any other part of America. They are named by the inhabitants *Katy did's,* from their note, which is loud and strong, bearing a striking resemblance to those words, ... one perpetually and regularly answering the other in notes exactly similar to the words *Katy did* or *Katy Katy did,* repeated by one, and another immediately bawls out *Katy didn't,* or *Katy Katy didn't.*"

P. 213—" They import many Black or Horned Cattle far and near, from *South-Carolina,* Southward, and from 300 Miles Westward, and from the Jersies."

Douglass, *British Settlements.* Boston, 1750, II, 333—" Of Pennsylvania."

P. 213—Near White's Tavern in 1793 was M'Allister's farm, of which Dr. Cooper has left a minute description, interesting as showing what the good eighteenth century method was. *Some Information respecting America.* Collected by Thomas Cooper, late of Manchester. Dublin, 1794, pp. 123-134.

P. 219—Among the most pronounced of these adventurers was the celebrated " Lord of Newburyport," Timothy Dexter.

P. 232—Apparently Dr. Schoepf was not familiar with Jeffery's Atlas (ed. 1768, 1775, 1776, 1782). Jeffery's map of Pennsylvania, (ed. 1782) after W. Scull 1770, delineates the mountains well, and should have been useful to the traveller.

P. 242—The journey seems to have been made from Nazareth to Pittsburgh in a chair, or chaise. The excursion to Wyoming was apparently by horseback.

Dr. Schoepf's visit to Pittsburgh is mentioned at p. 86 of Sarah H. Killikelly's *History of Pittsburgh,* Pittsburgh, 1906.

See also, Bulletin of the Carnegie Library of Pittsburgh, Vol. IX, No. 7, pp. 203-215.

P. 245—The figures used here were doubtless taken from *American Husbandry,* London, 1775, 2 vols., an extraordinary book, which owed a good deal on the political side to Governor Pownall's *Administration of the Colonies.*

P. 260.—See, ' A Narrative of the Incidents attending the Capture, Detention, and Ransom of Charles Johnston, of Botetourt County, Virginia, who was made Prisoner by the Indians, in the year 1790; together with an interesting account of the fate of his companions, five in number, one of whom suffered at the stake. To which are added Sketches of Indian Character and Manners with Illustrative Anecdotes.' New York, 1827, pp. 264.

P. 262—[Judge Richard Henderson, of North Carolina] "One of the most singular and extraordinary persons and excentric geniuses in America, and perhaps in the world. . . . . I beg leave to observe, that I do not presume to undertake his justification, but only admire his enterprising policy, and the vigour and activity of his mind."

Smyth, *A Tour in the United States of America.* London, 1784, Vol. I, pp. 124-128.

P. 263—" Upon occasion of the last war Dr. Mitchel [John Mitchell] was employed by the ministry to take an accurate survey of all the back countries of North America, most of them being then but little known, except to the French, who were in possession of a line of forts through all North America. No person could have been more properly appointed, for he was not only able to lay down the country with exactness, but being well acquainted with practical agriculture in Virginia and Pensylvania, he was able to understand the nature and value of those countries he should traverse. This was the origin of his map of North America [1755], the best general one we have had: at the time it was published, it was accompanied by a bulky pamphlet written by the Doctor, and entitled, *The Contest in America,* in which he enters into a full elucidation of the importance of the back countries, and of the fatal effects which must flow from leaving the French in possession of their encroachments. Among others he considers particularly the territory of the Ohio, and shews of how much importance it is to the planters of Virginia." *American Husbandry.* London, 1775. Under caption, " The Ohio."

P. 268—" A controversy has for a long time existed whether this animal [the Mammoth] were a species of *elephant* or not; and both the affirmative and negative sides of the question were confidently maintained by eminent zoölogists. It is probable the dispute is now nearly being terminated, as, in the estimation of good judges, proof little short of demonstrative has appeared, confirming the opinion of those who assign this far-famed animal to the genus *Elephas.*" *A Brief Retrospect of the Eighteenth Century.* By Samuel Miller. New York, 1803, Vol. I, p. 120.

P. 270—*Essai sur cette question, quand et comment l'Amérique a-t-elle été peuplée d'hommes et d'animaux* [par Samuel Engel]. Amsterdam, 1767, II, Ch. VI, p. 298 ff.—*Les Anges ont été les anciens habitans de notre globe.*

Dr. Schoepf has used De Pauw's *Recherches philosophiques sur les Américains.* Berlin, 1770, I, 321, where Samuel Engel's theory is the subject of pleasantry.

P. 278—Hugh Henry Brackenridge [Class of 1771, later on the Supreme Bench of Pennsylvania] in 1776 " went to Philadelphia, and supported himself by editing the United States Magazine." General Charles Lee would have been glad to horse-whip the editor. Brackenridge relinquished this work in 1781, going to Pittsburg.

Alexander, *Princeton College in the Eighteenth Century,* p. 140.

P. 278—" . . . . The principle which has been supposed to be recognised by all European governments, from the first settlement of America. The absolute, ultimate title has been considered as acquired by discovery, subject only to the Indian title of occupancy, which title the discoverers possessed the exclusive

right of acquiring. . . . . It has never been contended
that the Indian title amounted to nothing. Their right
of *possession* has never been questioned. The claim
of Government extends to the *complete ultimate title,*
charged with this *right* of possession, and to the *exclusive* power of acquiring that right."

Chief Justice Marshall's opinion, in Johnson and
Graham's Lessee *vs.* William McIntosh. (*Wheaton's
Reports,* Vol. 8.)

P. 290—General William Irvine, 1741-1804; and
Lt.-Col. Stephen Bayard, 3rd Pennsylvania. General
Irvine left this post Oct. 1st, and Colonel Bayard,
Nov. 3rd, of this year.

P. 291—See also, *Gentleman's Magazine,* 1786, Vol.
56, p. 801, "A letter from New York mentions the
discovery of a spring in the county of Fincastle in
Virginia, the waters of which have a singular quality
unparalleled in any country in the world, for by flash-
ing a little gunpowder over it, the water will take fire
and burn like spirits." The county of Fincastle had
lost its name and been subdivided several years before
1786.

P. 293—Dr. Thomas Burnet's *Telluris Theoria
Sacra,* 1680; and Woodward's *Essays towards a Natural History of the Earth.* 1695.

P. 296.—For an account of Husband's earlier career,
(he was a relative and correspondent of Franklin's),
see, Fitch, *Some Neglected History of North Carolina.*
Washington, 1905, ch. III-V.

P. 302—In the *Gentleman's Magazine,* Vol. X
(1740), p. 104, a curious letter is given, written by

Morgan Jones, 'Chaplain to the Plantations of South Carolina,' dated New York, March 10th, 1685-6. Mr. Jones says he was captured by the Tuscorara Indians, from whom a tribe of Doegs ransomed him. These Doegs spoke Welsh, and Mr. Jones 'did preach to them three times a week in the British language.'

P. 311—There are not many records of visits to Bath-town at this period or even much later.

See, Bayard, *Voyage dans l'intérieur des Etats-Unis, à Bath, Winchester, dans la Vallée de Shenandoha*, &c. *Pendant l'été de 1791.* Paris, 1797, pp. 75-105.

Also, James K. Paulding, *Letters from the South written during the Summer of 1816.* New York, 1817, II, 224-245.

P. 313—A few years later, in 1796, Isaac Weld found Winchester the largest town in America west of the mountains.

P. 314—This is doubtless a mistake, not *Delancy*, but *Dulany*.

See, *One Hundred Years Ago or the Life and Times of the Rev. Walter Dulany Addison, 1769-1848.* By Elizabeth Hesselius Murray. Philadelphia, 1895, pp. 66, 67.

P. 320—"The assembly, or parliament of North Carolina rewarded him with his freedom and two hundred pounds." Smyth, *Tour &c.* London, 1784, I, 109.

P. 340—For some account of Dr. Wiesenthal, 1726-1789, 1st President and prime mover of the German Society of Maryland, see, Hennighausen, *History of the German Society of Maryland.* Baltimore, 1909.

P. 345—Cf. Letter of Henry Lee, of Prince William County, Virginia, to William Lee of London, March 1st, 1775—

" We are making large Quantitys of Salt Petre from the Nitre in the Tobacco Putrified with Urine and have made some very strong well grained Powder in this County therefrom wch ketches quick and shoots with great force, so that we shall be able in Future to supply ourselves with Salt Petre and gunpowder without Importing any."

Lee of Virginia. Edited by Edmund Jennings Lee. Philadelphia, 1895, p. 293.

See also, *Work of the Ordnance Bureau of the War Department of the Confederate States, 1861-1865.* By Professor Mallet [Alumni Bulletin of the University of Virginia, III, 387]—" As regards the materials for making gunpowder, search was made for nitre earth, and considerable quantities were obtained from caves in Tennessee, Georgia, and North Alabama, as also from old buildings, cellars, plantation quarters, and tobacco barns."

P. 374—The old style was, " The Government of the Counties of New Castle, Kent, and Sussex upon Delaware." By the Constitution of Sept. 1776, the style became, " The Delaware State." See, Conrad, *History of the State of Delaware.* Wilmington, 1908, I, 150.

P. 379—Scharf, *History of Philadelphia,* II, 966-967, makes no mention of Reyan, but gives a brief account of Lewis Hallam's company, whose vicissitudes and stratagems at this time were very similar.

27

P. 382—See, *Freeman's Journal* (Philadelphia),
Dec. 24, 1783—
> " At the French Academy
> In Lodge Alley
At the particular request of a number of ladies &
gentlemen will be danced a second time on Saturday
the 27th instant by five & twenty scholars of the said
Academy
> A Ballet
Representing the return of peace and the coronation of
the success of America

*   *

There will be also decorations & transparent scenes
emblematical of the occasion, with an addition to the
figures and the scenery

*   *

N. B.   No admittance without tickets."

P. 385—This communication appears in the *Freeman's Journal* for Nov. 26, 1783, signed ' A. B.' who
quotes the Voyage to the Moon of Cyrano de Bergerac.

Francis Baily was the publisher of this very good
newspaper, ('in *Market-Street* between *Third* and
Fourth-Streets '), of whom Bayard remarks—" C'est
un homme bon, dans toute l'énergie de l'expression
anglaise, qui, pour être sentie, doit être accompagnée
de la valeur que lui donna Pope."

Voyage dans l'Intérieur &c., p. 115.

P. 393—Priscian, the first of Latin grammarians,
although in point of time one of the latest—The phrase
once current, " To break the head of Priscian."

P. 395—What Schoepf himself had attempted to do
was not understood as early as 1798. See, Benjamin

Smith Barton's *Collections for an Essay towards a Materia Medica of the United States.* Philadelphia, 1798, p. 2.—" Mine is not the first attempt of this kind. . . . . Dr. Schoepf of Erlangen in Germany has favored us with a specimen of such a work. . . . . The author arranges the articles according to the sexual system of Linnaeus. This, though an objection, is not the greatest. He has given us nothing from his own experience. . . . . But as the effort of Schoepf is the best of its kind, so we ought to tread lightly on his work. He is at least a man of learning, and learning should always claim indulgence " &c.—Almost simultaneously with Schoepf's *Travels* appeared the first of Dr. Morse's numerous American Geographies and Gazetteers.

P. 397—In the copy of Schoepf's Travels in the Library of the Historical Society of Pennsylvania there is pencilled a note, " Robert Hare, brewer, Callowhill." And in the Philadelphia directory for 1785, the first directory published there, the entry appears, " Hare & Twelves, porter brewers, Callowhill Street, between Front and Second."

Therefore Dr. Schoepf's fellow-traveller was the father of the late distinguished man of science, Dr. Robert Hare of Philadelphia.

Citations

Bloch, M.:

Ichthyologie ou histoire naturelle des poissons. XII vols. fol. Berlin, 1785-87.

Carver, Jonathan, 1732-1780:

Travels through the Interior Parts of North America in the years 1766, 1767 and 1768. By J. Carver, Esq. Captain of a company of provincial troops during the late war with France. London, 1778. [2nd ed. 1779, 3rd 1781.]

Catesby, Mark, F. R. S.:

The Natural History of Carolina, Florida, and the Bahama Islands, containing the figures of Birds, Beasts, Fishes, Serpents, Insects, and Plants: particularly the Forest-trees, shrubs, and other plants, not hitherto described, or very incorrectly figured by authors. Together with their descriptions in English and French. To which are added observations on the air, soil, and waters; with remarks upon agriculture, grain, pulse, roots &c.

London, 1731, 2 vols., folio, 2nd vol., 1743.

v. Crell, Lor. Flor. Fr.:

Die neuesten Entdeckungen in der Chemie. Leipzig, 1781-84.

Düroi, Jh. Ph.:

Harbkesche wilde Baumzucht, theils nordamerikan. & theils einheim. Baüme Straücher und Pflanzen &c. 2 Bd. Braunschweig, 1771-72.

Forster, John Reinhold:
*Beyträge zur Völker- und Länderkunde, gemein-
schaftlich herausgegeben von J. R. Forster und M. C.
Sprengel.* Leipzig, 1781-83.

Gronovius:
*Flora Virginica exhibens Plantas quas nobilissimus
Vir D. D. Johannes Claytonus, Med. Doct., etc., etc., in
Virginia crescentes observavit, collegit, et obtulit. D.
Joh. Fred. Gronovio.*
Lugduni Batavorum, 1762.

Hasselquist, Frederic, 1722-1752 [Pupil of Linnaeus,
who published his Travels]:
Voyage en Palestine. Stockholm, 1757. 2 vols.

Kirwan, Richard [1733-1812], President of the Royal
Irish Academy:
1] *Elements of Mineralogy.* 2 vols. London, 1784.
2] *Estimate of the Temperature of different Lati-
tudes.* London, 1787.

Knoll, Hnr. Eph. Fr. [d. 1786]:
*Unterhaltende Naturwunder, Aeolus-Höhlen, Don-
nerdämpfe, entzündbares Gewässer &c.* Erfurt, 1786-
88.

v. Schlözer, August Ludwig [1737-1809]:
Briefwechsel meist statistisches Inhalts. 1774-75.
Briefwechsel meist historischen u. politischen Inhalts.
10 Bde. Göttingen, 1778-82. [Several American
items of interest.]

Schneider, J. G.:
Naturgeschichte der Schildkröten. Leipzig, 1783-
89.

v. Schreber, J. C. D. [1739-1810]:
Saügthiere, in Abbildungen nach der Natur. Erlangen, 1774-1823.

Sparrmann, Andr.:
Reisen in Afrika. Berlin, 1783. [German edition.]

Pennant, Thomas, 'of Downing' [1726-1798]:
1] *British Zoölogy.* 1766.
2] *History of Quadrupeds.* 1781. &c. &c. His memoir written by Cuvier, in the *Biographie Universelle.*

Plukenet, Leonard [1642-1706]:
1] *Almagestum Botanicum sive Phytographiae Plukenetianae methodo synthetico digestum &c.* London, 1696.
2] *Phytographia sive Stirpium illustriorum & minus cognitarum Icones, Tabulis aeneis &c.* London, 1691-92.

v. Wangenheim, Fr. Adam Julius [1747-1800]:
Beschreibung einiger nordamerikanischen Holzarten, mit Anwendung auf deutsche Forste, mit 36 originalzeichnungen. gr. fol., Göttingen. 1787.

v. Zimmermann, Eberhard Aug. Wilh. [1743-1815]:
1] *Geographische Geschichte der Menschen und der vierfüssigen Thiere.* Leipzig, 1778-1780.
2] *Ueber die Verbreitung und Ausartung des Menschengeschlechtes.* Leipzig, 1778.
3] Among his works, an ethnographical and geographical comparison of France and America, published in two volumes. 1795, 1800.

Index

Printed in the United States
123858LV00002B/127/A

9 780548 494103